FOURTH EDITION

LANGUAGE AND LITERACY IN THE EARLY YEARS 0-7

Education at SAGE

SAGE is a leading international publisher of journals, books, and electronic media for academic, educational, and professional markets.

Our education publishing includes:

- accessible and comprehensive texts for aspiring education professionals and practitioners looking to further their careers through continuing professional development

- inspirational advice and guidance for the classroom

- authoritative state of the art reference from the leading authors in the field

Find out more at: **www.sagepub.co.uk/education**

Marian Whitehead was formerly a Senior Lecturer in Education at Goldsmiths College, University of London, with responsibility for organizing and teaching MA degrees in Language and Literature and Early Childhood Education. She has published extensively on literacy, literature and bilingualism and was for many years an editor of the journal *Early Years*. She now combines writing with language and early years consultancy work.

LANGUAGE AND LITERACY IN THE EARLY YEARS 0–7

MARIAN WHITEHEAD

Los Angeles | London | New Delhi
Singapore | Washington DC

First published 1990
Reprinted 2002
Second edition published 1997
Reprinted 2003
Third edition published 2004
Reprinted 2005, 2006, 2007
This edition published 2010

SAGE Publications Ltd
1 Oliver's Yard
55 City Road
London EC1Y 1SP

SAGE Publications Inc.
2455 Teller Road
Thousand Oaks, California 91320

SAGE Publications India Pvt Ltd
B 1/I 1 Mohan Cooperative Industrial Area
Mathura Road
New Delhi 110 044

SAGE Publications Asia-Pacific Pte Ltd
33 Pekin Street #02-01
Far East Square
Singapore 048763

Library of Congress Control Number: 2009932917

British Library Cataloguing in Publication data

A catalogue record for this book is available from the British Library

ISBN 978-1-84920-007-3
ISBN 978-1-84920-008-0 (pbk)

Typeset by Dorwyn, Wells, Somerset
Printed in Great Britain by TJ International, Padstow, Cornwall
Printed on paper from sustainable resources

Mixed Sources
Product group from well-managed
forests and other controlled sources
www.fsc.org Cert no. SGS-COC-2482
FSC © 1996 Forest Stewardship Council

CONTENTS

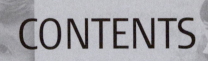

LIST OF FIGURES

Remembering Jim with love
1936–2003

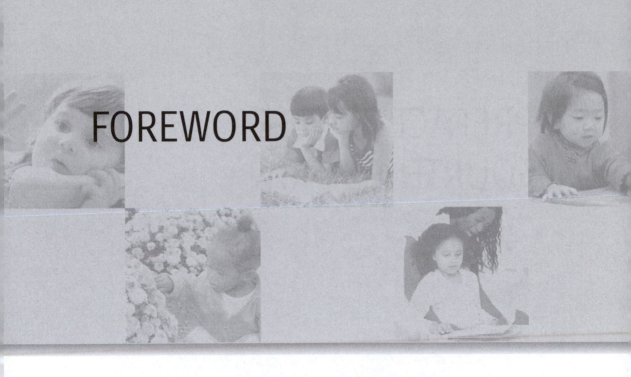

FOREWORD

This beautifully written book is an example to all of us – authors, teachers and tutors as well as students – of how to present complex ideas so that they are both accessible and useful to readers. Marian Whitehead pulls off the feat of describing competing theories of language acquisition, and of the development of children's minds through verbal thinking, in ways which make 'human sense', aided by numerous examples of snatches of children's thinking, language and mark-making. Her examples ably demonstrate not only children's competence and creativity in communicating, from early infancy onwards, but their absolute intentionality. Having established the immense capacities of children for learning from their environment, and from their interactions with adults and peers, Whitehead applies this knowledge to the question of how we can provide environments which respect and build on the strengths and skills which children bring with them into their early group care settings. The story of children's astonishing efforts to communicate – non-verbally, verbally and then through writing – as they develop from birth through to the early years of school should inspire everyone working with children to look again, and listen again, to the evidence of their own classrooms. No one reading this book, it is to be hoped, will ever again describe a child as 'not knowing how to talk' or 'not having a clue about print'. Instead, Whitehead demonstrates the logical thinking and problem-solving which can be seen to underpin children's utterances and their early interactions with print, if only adults pay proper attention. She shows, too, that children's own creativity in playing with sound and symbol can be the most productive basis for extending their learning in the classroom. This is a book to make readers feel wiser and stronger, and to inspire a respect for children's minds and potential which is grounded in solid theoretical argument.

Liz Brooker

PREFACE TO THE FOURTH EDITION

It is 20 years since the first edition of this book and the number and quality of 'language and literacy in the early years' books continue to increase steadily. This sustained interest in communication and language and its crucial role in children's development is heartening and I am pleased that the first edition of this book was at the start of such a significant development.

During the past 20 years research studies of communication, language, literacy and child development have continued to emerge and many of their insights are reflected in this fourth edition. But the greatest changes in the UK since this book was first published have occurred in the organization and regulation of early years care, education and schooling. The world of care and education has changed dramatically and is still going through many upheavals.

In England, as in the other countries and province of the UK, a statutory national framework for children from birth to 5 has been introduced. The ground-breaking English framework for supporting young children from birth to 3 in care and education settings (*Birth to Three Matters*, DfES and Sure Start Unit, 2002) has evolved into an Early Years Foundation Stage (birth to 5 years). A folksy passion for phonics has produced the officially sanctioned 'simple' approach to reading, which influences literacy work with the youngest children in group settings.

These curriculum frameworks and related training initiatives contain detailed requirements and guidelines for communication, language and literacy and make this book, with its emphasis on practitioner knowledge about language, more relevant than ever before – and in need of considerable modifications. It must also speak to a wider range of practitioners and early years settings, and cannot assume a readership of teachers working in schools.

This widening of the notion of what constitutes an early years practitioner and an early years setting can be a liberating challenge and I have approached it as such. However, the dangers of settling for oversimplified views of communication, language, literacy and early years education are still in evidence. This fourth edition still rejects quick-fix approaches to language and narrow prescriptive rules for teaching it – and teaching children – and continues to celebrate the complexity and the joy involved in supporting young children's development as innovative communicators, speakers, writers and readers. The call for a fourth edition indicates that early years practitioners in many settings, and with many different backgrounds, agree with me about the complexity of their task and approach it with undiminished professionalism and commitment. I am proud to count myself one of them.

Marian Whitehead
Norwich
July 2009

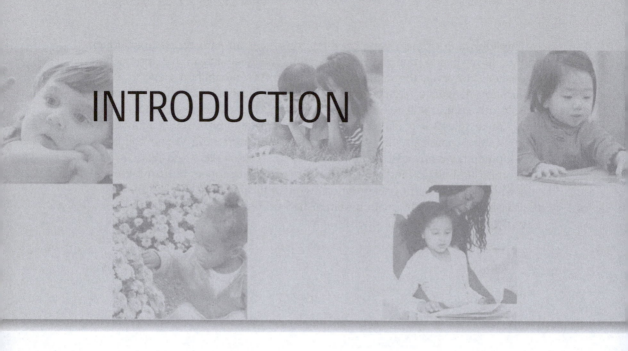

INTRODUCTION

The focus of this book is on children from birth to 7 and particularly on those attending a wide range of early years group settings providing care and education. In the terminology of the current legislation for England, this covers the communication, language and literacy curriculum for the Early Years Foundation Stage (birth to 5) and Years 1 and 2 of the National Curriculum. However, the early years of learning and education are not restricted to group settings and schools, and books about this stage must also focus on children's informal learning and experiences in homes and communities. Furthermore, no worthwhile study of communication, language and literacy should be restricted by the narrow legislation for England.

Communication, language and literacy are areas of study that continue to produce new research findings and stimulating theories, and certainly justify regular review and reappraisal. Early communication and language learning are often seen as patterns or 'models' for a great range of human learning strategies and achievements. Language and literacy demonstrate the complex interweaving of the personal and the public, the private and the social, the idiosyncratic and the conventional, that characterizes all learning. Communication and language also affect the whole of care and education for, even when they are not the particular focus of planned provision and activities, they are the means and the channel for teaching and learning.

The role of the early years practitioner involves looking at the theories put forward by linguists, reviewing some of the trends in linguistic research and making informed decisions about their possible implications for practice. Practitioners have to be their own researchers in their own settings, their own policy-makers and their own curriculum planners. It is never a simple matter of transferring carefully controlled laboratory findings to busy, complex group settings. Nor is it a simple matter of doing whatever the latest legislation dictates. Early years practitioners need the appropriate information and insights to begin to answer such difficult questions as: 'What is educational linguistics?' 'What use is it?' 'What do we do about the claims of the researcher?' These are practitioners' questions and they must be answered by practitioners. This book attempts to outline the kinds of knowledge about language from which practitioners might evolve sound and appropriate educational practices.

Early years care and education continues to be an undervalued area of specialism threatened by narrow curriculum control, economizing and bureaucracy, but its particular contribution to many research areas and to education in general should be recognized. Much of the work in early years care and education has been a source of original thinking and flexible practices. Studies of the development of the infant brain and the origins of children's later achievements in mathematical and scientific thinking, logic and topology began in early years research. In particular, the roots of language and of literacy have been investigated in research based in kindergarten, nursery and early years classes in several countries. Good early years practices are more likely to be grounded in educational theories, passionate commitment and rigorous research than in pragmatic responses to political, economic and social pressures.

Part I of this book describes contemporary approaches to the study of communication and language. Chapter 1 is an introduction to modern linguistics and Chapter 2 outlines sociolinguistic approaches in some detail. Chapters 3 and 4 are concerned with language and thought and the acquisition of language in infancy. Chapter 5 relates the topics of the first four chapters to the early years practitioner's planning and provision for the language curriculum.

Part II of the book focuses on literacy and sets the scene with a chapter on narrative and stories (Chapter 6). Chapter 7 discusses books and literature and the part they play in early literacy learning, particularly reading. Chapter 8 explores the development of writing in the early years. Chapter 9 is similar to Chapter 5 in that it brings together the topics of the preceding three chapters and relates them to the early years practitioner's planning and provision for literacy development.

Each chapter ends with a list of key terms that reflects the language and the concepts of the topic and extensive lists of further reading. Chapters 1, 2, 3, 4, 6, 7 and 8 contain specific learning and teaching suggestions for the practitioner, but Chapters 5 and 9 omit these because they are entirely focused on the professional implications of Parts I and II of the book.

ACKNOWLEDGEMENTS

My warmest thanks go to the children, staff and families of Earlham Early Years Centre, Norwich, and St John's Roman Catholic Infant School, Norwich, for many of the photographs and examples of good practice in this new edition. Special thanks and love to my daughters and grandchildren for their photographs and inspiration.

PART 1

LANGUAGE AND LEARNING

CHAPTER 1

LINGUISTICS: THE STUDY OF LANGUAGE

This chapter includes:

- a brief introduction to linguistics
- modern approaches to understanding grammar
- brief comments on signs, symbols and cultural systems.

This book hopes to establish a healthy respect for the mystery, complexity and beauty of language. It is focused on early childhood because early years practitioners are privileged to be the professionals closest to young children's discoveries and happy inventions in their first language learning. Indeed, early childhood practitioners are well placed, like parents, to appreciate children's language learning, particularly the determination and ingenuity with which they set about tackling the linguistic unknown – sometimes head-on and sometimes by devious routes. One way for all of us to comprehend the sheer scale of young children's linguistic achievements is to attempt a little linguistic learning for ourselves. Other gains include the clearing away of some common misunderstandings about language and the establishment of ground rules for further talking and reading about the nature of language. Furthermore, if we are at ease with some of the main concepts and specialist terminology of linguistics, we are less likely to be misled by dubious claims about language and learning and by questionable childcare and education interventions. So here are some working generalizations about linguistics and modern approaches to grammar.

Linguistics

The study of language (one simple way of defining linguistics) has probably been pursued in various forms for thousands of years. Humankind has puzzled over the proliferation of many different languages: we might call this the Tower of Babel problem. Earlier generations were fascinated by what we could call the 'roots' issue – when and where did human language originate? People have even speculated about which language God, or the gods, spoke and which language totally isolated and untutored babies would first utter naturally. Clearly, ordinary people as well as philosophers, teachers and linguists have persistently asked, what is language and how does it work?

For centuries the proposed answers to these questions were highly prescriptive, that is, they were cast in the form of rules and assertions about which language was best, the ways in which it ought to be used, and which ideals and models of linguistic perfection should be emulated. It is not surprising that traditional prescriptive linguists frequently promoted the superiority of their own particular form of language use. As we will see later, this tradition of linguistic partiality is deeply rooted in communities and in the attitudes of individuals. For example, it is noticeably difficult for many monolinguals (people who speak only one language) to take seriously other ways of naming, organizing and thinking about the world, apart from their own linguistic practice. Furthermore, any attacks on these language loyalties can lead to passionate and violent reactions, as linguistic conflicts all over the world often demonstrate.

At the personal level, the language of home and early socialization is an intimate part of our sense of self, and any attack on our first language can be insulting, disturbing and alienating. One of the reasons for the huge numbers of bilingual and multilingual speakers in the world is the desire to preserve the languages and the traditions of the home and cultural group, while living and working within another language community.

Saussure and modern linguistics

Modern linguistics originated alongside the other modern social sciences (notably psychology and sociology) in the latter half of the nineteenth century, although it had little impact until the twentieth century. One man, Ferdinand de Saussure, is usually credited as the founding father of linguistics but his ideas were only published in 1915, after his death, as reconstructed lecture notes (Saussure, 1974). Despite this haphazard publication, Saussure's work radically challenged traditional approaches to language studies and outlined a methodology and an analysis of linguistics that remains the basis of modern linguistic science.

Saussure's work proposed a complete rejection of prescriptive judgements and unfounded and fruitless speculations about the origins of language. In their place he suggested a scientific approach to analysing and understanding the nature of human language as it exists and as it is used. In order to clear the ground for this more scientific study of language, Saussure formulated a set of linguistic distinctions, or definitions.[1]

What has emerged most clearly from Saussure's radical reshaping of the study of language is a scientific concern to observe languages objectively, to propose theories about their systems and to attempt to reconstruct and describe them accurately. This descriptive linguistics, as it is sometimes called, created new scientific procedures for collecting unknown languages 'in the field', using phonetic systems of notation as well as recordings and photographs. The work also developed a useful technique of relying on the ordinary 'insiders' of a language and culture as linguistic informants.

Saussure's linguistics

- Linguists must clearly distinguish in their studies between the concept of language as the known system of rules of a specific tongue (for example, Welsh or Gujerati), and actual instances of language in daily use – that is, utterances or written examples. Saussure happened to be a French speaker and his original choice of French terminology for these distinctions, *langue* for language system and *parole* for specific usage, are still commonly used by linguists. Any book about grammar or modern linguistics is generally a study of *langue*, but an investigation of the languages and dialects used by inner-city schoolchildren would be predominantly a study of *parole*.

- Any language is a total system – a *structure* of elaborately interrelated elements and relationships. This emphasis on the relationships and the rules that link the elements of a language has led to all approaches since Saussure being broadly defined as *'structural linguistics'*.

- Linguistic studies should distinguish between descriptions of the current state of the language (synchronic language study) and accounts of the historical evolution of a language (diachronic language study). Synchronic approaches with their emphasis on describing how the language is 'now' tend to dominate modern linguistics.

This kind of approach has been taken up by most later researchers and used in the study of child language and language variety. The modern researcher tests the plausibility of any hypothesis about the nature of an utterance or a linguistic form by trying it out on a native speaker. In other words, the ordinary speaker–listener's knowledge of the particular language system they use is the reality against which the professional linguist must test any theories.

In emphasizing the existence of ordinary knowledge of language, linguists simply claim that the native speaker (adult or child) knows one or more language systems at a deeply intuitive level. We know that we 'know' language because we produce it and comprehend it fairly effortlessly and, frequently, under many different circumstances and in a great variety of situations. Furthermore, we self-correct our own minor slips of the tongue, the pen and the keyboard, and confidently reject any ungrammatical forms of our languages that we happen to encounter. Faced with foreign speakers or infants, we strive to make sense of their intended meanings despite errors, misunderstandings and inaccurate pronunciations.

Psycholinguistics, sociolinguistics and applied linguistics

Psycholinguistics

Psycholinguistics is the shared area of psychology and linguistics, and it studies language as a major expression of human thinking and learning. It is of central interest to early years practitioners and explains how language is first acquired in infancy and how language, thinking and learning are related. Most people are clear that language is for communication with others and that it has an obvious social dimension, but they are often less consciously aware of its personal function in our thinking and self-organization.

Sociolinguistics

Language is, of course, a crucial method of social communication, cultural cohesion and dissemination. It is the tool, the manner and the matter of much of our socialization in infancy. Linguistics cannot ignore the totality of the human settings in which language is shared with others and learnt in interaction with them. Sociolinguistics is the branch of language studies that seeks to explore these complex areas of linguistics and sociology. Language and its social contexts are of major significance in child development and educational studies, particularly because homes, early years group settings and schools are very different contexts in which children learn to use and develop their languages appropriately. Language is a social creation, the voice of a community, but it becomes a highly personal possession for each of us and a way of thinking. We cannot understand language, learning and thinking, unless we keep both the social and the psychological factors in focus.

Applied linguistics

The above comments are an example of 'applied' linguistics: using linguistic findings for practical social activities like education. Pure linguists pursue strictly linguistic ends, such as refining even more detailed and accurate descriptions of language or languages, but there are many other applications of linguistics, apart from the educational.

In the medical sphere, linguistics provides help with the study and treatment of language disorders caused by congenital or accidental brain damage or disease. Language disorder and retardation also occur in children and adults who have a variety of abnormalities in the organs of voice production or have some specific sensory impairment such as degrees of deafness. These complex problems can only be touched on in this book but progress in dealing with them has been enhanced by detailed linguistic knowledge of non-verbal communication, phonology and verbal thinking.

The application of linguistics has always been associated with the work of anthropologists, who study remote and unknown languages and cultures, but this approach has in recent decades been adapted to support the long-term and in-depth study of distinctive groups and communities existing within a larger community or society.

Another aspect of applied linguistics is the study of artificial languages and the creation of voices for robots and computers. In the past, ideological and pedagogical theories also promoted artificial languages, such as Esperanto and 'basic' forms of English. The best-known application of linguistics is also the most obvious: the use of linguistic knowledge in the teaching of natural languages to adults and children in a variety of educational institutions.

Summary

- Linguistics is the study of language.
- Modern linguistics is descriptive and scientific in its approach and can be contrasted with traditional approaches that were prescriptive.
- Prescriptive linguistics emphasized notions of correctness and ideals for good language use that were often based on a respect for classical languages and formal written texts.
- Modern linguistic science primarily studies spoken language forms; it describes a language in terms of its structures and relationships. These are the internalized sets of rules that govern its use by native speakers.
- Psycholinguistics is the study of language as it relates to human thinking and learning, particularly the capacity to learn a first natural language in infancy.
- Sociolinguistics is the study of language as it is used and modified by varied social contexts.
- Applied linguistics is the use of language knowledge in practical social settings: educational linguistics is one example, although there are significant applications for linguistics in medicine, information technology, criminology and anthropology.

Grammars

Grammar is not a popular topic with the majority of people, apart from professional linguists and language teachers. This is nothing new and many attempts have been made to sweeten the pill. In the early 1800s the paths of grammar were 'strewed with flowers' (Opie and Opie, 1980: 46) as well as jolly rhymes and exquisitely colourful engravings. In the latter part of the twentieth century there was a steady flow of books, as well as radio and television programmes, that assured us that grammar and language study could be funny, fascinating and even sexy! The humorous approach has continued to be surprisingly popular in the current decade (Truss, 2003). These guides are nearly always well researched and linguistically serious, but they have to combat a general fear of grammar by using such devices as cartoons, jokey sentences and glossy formats. Boredom and anxiety are, in fact, reactions to the half-understood prescriptive grammar referred to in the previous section. This traditional grammar may be a largely discredited ideal based on Latin, but it is only fully rejected by linguists and students of linguistics. The identification of learning, high culture and power with grammar and classical languages has deep roots in Britain's history, political life and establishment culture (see Chapter 2).

Modern linguistics describes a rich and complex range of grammars. There are several differing theories about the structure or grammar of human languages, but it is possible to identify two important characteristics they all share.

- The grammars are all descriptive: they set out to describe the complex sets of relations or rules that link the sounds of a language, or its written symbols, with the meanings or messages intended. In attempting to describe a grammar, the linguist behaves like a scientist, or even an early years practitioner, and observes, records and hypothesizes.
- All modern grammars describe far more than the surface of a language – that which is heard or seen in writing. The traditional prescriptive approach placed great emphasis on the surface written form and analysed that into categories derived from Latin. Modern descriptive grammars identify and describe at least three major levels of a language and, thus, they can be said to be richer and more complex models of language than the traditional prescriptive ideal.

Phonology, syntax and semantics

The three major levels of a language that modern grammars describe are,

- phonology
- syntax
- semantics.

Lexis, more commonly referred to as vocabulary, is sometimes added to this list. Lexis refers to all the words in the definitive dictionaries of a written language or the stock of words available to an oral-language community. This does not mean that we all know all the words of our first languages; nor does it follow that measuring or assessing anyone's vocabulary is an easy matter. We all operate an active vocabulary of words we use regularly and confidently, as well as having a passive vocabulary of words and meanings we understand but are not likely to use frequently. This is a sobering and significant thought for practitioners, educators and administrators who talk glibly of assessing a child's vocabulary.

Learning and teaching suggestions

- Write down some of the favourite words used by younger children on boards, large sheets of paper, wall spaces or hard ground surfaces – outside as well as indoors.
- How do dictionaries work and why do we use them? Create flexible loose-leaf dictionaries with index cards or postcards (based on the children's questions and interests).
- Use the spellchecker on a computer word-processing program. How has it been organized and what must you know to be able to use it?

Phonology

Phonology is concerned with the organization and patterning of sounds in a language. It includes such important indicators of meaning as intonation and the use of stress or emphasis. This patterning of sounds and stress occurs in all languages, but the actual patterns vary greatly between languages. Most of us become aware that different languages have very different 'tunes', and it is possible to recognize a language by its sound, pitch and rhythms without identifying, or even being capable of identifying, any of its words. We use this skill on a daily basis to identify questions or statements in shared conversations: the distinctive rising tone of questions and the drop in pitch at the end of a statement are common features of English phonology.

The stressed parts of an utterance may be of considerable significance in early language learning: important words are often stressed particularly in conversations with foreigners, infants and young children. Among the words most likely to be emphasized are nouns, verbs and adjectives, and these powerful language labels emerge frequently and very early in a child's first language learning.

Phonology also describes and charts the possible varieties of speech sounds, for example, the pronunciation differences between speakers of the same language, known as accents. In the social sphere this often ceases to be merely a matter of objective scientific description, and the values, attitudes and prejudices that surround accents are returned to in the next chapter.

One of the most valuable achievements of modern phoneticians has been the gradual evolution of an International Phonetic Alphabet (IPA), which is used throughout the world to write down the sounds of any language and which is particularly useful in transcribing the speech of young children and infants.

The inclusion of phonology as a major element in modern grammars emphasizes the primacy of the spoken forms of language in modern linguistic science. However, it is important that pedagogical ideas about 'phonics' and 'phonetics' are not confused with the study of phonology. Phonetics is closer to being a form of applied linguistics and focuses on the actual production of sounds by the physical vocal system. Knowledge about what the tongue, palate and vocal cords can do to shape the outgoing breath can be used to help second, and subsequent, language learners articulate a new set of sounds. However, we might note here that distorted versions of phonetic knowledge have also been applied to the teaching of initial reading for many years. This limited approach can be replaced by carefully researched insights about young children's development of phonological awareness (Chapter 7).

Syntax

Syntax is that level of language concerned with words and the modification of their forms, such as adding '-s' for many plurals and '-ed' for some past tenses of verbs, as well as the organization of words in meaningfully ordered combinations. This is, of course, the area with which traditional prescriptive grammars were concerned, and some modern studies still use the word 'grammar' in a very specific way when referring only to syntax. Traditional views of syntax are still very influential in non-specialist discussion about grammar. However, rash claims that some children have no grammar are meaningless, as a child without grammar would not only be speechless but also incapable of communicating meanings by any other method.

Studies of syntax also highlight the possible variations within the same language that can exist in vocabulary, word order, and ways of indicating tenses, possession, number and so on. These meaningful grammatical varieties of a language are known as dialects and are discussed in the following chapter.

Learning and teaching suggestions

- Share published collections of nonsense verse with the older children and help them create and record their own versions (filmed, electronically recorded, written down, bound into books).
- Let everyone (adults and children) enjoy the almost meaningful nonsense language of verses such as, "Twas brillig, and the slithy toves/Did gyre and gimble in the wabe', or terms like 'Reeling and Writhing' (Carroll, 1872). How does this work? How can we make up our own versions?

Semantics

Semantics is the study of meaning in a language and it touches on the most complex issues, even to the extent of bringing linguistics closer to a form of philosophy. At the simplest level, however, it is clear that meaning in language is partly derived from the syntax – the literal meaning of these words in this order: 'I am wearing a pink T-shirt.' On the other hand, an utterance's meaning can be clear in context but its literal meaning very strange. Thus a specific setting (for example, an early years classroom) makes the following extraordinary request perfectly meaningful: 'Would green table line up at the door, please?'

Semantics is also affected by historical changes in human relationships and circumstances, as well as changes in word usage and syntactic patterns. This only becomes obvious when we consider the dramatic changes in word meaning affecting such terms as 'nice', 'mistress', 'gay' or 'ain't'. Indeed, the chequered histories of these terms are often only known to historical scholars, students of literature and linguists.

There is a tendency for most people of a particular generation to believe that words and phrases have always meant what they currently mean. The complexity of semantics increases when we consider differing cultures and languages, and realize that the world can be classified, labelled and described in many ways. Cultures even divide up the colour spectrum differently and they vary enormously in the ways in which they classify and name food, homes and ideas about time.

Learning and teaching suggestions

- How could we begin to help a space alien understand our language/ languages?
- Do you have pets at home or in the early years setting? Do you talk to them? What makes you think that they understand you?
- Read *The BFG* (Dahl, 1982) and work out the language system of the giants. Use it for extending the story or creating a class/group BFG dictionary.

Language and mind

The important point to remember about the complex sets of relationships and rules known as phonology, syntax and semantics is that they are all involved in the modern linguist's approach to describing the grammar of a language. Furthermore, there is one very significant reason for asking early years practitioners to take a general interest in modern grammars: when linguists attempt to describe the grammar of a particular language, or make claims about the basic components of all human languages, they are trying to describe the human mind. Modern linguistics is, in essence, a tentative science of thinking and learning. It is tentative because it is not suggesting that it has any absolute answers.

Chomsky

The boldest claims about language and the nature of the human mind have been made by the American linguist, Noam Chomsky, and, although his work has inspired a considerable body of research, it is still the subject of disagreements and counterclaims. Chomsky's approach is based on his view that some kind of universal grammar is genetically pre-programmed in the human mind. This claim implies that all human languages share some deep underlying similarities and these 'universals' are reflected in the individual's linguistic 'competence' or innate ability to use and understand language. It would be hard to dismiss this claim in the face of the remarkable acquisition of language by all infants in all times and in all cultures and countries. Barring appalling cruelty or massive physical impairment, babies become skilled linguistic communicators in the first two or three years of life, without professional structured teaching.

Current research, now disseminated in a witty and informal style by Steven Pinker (1994; 2002), supports this innate hypothesis with the bold claim that there is a 'language instinct' in the human species.

Of course, this innate linguistic disposition, originally described by Chomsky as a Language Acquisition Device (LAD), must be triggered into activity by the child's involvement in a particular social and linguistic world. Chomsky has used the term 'performance' to describe the actual utterances and written manifestations that demonstrate our 'competence' in various languages. As individuals, even as linguists, none of us is able to analyse fully and describe all the rules and structures of our linguistic knowledge, but we use and operate this knowledge effectively and comparatively effortlessly. Indeed, linguists claim that our daily 'performances' are only a very partial reflection of our competence and this holds a salutary warning for carers and educators! It is all too easy to believe that children's linguistic performances in group settings and schools are the sum total of their competence. There is a body of educational research evidence that suggests that the early years group situation rarely taps as much of young children's linguistic competence as a routine day at home with an adult caregiver and siblings (Serpell et al., 2005; Tizard and Hughes, 2002).

Summary

- Language is governed by rules: it is organized, produced and made meaningful by the rules of grammar. A grammar is a set of rules that describe but do not prescribe language.

- Language is creative: we can put together the basic elements of sounds, words, meanings and letter symbols, according to the rules or grammar of the language, and produce an infinite number of original, appropriate and even fantastical utterances and written sentences.

- Modern grammars describe three major levels of language: phonology, syntax and semantics.

- Language is to some extent re-created by every infant, working on the above principles, and in interaction with more experienced language users.

Systems and signs

According to most estimates, there are between 4,000 and 5,000 languages in use in the world – the wide margin of variability reflects the many complicated overlaps between discrete languages and dialects. But this amazing variety of spoken languages should not be allowed to obscure what they have in common. A language is a system for communicating meanings using the human voice (vocal-auditory tract) and verbal grammatical symbols.

Human verbal language is a systematic and symbolic means of communication and, as such, it shares some similarities with clothes, movement, music, graphic art, flowers and, even, food. All these can be said to communicate symbolically: they convey messages by using varied means and objects that stand for whole ranges of feelings, meanings and values. Consider the possible 'messages' we communicate with a bunch of red roses, wearing an academic gown, or a simple handshake. These are cultural signs only fully understood within particular societies.

Semiotics and signs

What of the many mundane objects and events that communicate – for example, international road signs, traffic lights, musical notation, chess, mathematical signs, fish and chips, football matches and horse racing? They, too, are signs and can be said to communicate messages just as subtly and precisely as the more obvious and well-known systems, such as the signing and touching used by the deaf and the blind. Signing is not merely a compensation for major sensory handicap – visual signing is relied on by people in many occupations. The daily work of auctioneers, television and radio producers, bookmakers, airport run-way controllers, dancers and actors is based on elaborate and systematic gestures and body movements. The study of these cultural sign systems is called *semiotics*, or sometimes *semiology*. It studies a vast area of human activities including advertising and food, literature and fashion. Some sign systems are fairly cross-cultural, for example, diagrams, pictures, chemical formulae, mathematical symbols, the movements of chess pieces and musical notation. But other systems, such as gestures, clothes and food, are very specific to a culture and rely on intimate involvement and early socialization. Even in a relatively small area such as Europe, the cultural differences in sign systems can lead to unintentional insults and to misunderstandings about such apparently minor details as facial grimaces, hand gestures and the distance between speakers in face-to-face conversations. These cultural differences, particularly as they concern the systematic patterns for organizing proximity, relationships, food, clothes and pastimes, are the special concern of anthropologists and sociologists.

Learning and teaching suggestions

- Make laminated wordless signs for the outside area and involve all the children in choosing appropriate symbols (for example, for the sandpit; the pond; the digging area; the fruit and vegetable patch; the parking spaces for bikes, trucks and buggies) (Figure 1.1).
- Collect examples of signs and logos to bring into the setting/classrooms (use photographs and include different languages if possible/appropriate).
- Take the children on sign-and-print-hunting walks. Follow up with displays and plenty of talk and language play and experiments (such as creating their own names, signs, logos, notices and banners).

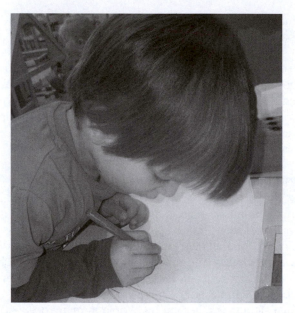

Figure 1.1 **A young boy creates his own marks and signs (3 years)**

Unique features?

Linguists study non-verbal systems of communication (sounds, gestures, facial expressions, and so on) in order to clarify the unique characteristics of verbal language. In particular, they analyse the paralinguistic features that accompany the production of all verbal language, as well as the pre-linguistic communications between infants and their caregivers. The characteristics of animal communication systems are also studied in order to clarify the differences between animal and human systems of communication. These differences actually highlight the unique features of human language.

Some unique features of human language

- A highly creative ability to produce, or generate, novel utterances and written sentences.
- The arbitrary or independent nature of words as signals: there is nothing horse-like about the word 'horse' and nothing sweet about the word 'miel'.
- Essentially meaningless 'sounds' are combined to create sets of sounds we recognize as meaningful words.
- Language is transmitted culturally: we have to learn our language in a language community.
- We can communicate about events and things that are remote in time and space, or totally imaginary. We can communicate about the 'not here and not now' – and the never!

Non-verbal communication

Paralinguistics

Human verbal language is also closely linked to another range of communicative systems that exploit subtle and flexible uses of the voice and the body. Paralinguistics is the term for the great variety of phonetic features available to every speaker, features such as intonation, speed and quality of voice tone, and the richly varied characteristics of accents. This system includes a range of noises, such as 'mm', 'uhu' and 'ah' that oil the wheels of conversation and assure speakers that they are being listened to and understood. In fact, these features form a special system known as phatic communication. This has particular importance in sustaining telephone communications: the phatic 'noises' used vary from culture to culture because they reflect the particular ranges of sounds that occur in specific languages.

We all know that the meanings conveyed by a particular utterance can be changed and varied by the skilled use of voice tone, speed and, even, accent switching. Thus a fairly bland statement can be laden with overtones of threat, irony, frivolity, gloom or erotic innuendo. Very few educators and carers need to be reminded of the power and subtlety of the human voice in group or classroom interactions and management. Similarly, most people who care for babies are aware of the great sensitivity with which infants respond to changes in emotional tone and pitch in adult voices.

Kinesics

We can also add another support system of non-verbal communicative signals to our use of the linguistic and paralinguistic: the huge range of body 'language'. This idiom is known as kinesics and includes facial expressions and head gestures, the use of the hands and arms when communicating, whole-body movements including walking and sitting, and, of course, subtle judgements about distances between speakers and the rules for touching others. It would be difficult to overestimate the importance for interpreting meanings, moods and responses of our reliance on the body messages we receive from our conversational partners, or large groups and audiences.

Again, early years practitioners are experts at reading the silent language of dropped eye contact, smiles and frowns, head nods, slouched bodies and fidgety hands and feet. However, it is equally certain that infants and children of school age are also experts at reading the kinesic messages given out, quite involuntarily, by their parents, minders and teachers. These systems are very much a matter of culture and, although they exist in all language communities, they vary enormously. The potential for offence is great, and our spontaneous responses may sometimes need a little conscious thought and modification in multicultural communities, group settings and schools.

Clearly, these human non-verbal communication systems have some relevance for early years practitioners and educators because they are major ways of conveying messages in group settings and classrooms, from children to adults and from adults to children. But these systems are also of great significance for first language acquisition in infancy. It now seems fairly clear that the paralinguistic and kinesic systems are established in earliest infancy, long before speech. The significant features of this pre-verbal communication in most cultures are the establishment of eye contact as a preliminary to interactive talk and play; the placing of gaps or pauses in the adult's talk so that the child can potentially be drawn in; the use by the adult of rather exaggerated intonation and stress patterns; and the adult use of body tickling, bouncing, bold gestures and rather dramatic facial expressions. The gestures and subtle body movements of their carers are very important factors in babies' successful early language learning.

It is clear that this elaborate use of paralinguistic and kinesic behaviour by an adult partner is natural and unselfconscious and this very heightened use of non-verbal systems is also noticeable in the interactions of professional carers and educators with very young children.

Learning and teaching suggestions

- Families and early years professionals should use helpful and informative gestures in their play and talk with babies.
- Practitioners can teach hearing babies and toddlers (and their families) some useful signs from British Sign Language (BSL) and use them to accompany speech when playing, singing and eating, etc.
- Use role play and drama to explore other ways of communicating without speech. Help older children to think about animal communications, sheepdog whistles, flags, human signing (BSL, Makaton), touch systems (Braille) and other cultural symbols (Mendhi patterns) and signals (road signs, traffic signals, and so on).

Summary

- Human language is a system for communicating meanings using the vocal-auditory tract and verbal grammatical symbols.
- Language can be compared with other cultural, communicative systems of symbols, such as music, clothes, road signs, mathematics and food.
- The general study of all these cultural systems of signs and symbolic communications is known as semiotics.
- Human language is developed on an earlier foundation of nonverbal signs and communicative strategies: the paralinguistic, involving voice tone, pitch and emphasis, and the kinesic, which includes the whole area of gestures and body language.

⊶ Key terms

Grammar: rules governing languages and the study of such rules.
Linguistics: the study or science of language.
Phonology: the study of the organizing and patterning of sounds in languages.
Psycholinguistics: the study of the role of language in thinking and learning.
Semantics: the study of meaning in language.
Sociolinguistics: the study of language in use in all possible social contexts.
Syntax: the organization of words into meaningful combinations and the small changes made to words to indicate, for example, plurals and tenses.

📖 Further reading

Aitchison, J. (2000) *The Seeds of Speech: Language Origin and Evolution*. 2nd edn. Cambridge: Cambridge University Press.

Crystal, D. (2005) *How Language Works*. London: Penguin Books.

Pinker, S. (1994) *The Language Instinct: The New Science of Language and Mind*. Harmondsworth: Allen Lane/Penguin.

Pinker, S. (2007) *The Stuff of Thought: Language as a Window into Human Nature*. London: Penguin Books.

Note

1 For part of this summary, I have drawn on Jonathan Culler's introduction to Saussure's *Course in General Linguistics* (Saussure, 1974).

CHAPTER 2

SOCIOLINGUISTICS: LANGUAGE AND CULTURES

This chapter includes:

- language variety, accents and dialects
- issues around power, gender and Standard English
- language change
- multilingualism and inclusive educational policies.

Sociolinguists study the language worlds of communities, homes, factories and schools, and their work reveals the chameleon-like characteristics of human languages. Remarkable variety and continuous change are the norms, not just among different languages but within language communities. Sociolinguists have always added to the more abstract descriptions of the 'pure' linguists with their own richly diverse accounts of the relationships between languages and cultures. This chapter outlines the ways in which language variety and change are usually described and includes some consideration of the social and personal value systems involved. Any account of the human contexts in which language occurs must try to reflect as vividly as possible the complex inter-weaving of values, prestige, power and individual identity.

Language variety

The topic of language variety can be discussed in two ways:

- the practices of distinct language communities
- personal and idiosyncratic usage.

The latter emphasizes the highly individual nature of language use, including the effects of different styles and linguistic choices. The former reveals the huge number of human languages that exist as well as the immense variations of accent and dialect found in any one apparently uniform language community.

Variety within a language community: accents and dialects

Accents

Accent refers simply to pronunciation: the sound of the language as it is shaped and articulated by a speaker. Discussions about English phonology tend to focus on such differences as the sounded length of the vowel '*a*' in '*bath*', '*path*' and '*class*'. This well-known variant is associated with a north–south geographical divide, the short '*a*' sound (as in 'cat') being commonly used from the Midlands northwards and the long '*a*' (as in 'car') being a typically southern form.

However, geography is not the only explanation for accent variation in Britain: social class and notions of educated speech complicate the picture. Our voices are the immediate and most obvious indicators of our origins because in infancy we begin by speaking and sounding like those around us. However, regional accents are subjected to the most extraordinary non-linguistic judgements: basically, our personal likes and dislikes.

We are all aware of, or have even been the victims of, the many self-styled guardians of linguistic standards who express strong disapproval of such characteristics as the dropping of sounds at the ends of words in casual rapid speech. Similarly, the glottal-stop feature found in London dialects that replaces the sound '*t*' in such words as '*butter*' and '*bottle*' with a throaty 'uh' sound, is regularly condemned.

A more objective appraisal of these kinds of issues reveals some interesting facts. For example, the pedantic sounding of all terminal sounds would make many English utterances slow and stilted. Indeed, many other languages feature regularly unsounded terminal letters. The juxtaposition of words in English utterances affects phonetic patterns and ease of articulation, frequently resulting in the dropping of terminal sounds. Try listening for the final '*t*' sound in '*last*' when it is part of an everyday expression such as 'that's the las*t* straw!' The relative pleasantness, ease, or even physical possibility involved in the production of the sounds of a language, are significant factors in the spoken form.

However, ease is only one among many elements: some apparently very difficult sounds, such as clicks, glottal stops and the English '*th*', are standard features of particular languages and dialects and 'natural' to their speakers. The glottal stop is much maligned by some speakers of British English, yet it is a distinctive standard feature of the German language. As for the dropping of the initial breathy (aspirated) 'h' in English, it can be a sign of aristocratic birth as well as of working-class origins.

All these strange contradictions indicate that careless pronunciation or even phonological limitations are *not* the major issues in discussing accents. Social judgements and cultural myths are usually being aired. We hear the voices of the people we meet – children and adults – through a filter of cultural beliefs, personal experiences and social values. It is not surprising then, that in the course of their lives, many individuals effect a blurring or weakening of their localized accents until they approximate to a more standard and prestigious variety. These changes are influenced and facilitated by such life experiences as extended education, membership of the professions, social-class mobility and personal ambition.

The most prestigious accent in the UK has been Received Pronunciation (RP), and it is also associated with the most influential dialect, Standard English (SE). These two special cases of variety will be discussed in the context of power and influence in language issues, as well as in the following discussion of dialect. Before moving on to consider dialect, it is important to re-emphasize the emotionally charged and value-laden nature of our responses to the sounds of voices. All kinds of feelings and prejudices may be aroused simply by the sounds of vowels and consonants. The accents of our childhood can evoke powerful memories of warmth or community, but their reception by others at a later stage may have caused us either to exaggerate or to modify them. We may even have rejected them completely.

Dialects

Dialects are usually associated with specific geographical regions and, therefore, involve the use of regional accents. The concept of dialect regions is complex and variable (see Trudgill, 1994). We may find that sociolinguists are referring to areas as vast as the USA, or as specific as the city of Norwich or the Harlem district of New York. However, the notion of dialect is clear and is not restricted to the sounds of a phonological system. A dialect is a true variety of a language and it includes distinctive vocabulary and syntax systems.

We are usually first aware of a dialect because of the lexical choices speakers, and sometimes writers, make, for example, 'bairn' and 'greetin', 'mither' and 'flit', 'faucet' and 'pocketbook'. The regular use of the previous examples would identify speakers of Scottish English, Lancashire dialect and American English, respectively. The differences in syntax, such as the order of words in utterances and sentences and different ways of marking plurals, tenses and agreements are not always so obvious. However, some very distinctive forms of syntax are widely recognized: 'I kinda gotten used to' from the USA or the British variants, 'I dinna ken' and 'Tha's a reet proper good un'.

Dialects are regular, rule-governed systems of language and, just as it is impossible to speak at all without an accent, so it is impossible to speak without using a dialect. We are all dialect speakers and we all have accents. Judgements, preferences and views about these dialects and accents are social and cultural features of language in use, but not purely linguistic facts.

Received Pronunciation (RP) and Standard English (SE)

The issues become even more complicated when we take account of the influence on British English of two high-status language variants. In the matter of accent there is Received Pronunciation (RP). Outside linguistic circles it has been known variously as Queen's English, a public-school accent and even BBC English. Most of my own young pupils in south London neatly summarized it as 'talking posh'. The RP accent no longer reflects any geographical origins but it still has considerable social and political power and, in combination with Standard English (SE), it is an indicator of social class.

The really posh or affected form of RP appears to have lost favour in recent years and been abandoned by the BBC. It can only be heard among the older generation of royalty, certain politicians, senior military officers and public-school 'types'. Contemporary RP is still an establishment accent, suggesting a decent education while retaining some slight traces of regional affiliations. The accents of those who have experienced lengthy post-secondary-level education, entered the professions or the higher managerial levels of business and industry tend to be modified in the direction of RP by neutralizing any strongly localized sounds.

Received Pronunciation is the accent usually associated with the prestigious dialect of SE, but it is very important to understand that this dialect may be spoken with a range of accents. This fact is demonstrated by radio and television broadcasting: programmes of news, current affairs and the arts are now presented by speakers using SE dialect in a wide variety of regional accents. Apparently, many presenters are able to enhance their own personal popularity, as well as the programme ratings, because of their appealing accents, be they east London, southern Irish or Cumbrian. The appeal or otherwise of accents is an issue that will be returned to in the next section, but the dialect of SE dominates broadcast media, the printed forms of the language and education. It is also the dialect taught to foreigners and to British children and their families who have other first languages. These important uses of SE indicate that the prestige of the variety springs from its significant social and cultural functions rather than from any inherent linguistic superiority.

It is not difficult to see that in a complex democratic society, command of one fairly standard form of the language is important for unambiguous national communications, access to information and education and full individual independence and participation in the community. This does not mean that SE is the best dialect for all of us, for all purposes and all personal needs, although for some groups and individuals it may well be their first dialect.

Learning and teaching suggestions

- Organize visits to distinctive language community areas (shops, markets, old people's homes, clubs and places of worship). These experiences can be recorded electronically, or in photographs, or in class and group books/folders/posters.
- Invite speakers of different languages and dialects to visit the setting and share something of their language and culture (this must be handled sensitively but potential language visitors may be found among the parents and families of the children and the practitioners in the setting).

Variety in individual language use: idiolects and registers

Idiolects

If variety is the norm at the level of world languages and the diverse forms within them, it is also the case at the level of individual language use. Just as there is a multitude of world languages, so there are as many different ways of using language personally as there are individuals in a language community. This may seem a wild claim but we each have a unique way or ways with our language or languages. This individual linguistic style is called 'idiolect' and is made up of the very slight differences in phonology, syntax and vocabulary that are normal in individuals and give us our instant linguistic identity among family, friends and acquaintances. Within our own idiolect range we all switch language styles and this again includes changes in phonology, vocabulary and syntax. Many people use at least two distinct dialects and many are operating two or more distinctive languages. This bilingual feature will be looked at separately but the regular use of more than one dialect has already been implied in the comments on SE dialect. Children and adults whose home or regional dialect differs from SE still hear it on the media, and read it and see it in books, newspapers and other written materials. Children also see, hear and read SE in group settings and schools, and become expert at negotiating the dialect switches involved in moving between nurseries, playgroups, classrooms, playgrounds, streets and homes.

Registers

There are no single-style speakers in any dialect and we all have a wide repertoire of sociolinguistic responses. These ideas are usually described in terms of 'communicative competence' (Hymes, 1972), which is one of the central concepts in modern sociolinguistics. The theory states that grammatical competence alone is not an adequate way of explaining the linguistically appropriate ways in which we respond to a total social and cultural situation. We change our ways of speaking according to the who, where, when and how of the situation.

This kind of communicative competence is specific to cultures and societies and their differing value systems, but the end result is that competent communicators anywhere employ a wide range of linguistic styles. These styles, which are tied to certain situations and activities, are usually called 'registers' and can range from the very formal to the very casual. Registers are usually indicators of interpersonal relationships, status and power. Thus we find that there are different but appropriate registers operating in talk between, for example, teachers and pupils, doctors and patients, customers and shop assistants. Social settings call for varied registers, and people switch styles as they move between homes, schools, shops, factories, offices and so on.

Learning and teaching suggestion

• Set up telephones in your various role-play areas, as well as providing pretend mobile phones for the outside and inside environments. Attempt to record some of the children's conversations (video/audio). How do young children 'create' their non-existent language partner? What kinds of topics and issues occur in these 'conversations'? Add your observations to the children's individual records of progress in speaking and listening (see Gillen and Hall, 2001).

Among our repertoires of registers all of us will be able to call on some elements of that extremely informal style known as slang. On the whole, slang tends to rely on a special range of vocabulary, for example, 'cool' and 'laid back' from the world of jazz. Slang is usually closely tied to a place and a lifestyle, and has often been associated with racy street language.

Slang is ephemeral and easily dates overenthusiastic users who fail to move with the times. We probably cringe now at an exclamation like 'gosh' but some slang does enter the fairly permanent stock of the language. Perhaps this status has been achieved by such terms as 'cool', 'super', 'OK', 'sleaze' and 'wally'. Slang is not a modern deviation from some golden age of language – it has always been used and recorded by historians, diarists, novelists and amateur and professional linguists. Furthermore, it is ordinary evidence of the vitality and creativity of language in daily use. Just as we delight in the linguistic inventiveness of very young children, we can savour in slang the language play of adults, particularly young adults. Slang is often richest and most diverse in youth subcultures.

There is a darker side to slang: it has always been used to mask activities involving crime and violence. When slang is a secret criminal language it is called '*argot*', and many claim that one of the most famous slang dialects, Cockney, began as an argot used by London's criminal underworld. The traditional use of Cockney rhyming slang requires reference to just the non-rhyming half of the word pair. Thus, only those in the know would understand the intended meaning of 'Wash your boat and put your titfer on. We'll 'ave a butchers at me old China'. Cockney is now more accurately described as a social-class dialect rather than an argot or a slang.

One other language register frequently confused with slang is jargon. Again, most of us have some jargon in our repertoires and we use it appropriately. There are hints of criticism and disapproval in most references to jargon but it can be a useful linguistic tool. Jargon tends to come into a language as new technologies, occupations and pastimes enter and permeate the society. Like slang, jargon is a source of enrichment and creative usage, and we would all be linguistically diminished by the loss of some contributions from space exploration, information and communication technology, science, medicine and the media, to name but a few sources.

The jargon of occupations and professions also fulfils a very positive role. 'Talking shop' enables us to communicate efficiently and accurately with our colleagues and can be absolutely vital in the context of hospital operating theatres, airport control towers and the factory floor. It is just as important, if a little less dramatic, in educational settings when we talk of 'fours in Reception', 'special educational needs children', 'concrete experiences' or 'emergent writing'. There is, however, a negative side to jargon and this probably gives it a bad name. When jargon is persistently used outside the appropriate setting in which it makes good sense, it functions as a barrier to exclude outsiders. 'Talking shop' then becomes a way of intentionally limiting communication to a chosen few. Although it certainly enhances their sense of group solidarity, it tends to infuriate outsiders.

Summary

- Language variety is reflected in the different languages of the world but it is also a feature within apparently uniform language communities.

- Two major aspects of variety within a language are accent and dialect. Accent refers solely to differences in pronunciation – the sounds of a spoken language. Dialect is a variety of a language with distinctive variations in syntax and vocabulary, as well as pronunciation.

- Standard English is the high-status dialect of English that is used in the written form of the language. It is also used widely in business and professional circles, the media, education and the teaching of English as a foreign language. Standard English dialect may be spoken with any accent.

- Received Pronunciation is a prestigious non-regional accent associated with higher education and, traditionally, the private school system in the UK and Oxford and Cambridge universities (Oxbridge).

- Variety is also found in every individual's linguistic repertoire because we all switch registers, changing the degrees of formality in our language, according to the social context. Individuals use a variety of other forms, including other dialects, slang and jargon. We all develop a unique idiolect that makes our voices and language styles instantly recognizable.

Power and influence

The old advertising slogan, 'how to win friends and influence people', is still a useful tool in the hands of those who take advantage of the networks of power and influence that permeate language use in Britain. Think of the so-called language teachers who still advertise their services in the pages of daily newspapers, for example, 'Why Are You Shamed By Your Mistakes In English?' The private speech teachers and the steady output of magazine articles, books and DVDs that claim to be able to increase our word power, our influence over others and our business and social success, are evidence of the power of social judgements about language.

With respect to children and education, it is clear that one of the 'good things' families buy when they pay for their children's education in private schools is fluency in 'good English'. Evaluative judgements of this kind about English have little place in purely linguistic descriptions of the many varieties of English. However, British people do understand and use such phrases as 'good English' or 'talking properly', and they know that these expressions refer to SE spoken with an RP accent, although not necessarily a posh or affected form. The decent education suggested by the consistent use of RP and spoken SE is often synonymous with private schooling or a state schooling topped off with an Oxbridge degree. These comments may sound like unfounded generalizations, but there is something to be said for accepting the existence of linguistic prejudices, noting their power, and evolving clear and principled responses to their influence.

Although the prescriptive tradition in linguistics has been weakened (if not fully replaced) by a more scientific descriptive approach (see Chapter 1), its influence in the social and cultural spheres has not diminished. Yet it is in the daily use of spoken and written language throughout society and in many influential institutions that people's life chances may be deeply affected. It is the case that people may still fail to obtain jobs, accommodation or even places in higher education because the sounds of their accents and the dialects they use trigger in others immediate reactions that equate some voices with stupidity, dishonesty, lawlessness, poverty and the general condemnation expressed as 'common'. The fact that these judgements are direct reflections of power and status, and not inherent in accents and dialects as such, is obvious because they only occur when the weaker partner, the applicant, speaks a low-status language variety. However, if you have become a successful employer, property owner or college principal you can be as broadly Cockney or Glaswegian as you choose, within the limits of intelligibility. This now happens in the broadcast media where the whole irrationality of it becomes obvious. A very popular and highly paid chat-show host, business entrepreneur or television chef can use a low-status, south or east London accent and dialect, but a female newsreader with a Scottish accent speaking SE is subjected to abusive and complaining letters!

Most people cope with these situations by becoming bi-dialectal in their professional and personal lives and making the necessary switches according to the current state of the particular power game in which they find themselves. This means that if we are not native speakers of SE dialect, we may choose to add it to our spoken repertoire and use it in those situations where our home dialect may put us at some social, political or cultural disadvantage. In practice this is what many of us do, but some sociolinguists would deplore this on ideological grounds and urge us to set about changing the attitudes of society. In the long term this may well be the aim of all informed and concerned linguists, academics, lawyers, politicians, employers and so forth. But early years practitioners have a professional commitment to the young children who are in schools and group settings now. We not only plan for the futures of all our children, we must also have a response and a policy for next Monday morning. It is for this reason that the role of the SE dialect in care and education must be clarified.

Standard English

As long ago as 1988 the National Curriculum English Working Group set out some perceptive general principles for educational policies on Standard English (DES, 1988: 13–16), emphasizing the sensitive nature of the issues. These are still worth consideration in the early decades of the twenty-first century.

- Access to SE: children have an undoubted entitlement to learn to use the standard form. This argument rests on the role of the standard variety as the common and shared communicative and cultural basis of British society, particularly in its public, commercial, industrial, professional and educational spheres. The role of SE extends beyond the UK and its competent users have automatic access to a world language.
- Standard English must be learnt and taught in ways that do not denigrate the non-standard dialects spoken by many children and adults. Educators need to be aware of the powerful symbolic and emotional charge non-standard dialects carry. They also need to recognize the damaging impact on children, their families and their communities of a too premature or forceful imposition of SE in group settings and schools. Early childhood educators need to be particularly sensitive to the confusion, distress and lack of progress an excessive zeal for standard forms in talking and writing may produce. Much older children can choose if, when, and how they will use SE in their lives, because they are able to judge its limitations and its power and set it alongside their home dialects as yet another option. Very young children are emotionally and socially vulnerable, and experience language forms as intimately bound up with the people who use them. At its most positive, this is revealed when they are playing and dramatizing roles and they slip easily into talking as a posh or pompous person, or even imitate the ways in which their carers and teachers tell stories or deliver reprimands. An amazing command of SE is frequently demonstrated on these occasions!
- Teaching SE in schools is most fruitfully and positively focused on the

teaching of the written form. Standard English is the language of non-regional public communication, and children need to be able to communicate and have control over their lives beyond the limits of family and local culture. This aspect of political and democratic power may be years away from small children in playgroups, children's centres, nurseries and primary schools, but the foundations of literacy are laid in the early years. We all learn a new form of the language when we begin to read and write, and this gives a sensible, shared focus for literacy in the early years. The written SE dialect can be taught well without undermining children's pride and involvement in the personal and cultural worlds of family, faith and race. Indeed, families and local communities look to schools to advance their children's literacy; they also teach them many things about reading and writing themselves and they take a pride in their children's early mastery of literacy.

If insisting on the use of spoken SE at all times can be a dangerous game, how much more so is rash interference with accents. Regional and class accents are intimately bound up with early infancy, personal identity and community. Furthermore, the complexities of phonology are such that any artificially imposed changes may be totally negative in their effects. We choose to vary our accents, we choose to sound like the people we admire or wish to be associated with and, conversely, we can use our accents as clear markers of resistance or dissent. It has already been noted that accents are often the focus for extraordinary and instant sets of prejudices, assumptions and aesthetic judgements. Nowhere is this more so than when the accent indicates foreign origins or non-British varieties of English. The totally unpleasant nature of these discriminations can be appreciated if we contrast the generally positive status accorded to some European accents, for example, French or Spanish, with responses to Asian or Chinese accents. Racism and prejudice are often linked with ignorance, fear and competition for limited resources such as wealth, good housing and education. In the USA, a Spanish accent is frequently linked with deprivation of all these good things and provokes some very negative responses. This is in marked contrast to positive British feelings about Spanish accents: they can evoke the passionate Latin temperament, images of cities like Seville and Granada, as well as the glorious Iberian climate! The implications are clear: people's initial responses to each other are strongly influenced by the feelings, assumptions, experiences and ideas they and their cultural group attach to certain dialects and accents.

Learning and teaching suggestions

- Create a group/class/setting dialect inventory by listing all the dialects known and used by the children and adults. Try to discover where they come from and also start to investigate the nature of accents (draw on the children's television viewing for a wider range of dialect and accent experiences).
- Choose a range of stories, poems, rhymes and songs which use a range of dialects and accents (including both the familiar and some new to the

children). Listen to nursery rhymes, poetry and stories spoken in a variety of dialects and accents (on CDs and DVDs).

Language and gender

The complicated issues of discrimination and bias have also been linked with language and gender studies in recent years. It has long been known that in many cultures there are differences in the language forms used by women and men. In English language cultures and in the West generally, these differences are stylistic tendencies rather than clear language varieties. The impression has been that women spoke 'nicely' in their social contacts, even if they were not speakers of high-status varieties by regional or social-class origin. In the recent past this impression was further reinforced by the general absence of swear words and taboo references in women's habitual talk.

Some observations of women's talk also noted a greater use of tentative and deferential forms: 'If you don't mind … ?' 'Would you like to … ?' 'Is it alright if … ?' But these tendencies are fairly general and they can be true of the weak, the insecure and the dominated of either sex. The language forms mainly associated with women can be seen as the appropriate deferential responses of any powerless group. Until recently it appeared that women regularly used these subservient forms rather than resisting by exaggerating their non-standard and low-status varieties, or choosing positive and even aggressive language. The reasons for this are not linguistic but reflect social training and habitual roles. Women appear to be very status conscious: they tend to 'set a good example' to the children they are raising. Furthermore, their own earlier socialization may have emphasized that low-status, aggressive or rude language is masculine and tough. However, this state of linguistic affairs has changed dramatically and the tendencies mentioned here are disappearing rapidly, particularly among women who are employed and the younger generations of women and girls. This points to the really important factor: language primarily reflects and also emerges out of social practices and situations, not gender differences.

Gender issues are also very obvious in the linguistic area of word choices in texts and the conventional and unthinking use of the written language system. These issues have particular significance in education and the teaching of literacy, and should be the focus of a continuous, sensible and sensitive consciousness-raising approach. This applies to apparently unintentional bias as well as to specifically sexist usage. The matters to be addressed have received considerable attention in recent years but should still be in the forefront of the concerns of thoughtful language users, professional carers and educators. Careless and frequent references to 'mankind' or 'the history of man' may not be as sex-neutral as is traditionally claimed, particularly for young and unsophisticated early readers, viewers and listeners. Also, do we need to be made a little uncomfortable about always automatically writing 'men and women' rather than 'women and men'? Some real changes in awareness are beginning to affect the use of such terms as chairman, postman and paper boy, but spoken and written references to barristers, consultants and professors often assume the appropriateness of the male pronoun, without first verifying the gender of the individual.

The use of the allegedly neutral male personal pronoun in the written forms has now been questioned so much that authors have to provide a gender disclaimer. But is this good enough? Sensitive usage adopts the plural 'they' whenever possible, or carefully specifies her or him, she or he. The books used in early years settings and schools carry considerable status and approval, so great care needs to be exercised over the messages texts and images carry about all forms of discrimination. With respect to gender, educators are now very much aware of the attitudes conveyed by narratives, photographs and illustrations. There has been a long tradition of reading primers that featured boys helping fathers service the car while girls helped mothers to wash dishes and make beds. Such obvious stereotypes are easily identified in reading books, but other textbooks and teaching materials that use drawings, photographs and apparatus need to be examined carefully. We must always ask, 'Where are the women and girls? What are they doing and saying?' and, 'Are the boys engaged in literacy activities?' Admittedly, the use of computers in early years settings and schools has drawn more boys into literacy activities (Figure 2.1) but this may sometimes reduce the contact girls have with information and communication technology (ICT).

Figure 2.1 **Josh (4 years 6 months) and his friends at the computer**

Schools, early years settings and individual practitioners also have to deal with attitudes that mainly associate art, literacy, books and sensitive or caring responses with girls and women, while such areas as mathematics, science, technology, physical courage and boisterousness are the prerogative of men and boys. These attitudes or prejudices are often deeply rooted in certain social classes and ethnic groups, and will only be modified by a long process of reasoned challenges, caring attitudes and continuous talk between schools, families and their communities. Policies and provision in early years settings should continue to raise gender awareness and challenge practices and stereotypes that devalue girls and restrict the literacy achievements of boys. Gender bias, like many other prejudices, is not primarily a language problem: language reflects and perpetuates existing social attitudes.

Summary

- The topic of language variety is bound up with sociocultural values and judgements about people as much as about identifiable linguistic features. Language variety reflects individual and group identity and loyalties, because it originates in geographical regions and close-knit communities.
- The SE dialect and the RP accent are high status because of their links with education, wealth and power in British society.
- Children have an entitlement to learn to use SE, particularly in the formal written mode, because it gives them access to national and international culture, education, democratic autonomy and employment.
- The teaching of SE in schools must respect children's home dialects and be sensitive to the social and developmental needs of young children.
- Language and gender studies highlight the links between power and language use in a community. It is obvious that submissive female language is not genetically ordained – it was the language of the insecure and dominated.
- In educational contexts great care must be given to avoiding written and spoken language forms that appear to marginalize or ignore girls and women and limit the literacy activities and aspirations of boys.

Language change

Human languages are in a constant state of change. Most of us are fairly sensitive to the changes that have occurred in our own first language lifetimes: we are aware of subtle differences in the language of old films and we may even sense that our grandparents' generation talk and use written language differently. In the case of English literature, we see and hear remarkable changes in Chaucer's, Shakespeare's and Pinter's language. Historical linguistics has always studied languages as they change over generations and centuries, but this perspective has now shifted to an interest in studying the subtle, ongoing processes of change in progress in contemporary language communities.

Change in language is mainly associated with the vocabulary and pronunciation of the spoken form because these features are so easily noticed; however, change affects other aspects of a language, such as semantics and syntax. Some linguists would claim that individual language-learning experiences and histories are a part of language change and modification. The misunderstandings and mishearings of infants in a language community are a source of variations that are sometimes retained in families and groups. Most of the non-standard sound patterns (past tenses and plurals or misunderstood word meanings) are gradually corrected but, in certain social situations, mature fluent speakers may switch to a lisped pronunciation, a 'foreign' accent, a babyish word or an ungrammatical plural or word order. Families frequently preserve and continue to use some expressive features of their children's first language experiments, for example, 'mapple' (apple), 'chimps' (shrimps) and 'annadent' (accident). But these are very minor features of change and more closely related to human linguistic playfulness and social sensitivity than the kinds of changes that affect a whole language community.

Major sources of language change

New technologies

The arrival of new inventions and the influences of new forms of mass communication lead to a sudden increase in the numbers of new words in a language. The effect in terms of vocabulary is particularly noticeable with respect to nouns and verbs. But words are not mere labels and the new terminologies provide ways of thinking about and using the new concepts involved in areas as diverse as ICT, psychoanalysis, space technology, medicine, television, environmental issues and so on. These words and concepts provide metaphors that pervade our language and our thinking (Figure 2.2).

It is interesting to note the everyday occurrence of terms that already distance us from our parents' and grandparents' generations, for example: 'psychosomatic', 'countdown', 'lift off', 'mobile', 'texting', 'click', 'mouse', 'download', 'the remote', 'software', 'cloning', 'green', 'credit crunch', 'global warming'. Perhaps the early twenty-first century will come to be 'dated' by all the language associated with emails, mobile/cell phones, iPods, interactive whiteboards and text-messaging systems. This is a reminder that languages are living and changing (Aitchison, 2001; Crystal, 2008): they are not as rigid, sacred or eternally true and perfect as is sometimes suggested by some commentators, policy-makers and textbooks.

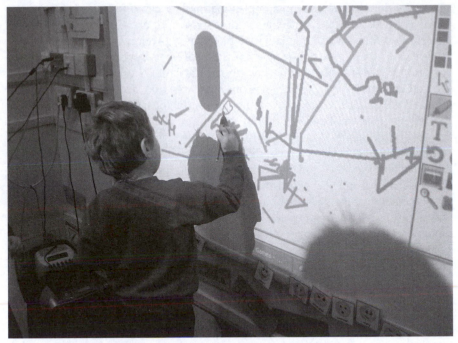

Figure 2.2   **Mark-making with new technologies (4 years)**

Group loyalties

The idea that languages are responsive to and shaped by the needs of their speakers brings us to a consideration of group identity as a source of language change. Within a single language community (although the concept of 'single' will have to be greatly modified in the next section), the various social, economic and regional groups or classes use varieties of the main language. These varieties are the dialects discussed earlier, and their distinctive grammatical forms and vocabularies are the means by which their speakers assert and maintain their group loyalties and identities. Group dialects also include such specialized registers as argots and slang and some of their variations in syntax and lexis also enter the general usage of the larger language community. Clearly, it does not do to become too solemn about careless slang ruining the language: after all, 'pram', 'buggy' and 'car' are today's standard words but they were slang only a few generations ago.

Group solidarity also provides us with good evidence for the changes in phonology that occur in a language. The subtle changes and value judgements associated with accents are very interesting in that they reveal two different and opposed tendencies. Accent change in a language community can be said, in a social-class sense, to pull two ways. First, there is the more generally known tendency for speakers with a low-status accent to shift closer to standard or high-status features of pronunciation when putting on a 'telephone voice', or talking to speakers with a 'superior' accent. This suggests that it is a rather conscious decision and such examples may reflect a bid for prestige in certain social contexts, or even a general admiration and envy of the lifestyle and affluence of those who habitually use high-status pronunciation patterns.

However, there are instances when the process is reversed and the change is from the high-prestige to the low-prestige accent. The paradox here is that, for certain social and cultural reasons, a low-status accent can become so admired and indicative of success that people want to imitate it. In the 1960s the influence of the Beatles elevated the Scouse dialect and accent to a status they have never quite lost. More recently, highly educated middle-class youngsters were integrating Cockney-style expressions into their speech, saying such things as 'get it sorted' and 'I was gutted'. Young people have also been using terms derived from Black British English, such as 'man', 'sister', 'brother' and, for absolute approval, 'it's da bomb'! The point of the paradox is that high and low status, as used to refer to accents and dialects, are sociocultural value judgements and subject to change and fashion, as are all tastes and values.

Historical and political developments

Generally, language changes caused by large-scale historical and political developments are greater and more dramatic than vowel shifts and accent switching. Imperial conquest and trade have been the major sources of changes and of enrichment in the English language. It is important to note that this is not just a matter of a few new words or borrowings, although much of Britain's imperial and trading past is preserved in such everyday words as 'tomato' and 'cocoa' (Aztec), 'pundit' and 'verandah' (Hindi), 'sofa' (Arabic), 'caravan' (Persian) and 'khaki' (Urdu). Borrowed words for particular items are easily and conveniently assimilated into a language and sometimes a whole area of cultural experience becomes dominated by a foreign tongue. Thus French is the traditional language of much European cooking and Italian is still used in musical notation.

The earlier history of the English language can also be traced in many words used and seen daily. Thus Latin, the language of the Church, the Court and the Law in the distant past, is still with us in such modern forms as 'referendum', 'exit', 'discipline' and 'language'. However, the accidents of history and politics have produced changes in language that go beyond the borrowing or retention of isolated words and phrases. New and distinctive varieties of English have evolved under the pressures of conquest, trade and basic survival. These varieties are known as *pidgins* and *creoles*.

Pidgins and creoles

Many misunderstandings surround pidgin or creole language forms: they are frequently condemned as broken, primitive or bad language. Once again, these pejorative terms are really social judgements and prejudices about the status and lives of the people who use these languages. The linguistic facts are more interesting and more complex. Pidgins develop under conditions of conquest and foreign domination. When two language communities and cultures are thrown together some form of basic language for trade and daily survival must be evolved. The simplified language that emerges is usually based on combining features of the new dominant language (sometimes English, Spanish or French) with vocabulary from indigenous languages in use in the area.

DEFINITION: A pidgin is no one's native language. A pidgin has limited vocabulary, reduced rules of grammar, a narrow range of functions and it is often temporary or short-lived.

Once a pidgin is used extensively, groups of speakers begin to elaborate its simple grammar and vocabulary because they are using it to meet needs and circumstances more complex than simple trading and survival. At this stage the pidgin is on its way to becoming a creole. A creole has a crucial definition: it is a pidgin that has become a genuine first language. It has developed the potential to meet the full range of human language needs, including children's early socialization.

DEFINITION: A creole has developed from a pidgin to become the mother tongue of a community. It has an expanded vocabulary, complex rules of grammar and satisfies an increasing range of functions.

Freezing languages

The desire to stop, or control, language change is found at national and at individual level. It seems that the idea of change in languages is deeply unsettling and provokes reactions whose strength and irrationality confirm that our sense of identity and personal worth is partly rooted in our language. Many of those who complain about language change are middle-aged or older, suggesting a general anxiety about change associated with growing old.

The desire to freeze language at a precise point in time persists and is even tackled nationally in some countries by establishing academies and committees to regulate the language. This has very little effect, particularly on the spoken forms, because language is constantly evolving to meet the needs of its speakers. Language change is never random and chaotic – basic patterns of syntax and phonology are very stable and only certain features alter in predictable ways. The addition of new words and new phrases is not a recipe for confusion: change is balanced by powerful and influential pressures for maintenance and stability. Among these stabilizing influences are the serious media, the formal education system, group pride, loyalty and identity. Fear of language change frequently masquerades as an attempt to protect and preserve the linguistic inheritance, but the fact remains that a language can only die with its last speaker. This process of language death (Crystal, 2000) appears to be accelerating and is driven by changes in worldwide communications, trade, education and traditional occupations, but it is not a sign of linguistic ill-health. Language change is evidence of growth and vitality.

Summary

- Human languages are in a constant state of change. Change can affect the areas of syntax, phonology, semantics and lexis.
- The major sources of change are new inventions and technologies, historical and political changes, and group identity and loyalty.
- The areas of vocabulary and the related conceptual ways of thinking are particularly enriched by new inventions and discoveries, and by historical and political changes.
- Historical and political changes and notions of group identity have led to the creation of new languages through the evolution of pidgins and creoles.
- Language change, like many other changes in life, can arouse deep feelings of anxiety and danger. But change may be seen as evidence of the vitality and growth of a language.

Multilingualism

Many individuals living in supposedly homogeneous monolingual societies use more than one language. Patterns of individual movement and settlement between different countries, as well as larger-scale group emigration caused by economic, political, religious and racial pressures mean that, in reality, true monolingual communities are exceptional. This fact comes as a surprise to many monolinguals in Britain, particularly because they speak what is fast becoming the acknowledged world language. But many British citizens are bilingual, using English and a different first language of their family's origin. This family language may be Urdu, Vietnamese, Hindi, Greek, Turkish, Cantonese, Italian, Polish or Arabic. The list could be extended but it is representative of the languages used by children in early years settings and schools in British towns and cities.

Many individuals and families operate more than two languages and can themselves be considered multilingual. It is not uncommon for children to grow up in families where three languages are in active use, including a variety of written forms, and a fourth may be latent but surfaces in songs, rhymes, old tales and memories. This is not just a hypothetical example but a summary of the linguistic home environment of my eldest grandchildren, who also learnt Welsh in school (Engel and Whitehead, 1993).

Learning and teaching suggestions

• With the help of families and community members, create notices in several scripts and languages for the inside and outside play and learning areas.

• Create group/class/setting language inventories by listing all the languages known by children and adults (include examples even if only one or two words are known). As appropriate, explore the use of these languages outside the setting and any knowledge of their societies and countries of origin. Explore any ability to write various scripts and languages among children, parents and practitioners. Involve the families and the community in displaying, discussing and updating the inventory.

Aspects of bilingualism

Definitions

Given the facts of multilingualism in the world, it is not surprising that the definitions of bilingualism for any individual or group are complex and need to be expressed with great flexibility. The definitions should attempt to reflect something of the degrees of competence in two languages, the manner and situations in which they are acquired and used, and whether competence is in the spoken forms only or includes degrees of literacy. Because of these dimensions of complexity, it is now usual for linguists to describe the bilingualism of individuals in terms of a continuum. A speaker's range of bilingual skills can be plotted with reference to oracy and literacy and the fluctuations attributable to age and circumstances. Thus it is possible for individuals to be anywhere between an ideal of complete fluency and literacy in both languages, and simply possessing dormant or very limited understanding of a second language.

Language mixing

Degrees of interchangeability and fluency in thinking, speaking, reading and writing with two languages are partly reflected in the 'language switching' and 'language mixing' typical of many bilinguals, particularly when they are speaking. 'Mixing' tends to be used to describe the combining of words and phrases from both languages in a single utterance, often by young bilingual children who are in the process of learning to separate their two languages. This should not, however, be equated with random muddle or inadequacy. Some very young infants appear to be associating one language with a particular person, activity or situation on a very regular and systematic basis. In the first two or three years of life, the use of particular words from a second language might on occasions be preferred because of their ease of articulation, particularly if the equivalents in the dominant language are phonologically more complex.

Language switching

This is frequent and usual among older and more fluent bilinguals and can occur at many points in utterances, readings and conversations. Sometimes words are switched, sometimes sentences and sometimes phrases within sentences – the permutations are probably infinite. Linguists explain these switches in terms of several possibilities: simple tiredness and distraction, the lack of a word or concept in one language, a sign of group solidarity and identity, a device to exclude outsiders, a means of emphasis and clarification or an association of certain activities and concepts with one language and culture only. The possibilities are many and complex and emphasize that language switching by bilinguals can be a powerful and subtle tool. There is no linguistic support for the misinformed assumption that this switching is a symptom of inadequate and confused understanding of either or both languages.

'Bucket' myth

Among monolinguals there are considerable misunderstandings about the nature of bilingualism and a readiness to associate it with problems and difficulties in personal, national and educational life. The most pervasive belief implies that the brain must be like a bucket, with a limited capacity for only so much language. To have it full of one language, that is, to be monolingual, must be the natural and ideal linguistic state. To have a second language involves an automatic reduction of the available brain capacity for either language. These naive misconceptions are mainly based on ignorance of how language develops in response to the experiences and the needs of individuals in communities. Such beliefs can, however, permeate and undermine educational policies and strategies for bilingualism and expose children to the damaging effects of institutionalized low expectations.

Bilingual development

Despite all the myths and popular misgivings about the brain's limited language capacity and its tendency for linguistic muddle, many children acquire two languages from birth and are bilinguals on entry to early years group settings and schools. Distinct stages of development can be identified in this process of *simultaneous acquisition* (Crystal, 1997: 363). Initially, the infant acquires a set of words, as in monolingual first language learning, but the words are from both languages. Sentences of two or more grammatical elements, when they appear, contain a mixture of words from both languages. This only lasts a short period of time and the child's increasing vocabulary in each language leads to a growing capacity for translation between the languages. Finally, around the fourth year, the different sets of grammatical rules are separated out (before this happens, one set of grammatical rules seems to be used for both languages). Young bilinguals reveal their awareness that their languages are different in the choices they make about with whom to use a particular language, as well as where and when each language is appropriate. Such subtle social and linguistic competencies are a far cry from muddle and confusion, and they are demonstrated by children who acquire their two or more languages successively.

Successive bilingualism is usually defined as occurring after the age of 3 and has, therefore, tended to be developed by children when they attend nurseries and primary schools. It is also stimulated by being old enough to play outside the home and of course it occurs among children whose families move between countries and linguistic communities. One positive advantage of successive bilingualism is the fact that the child has already learnt one language and has some general skill in handling people, the environment and linguistic concepts. Young successive bilinguals are also readily engaged in play activities (Figure 2.3) and playful language that supports second language learning linked with meaningful activities and key persons (Ruby et al. 2007). When bilinguals are acquiring other languages they may use a strategy of 'bridge-building' to get from a known language to a new language. This often involves using words from the new language, but they are organized by the grammatical patterns of the securely known language. This is a highly skilled temporary solution called 'inter-language' (Selinker, 1992). Very young bilinguals are also less likely to be self-conscious or upset about trying other language forms and pronunciations. Thus, they quickly get to sound like native speakers.

Figure 2.3   **Playful activities for a young bilingual (24 months): writing down a phone message**

Bilingual Britain

The dangers of accepting the general view that bilingualism is a problem or an abnormality are bad enough, but they are also added to by unthinking prejudices about certain languages. To be bilingual in French/English, German/English or Swedish/English can be considered a social and cultural gain in some circles. In Britain there is one nationally established precedent for the provision of a full education service through the medium of a language other than English. This is, of course, the use of Welsh as a first or second language in schools in Wales. However, these positive images of bilingualism do not, it seems, always extend to speakers of Bengali/English, Urdu/English or Turkish/English. This should force us to think about the social attitudes that so sharply differentiate some European languages from languages associated with old imperialism and exploitation.

Another strand in the web of irrational fears and attitudes surrounding these specific examples of bilingualism is a deep anxiety about all things foreign and strange. This dormant xenophobia about other races, religions and traditions sometimes emerges as a pseudo-linguistic fear for the survival of English language and traditional culture, particularly in areas of the country with noticeable minority groups and communities. This can have an immediate and damaging impact on local group settings and schools. Fear of a loss of linguistic and cultural dominance is frequently expressed in terms of objections to educational policies concerned with anti-racism, equal opportunities and bilingual instruction in schools.

Learning and teaching suggestions

- Invite families to bring into the setting examples of home language materials and literacy activities they share with their children. Ask the families to help you make these kinds of materials freely available in the setting.
- Organize regular 'teach ourselves another language' days. Make it a self-help effort with tutoring by child and adult speakers of different languages. This may be limited to greetings, counting, songs and rhymes, but it can be enriched by shopping, cooking and eating foods from the different language communities.

Educational policies

Educational policies for multilingualism and first language support teaching for young bilinguals in early years settings and schools highlight a dilemma that may not be peculiar to Britain, but is certainly aggravated by its traditional insularity, monolingual assumptions and linguistic status as the source of a major world language. Most children, whatever their degrees of bilingualism and multilingualism, will be cared for and taught for most of their educational careers by monolingual practitioners. The temptation to pressure very young children into being English speakers first and foremost is strong, but this may act against the children's best interests, both as learners and as English speakers. There is a general agreement among many linguists, as well as experienced and successful bilinguals, that some considerable element of first language support in early years care and education settings is highly desirable.

The reasons for this are:

- children's learning and cognitive development increasingly depend on the confident use of a human language that satisfies their personal needs for thinking and planning, as well as structuring their social and cultural inter-actions with others
- children's self-esteem and confidence, as well as their linguistic and cultural identity, may be undermined if they do not encounter their first language in some significant areas of early years care and educational provision
- if young children's languages are not respected and used in early years settings and school contexts, there is a danger that monolingual practitioners may unconsciously retain damaging lowered expectations and attitudes towards the development and achievements of young potential bilinguals.

Important as these justifications for first language support are, we do have to recognize that they are complicated by the nature of contemporary multilingualism. In most town and city early years children's centres, playgroups, nurseries and schools there are usually several minority languages and the clear identification of one or two dominant tongues is not easy. However, modern approaches to multicultural education emphasize the richness of the contributions linguistic and cultural diversity can make to the ethos and the curriculum of a group setting. There is also much to be said in cognitive and affective terms for putting children into the roles of language teachers and researchers for part of their day. That is to say, we can encourage them to share, investigate and demonstrate their knowledge of other languages. And, by extension, we can invite children's families into our schools, groups and classes to share with us their daily experiences of moving between the language worlds of the wider community and their homes. A determination to bring the children's languages and cultural lives into care and education settings may eventually help to combat the racism that afflicts many of our communities. Such an approach might also counter the misguided belief that there is something deficient or inadequate in languages and writing systems from distant countries.

Summary

- Multilingualism is the norm in many language communities: patterns of migration caused by economic and political pressures mean that truly monolingual communities are rare.

- Individuals are often bilingual although they, too, can be multilingual. Definitions of bilingualism need to reflect a range of degrees of competence in both spoken and written forms.

- Young bilingual children may use two languages from birth. This is simultaneous bilingualism. Alternatively, they may acquire their second languages after the age of 3 in a process known as successive bilingualism.

- The mixing of languages and the switching of languages are powerful linguistic tools for the bilingual. These skills should not be misguidedly attributed to inadequate and partial language learning.

- Educational policies for an inclusive society need to include provision for first language support for very young bilinguals in early years group settings and schools.

- Policies also need to avoid implicit notions of compensating for, or lessening the significant use of, children's languages other than English as soon as possible in early years settings and schools.

⚬━ Key terms

Accent: this refers to pronunciation – the sound of the language as it is spoken by an individual or a group. There are regional, social class and educational accents.

Bilingual: this refers to varying degrees of fluency and/or literacy in two languages. 'Bilingual' can refer to an individual or a community.

Dialect: this is a variety of a language, including distinctive vocabulary and syntax.

Idiolect: an individual's unique linguistic style.

Jargon: a specialist variety of a language, often associated with professions and occupations, or derived from areas of knowledge like science, technology and the arts.

Multilingual: this refers to degrees of fluency and/or literacy in several languages (in an individual or a community).

Received Pronunciation (RP): a prestigious British accent associated with upper-class influence and power, university education (Oxbridge) and private schooling.

Register: this refers to the repertoire of appropriate styles of language we all use for different social settings and occasions.

Slang: this is an informal language style and uses a distinctive range of vocabulary and grammatical forms particular to the 'in crowd'.

Standard English (SE): this is the 'norm' or standard dialect for communicating in English in public, educational, professional and commercial settings. There are a number of varieties of SE in Britain and other English-speaking societies.

Further reading

Aitchison, J. (2001) *Language Change: Progress or Decay?* 3rd edn. Cambridge: Cambridge University Press.

Baker, C. (1996) *Foundations of Bilingual Education and Bilingualism*. Clevedon: Multilingual Matters.

Crystal, D. (1998) *Language Play*. Harmondsworth: Penguin.

Crystal, D. (2000) *Language Death*. Cambridge: Cambridge University Press.

Crystal, D. (2004) *The Stories of English*. London: Penguin Books.

Drury, R. (2007) *Young Bilingual Learners at Home and School: Researching Multilingual Voices*. Stoke-on-Trent: Trentham Books.

Engel, D.M. and Whitehead, M.R. (1996) 'Which English? Standard English and language variety: some educational perspectives', *English in Education*, 30(1): 36–49.

Siraj-Blatchford, I. and Clarke, P. (2000) *Supporting Identity, Diversity and Language in the Early Years*. Buckingham: Open University Press.

| CHAPTER 3 |

PSYCHOLINGUISTICS: EARLY LANGUAGE ACQUISITION

This chapter includes:

- early language acquisition
- stages in speech and language development
- understanding sounds and meanings
- language functions and first words.

Psycholinguistics can be defined as the shared area of study of psychologists and linguists. This indicates that issues of speech and language (the concerns of the linguists) and of mental processes and learning (the concerns of the psychologists) will be involved in any introduction to psycholinguistics. The big questions of psycholinguistics are:

- How do we learn to understand and produce our first language or languages?
- What is the nature of the relationship between language and thought?

This chapter is concerned with early language acquisition, while the following chapter reviews the complex relationship between language, thought and culture, and the nature of concepts and words. One important idea about the development of language that must be grasped and understood is that we are concerned with two things – not simply speech but a language system. This relates back to the earlier references to *langue* and *parole*, or language and speech, discussed in Chapter 1 (Saussure's linguistics). So it is not surprising that studies in psycholinguistics frequently refer to the mind, the nature of thinking and ways of understanding the world.

Early language acquisition

Changing views

Explanations of early language acquisition changed dramatically in the twentieth century, particularly in the decades following the 1950s. The differing views and theoretical positions are best thought of as useful pieces added to a still incomplete puzzle. All have in their time answered some questions about processes in early language acquisition and revealed some developmental characteristics. In very general terms, the different views about language acquisition are the products of different schools of psychology and we can usefully distinguish between:

- behaviourist
- nativist
- cognitive
- social interactionist.

Behaviourist approaches

Behaviourist approaches dominated nineteenth- and even twentieth-century psychology and produced theories of learning often based on studies of animal behaviour and laboratory experiments. There is a tendency for such work to explain learning as the imitation of models and small segments of behaviour. The process of learning (whether it be of language or of anything else) is seen as being shaped and controlled from outside the learner by a process of reinforcement; that is, the correct responses are rewarded and the wrong ones are ignored or penalized in other ways. On the surface it would seem that behaviourist accounts of early language learning explain the useful social phrases and instructions very young infants are apparently imitating when they first start saying such things as 'bye-bye', 'ta' or 'up'. It is also obvious that very positive reinforcement is significant in early language acquisition. Adults and older children are immensely enthusiastic and supportive of babies as they begin to produce speech-like sounds and words. However, closer observations and reflections on the behaviour of infants and adults indicate that there are serious limitations to the traditional behaviourist view.

Apart from a few obviously imitated words and expressions, infants do not speak and use language in the same ways as older children and adults. Their first combinations of two or more words are very unusual and could not have been imitated. The child-language literature is full of examples: 'He's keying the door' (Clark, 1982: 402). We should, of course, bear in mind that imitation may be significant at different stages in acquisition: it may have some part to play in extending vocabulary in the pre-school and early school years, as well as helping considerably with the control and practising of the sound system, or phonology, of a language. The issue of reinforcement is also complicated because, at first, adults enthusiastically reward and support a child's every attempt to speak – even if the utterance is grossly mispronounced, socially inappropriate or untrue. Indeed, it often seems that the adults are the ones who delight in imitating the child in these early stages. The rule adults appear to be following is, respond with excessive enthusiasm and delight to anything the child tries to say and take it up and keep it going jointly as long as possible.

Perhaps an actual observation best captures the unbehaviourist behaviour of parents with their children.

The setting is a seaside café on a wet and blustery morning where a young couple with a small girl of about 18–24 months are waiting to be served. The mother leaves the child sitting on the father's lap while she goes to find the toilets. The little girl watches her mother intently as she crosses the long room, then she raises her arm and clenches and unclenches her fingers and shouts, 'bah, bah'. The mother laughs, turns round and calls, 'Not goodbye, I'm not going, I'll be back in a minute'. But she does go out of sight and the child repeats her 'bah, bah'. The father now sits the child up on the edge of the table, positioning her closely face to face with him. He says, 'Not goodbye, she's coming back, I promise you'. The little child appears very contented, nods her head enthusiastically and starts repeating her 'bah, bah', for sheer delight, along with rhythmic head nodding and leg swinging. The father now joins in this head nodding and chanting of 'bah, bah', and they play this musical game until the mother returns.

It is obvious that at some point this little girl has learnt to imitate 'bye, bye', along with the conventional arm and hand wave, although her articulation of the speech sounds is still an approximation. But she is rewarded with warm approval, as well as sensible explanations about the inappropriateness of the response in this particular social context. The child then proceeds to take full control of the misjudged situation by turning it into a game with her father in which she 'calls the tune'.

It is this kind of child-initiated behaviour and inventiveness, going well beyond basic linguistic responses, that makes traditional behaviourist explanations thin and inadequate. The sort of positive reinforcement that does occur in early language acquisition is a subtle concern for establishing and maintaining joint attention and conversations. The actual truth of a child's statements is more likely to be monitored and corrected by adults than are grammatical or phonological accuracy. What seems very clear to the most casual observer as well as the psycholinguist is that parents and other adult caregivers do not settle down at any point to teach young infants to speak, let alone to understand the language system. The task would be beyond the capabilities of most, if not all, of us!

Nativist approaches

This is the dilemma of early language acquisition: how is it that infants manage it when they are not obviously taught, and are not able to comprehend so complex a learning task? The nativist approach attempted to resolve these questions by returning to some seventeenth- and eighteenth-century theories that proposed the existence of innate and therefore universal features of the human mind. In the 1950s these ideas were revitalized by the American linguist and philosopher, Noam Chomsky, in what he likes to call the second cognitive revolution. This revolution gained a new lease of life as 'the language instinct' (Pinker, 1994) and this researcher has gone on to argue that our current knowledge of human biology and genetics in no way diminishes the nature and significance of the human mind (Pinker, 2002; 2007). The old order overthrown by Chomsky's revolution was the simple behaviourist explanations of language learning, and the new era he introduced has probably made possible all the developments and achievements in child-language study since then. Even those who dispute Chomsky's emphasis on studying the abstract rules of grammar would probably agree that at least he revealed what remarkable things children can do with language at a very early stage.

After Chomsky's (1957) attacks on behaviourism, researchers really listened to young children and began to note their innovative and unusual production of words and utterances, as well as their amazing sensitivity to rules, regularities and patterns in language. For example, children's grammatical mistakes are highly systematic and rather admirable: in English they overgeneralize the rules for making plurals and past tenses once they have deduced the add an '-s' or add '-ed' rules respectively. Around age 2–5, children talk of 'mouses' and tell us that they 'rided' a bike. Clearly they are demonstrating some degree of sensitivity to regular patterns and a possibly innate ability to make analogies with the regular forms, such as 'houses' and 'walked'. One thing is certain, they do not simply imitate adult speech and they are not taught explicitly that a grammar is a system of rules.

The nativist view is that children are pre-programmed to learn a language and are highly sensitive to the linguistic features of their environment. Chomsky emphasizes both the process of maturation in children's linguistic development and the essentially creative nature of all human language use. We are all continually involved in re-creating and generating new and appropriate utterances. But Chomsky's central concern is with the human mind: he sees linguistics as the study of mind and of the mental structures that make language possible. His suggestion that there must be some internal Language Acquisition Device (LAD) that enables the young infant to process all the language it hears and generate its own meaningful utterances, led to considerable research into grammatical systems in the 1960s and 1970s. But the approach has been criticized for its tendency to look at language and the mind in a vacuum, divorced from significant human relationships and social settings, and from all the other kinds of learning with which babies are actively involved.

Cognitive approaches

Cognitive psychologists in the 1970s criticized the Chomskyan preoccupation with the structures of language and its comparative neglect of the personal intentions and uses to which infants put their developing linguistic knowledge, along with all their knowledge of people and the environment. Language development was seen from this perspective to be part of general cognitive development. This view can be linked with Piaget's descriptions of the important mental structures, or schemas, created by the infant's interactions and explorations in the environment in the first 18 or so months of life and with modern studies of the developing infant brain. It can be claimed that early language acquisition must wait for certain synaptic links and sensorimotor strategies to develop.

This cognition hypothesis does not necessarily deny the existence of an independent linguistic system in human development, but it does reassert the significance of other cognitive abilities that must also mature and create a framework for early language learning. Furthermore, this approach indicates the eventual dominance of human thinking by language and by mental processes derived from language (Vygotsky, 1986). Studies of child language that were inclined towards this cognitive focus tended to highlight the complex meanings carried by children's early one- and two-word utterances. This implied that full understanding of children's words required detailed knowledge of the social context and the possible intentions of the children.

Social-interactionist approaches

In the late 1970s and 1980s, developmental psychologists with a deep interest in the nature and effects of human social interactions began to reassert the importance of the role played by adult and child relationships in learning. They also focused on the functions language fulfils for individuals and for groups. We learn a language because of the things it can do for us and the part it plays in making us social beings.

An emphasis on using language to get things done and to make sense of the world of persons and situations is generally associated with the linguistic theory of *pragmatics*. This view of early language was also supported by a body of research evidence that demonstrated the remarkable competence and social sensitivity of infants, including the newborn. Interlocking with these abilities is the finely judged and supportive tutoring in two-way communication that adult caregivers provide for their infants. Bruner (1983) has summarized these dis- coveries in a memorable way: the infant's language-learning capacities could not function without the help given by an adult, who provides a language acquisition support system and scaffolds the child's entry into a language (ibid.: 19). The great importance of these research findings may well be the descrip- tions they provide of the pre-verbal foundations for communication on which all later language and speech will build. This modifies the traditional cognitive view that language must simply wait for the prior establishment of essential gen- eral thinking skills and indicates that language has its own prior skills of pre-verbal communication to establish.

There is general agreement that early language acquisition has both a cogni- tive and a linguistic component, but one mystery still exists: how do infants move from pre-linguistic to linguistic communications? Part of the answer must be that infants do not wait around passively and are not left to go it alone, so the 'impossibly difficult to learn' dilemma of early language acquisition is less intractable. Children learn to be social beings and language users in close partnerships and collaborations with caring adults who participate eagerly with them in the adventure of reconstructing a language for communicating and getting things done.

Other people's minds

From birth babies learn in companionship (Trevarthen, 2002) with their carers, the key persons in their homes and care settings. The significance of one or two caring, attentive and consistent carers in a young child's life has been well researched and is the basis of the key person theory. Key persons (Elfer et al., 2003; Goldschmied and Jackson, 2004) provide the close and intimate relation- ships that babies and young children need if they are to thrive emotionally, cognitively and linguistically. This applies to children's care at home and, or, in group settings. The professional practitioner key person in a group setting can bridge the children's worlds of home and outside care because of their special knowledge of the child, the family and the setting. This can be described as a 'triangle of care' (Nutbrown and Page, 2008) and promotes the kind of emo- tional well-being that enables very young children to cope with changes, separations and frustrations (Brooker, 2008).

Infants need to feel a deep attachment to one or two carers and just as they need to be physically held in the arms of their carers, they also need to be 'held in mind' (Pawl, 2006; Siren Films, 2004). This is a way of feeling safe and con- tained during brief periods of separation and anxiety. This recent research ties in with psychological theories about how young children develop their own insights into what makes people tick. More formally known as 'theory of mind', or TOM, this research is beginning to reveal a complex picture of how infants and toddlers learn to infer mental states in others and predict their responses (Doherty, 2009; Meadows, 2006; Saxe and Baron-Cohen, 2007). Understanding that other people have feelings and thoughts is essential to forming and nurturing relationships and friendships. This is the folk psychology that permeates stories, picture books, folk tales and most art forms across many cultures. However, the fact that 'theory of mind' may be absent or underdeveloped in autism in childhood, has great significance for the families and practitioners who care for children on the autism disorder spectrum.

Summary

- Changing views of early language acquisition are the products of different approaches in psychology but none of these can claim to have answered all the complex questions surrounding the subject.

- Behaviourist perspectives placed great emphasis on the child's imitation of the language of others, supported by adult reinforcement. Later research has tended to discredit this view.

- Nativist approaches emphasize the existence of innate and, therefore, universal abilities in the human mind and claim that the child is pre-programmed in some way to learn a rule-governed language system.

- The view of cognitive psychologists is that language development is an aspect of general cognitive growth and depends on the maturing of these general structures of thinking for its development. This approach also stresses the intentions and meanings of children and the uses to which they put their developing language ability.

- Social-interactionist approaches view the total social and cultural setting in which language is learned as just as necessary for its emergence as grammatical competence. This work emphasizes the social skills of newborns; the need for attachment to a key person or persons; the development of theory of mind; the tutoring role of the adult carer, and the importance of the establishment of a pre-verbal communication system from which language emerges.

Learning and teaching suggestions

- Ensure a rich language input for the babies in your care: respond verbally and with appropriate facial expressions, gestures and body language to all their attempts at communication.

- Repeat their attempts at words and always aim to keep conversational exchanges going.

- Turn regular care routines such as nappy changing, bathing, dressing and feeding into a language experience by talking about what is going on and inviting the babies' responses.

How do we do it? Stages in speech and language development

The first year of life is particularly significant for the development of phonology, or sound production, and for the establishment of the kinds of interpersonal communication skills discussed above. First words and grammatical utterances are built on these foundations in the ensuing months and years. There is a vast amount of research evidence that records the stages all children go through in their early development of speech and language, and the process is remarkably similar for any language (Crystal, 2005; Harris, 1992; Karmiloff and Karmiloff-Smith, 2001). The main speech and language challenges are:

- the production of language
- the understanding of language
- the functions of language.

Production: listening, watching and sharing

Listening

It is now clear that a lengthy period of listening, watching and playful social interactions precedes the first production of recognizable words by young children. Babies are born with exceptionally sensitive hearing and are able, within hours of birth, to discriminate human speech from all the sounds that bombard them. Furthermore, there is evidence that they find human speech so noticeable and pleasing that they will attempt to prolong its occurrence, even in preference to musical sounds. Some researchers even refer to the busy eavesdropper in the womb (Karmiloff and Karmiloff-Smith, 2001: 2) in order to emphasize the significance for speech perception of the last three months in foetal development. The newborn has already had considerable experience of hearing its mother's conversations and has acquired some sophisticated understandings of words, intonation and grammatical patterns.

These facts are interesting examples of infants' readiness for speech, long before it can possibly be produced and understood by them. Such research findings are also reminders that the production of speech sounds and the understanding of language emerge after many months of finely selective listening to human voices, particularly the voices of familiar and caring adults.

Watching

Listening to people is very important for babies but it is also accompanied by equally discriminating and intense observations by babies of those adults who consistently care for them. Studies of newborns indicate that not only are they highly sensitive to patterned sounds, but they are also as highly attuned to certain visual patterns. In particular, faces and eyes attract the most attention and babies gaze at the eyes of their carers. This normally elicits warm and responsive behaviour from the adults singled out for such rapt attention! Clearly this is most important in establishing the sort of human social interactions that will involve the infant and adult couple in lots of language, pleasurable joint attention and playful sound production (Figure 3.1).

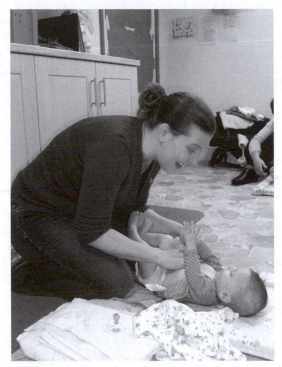

Figure 3.1 **Mutual delight in communication: baby (4 months) and mother at a baby massage session**

Eye contact is also essential to the ways in which all conversations are started, maintained and ended. Eye contact regulates the turn-taking so typical of our face-to-face conversations. We rely on catching someone's eye, holding their gaze, as well as dropping eye contact, to manage the to and fro of social talk. Mutual eye contact is an important method of gaining and maintaining joint attention – an essential for most social exchanges and conversations. Following the focus of another person's gaze is crucial to picking up clues about what they are thinking, concentrating on and likely to talk about.

Infants can and do signal their own wish to stop socializing and playing by dropping eye contact, lowering the head and even turning away. They also become fretful and restless if these important signals are ignored by an over-enthusiastic adult. The social and cultural significance of turning the face away from someone persists into adult life and conversations, but it begins here in the first few weeks of life, as do some other surprising skills.

Mimicking

It appears that infants can mimic closely the facial tricks and grimaces of their carers, such as tongue poking and lip pursing, as well as following an adult's line of gaze (Stern, 1977; Trevarthen, 1993; 2002). Although it might be thought that making funny faces is a silly thing to do with babies, it is well worth remembering that complex mouth, tongue and lip movements are essential to the production of speech and may be rehearsed in face mimicry and games. What we are able to say about all this surprisingly early watching listening and mimicking behaviour is that it makes the baby an active conversational partner.

Sharing

Mutual communication between babies and caregivers (sometimes called intersubjectivity) starts at birth when the newborn infant is welcomed into a community. Within minutes of the delivery the child is frequently addressed directly and its grimaces, movements and splutters are commented on, interpreted and even imitated by the adults present. The adult community does not appear to regard the newly born as immature organisms only capable of random physical responses, but attributes sociability and communicative intentions to them.

In the very early stages of an adult's relationship with an infant, the priority seems to be to establish turn-taking and conversational exchanges, although the infant partner is just a few hours, days or weeks old! These rituals may begin with a minimal contribution from the infant, but the adult still maximizes any of the child's burps, yawns or eye contacts by accepting them with courteous greetings, pauses and thanks, or with little invented story explanations about them.

The recorded commentaries of mothers, going back many decades, seem to reflect their belief that tiny babies have motives and intentions, and are capable of contributing to gossip and conversations (Snow, 1977). Mothers may even try to avoid putting questions to a pre-verbal child when it has its mouth full of food! Just as extraordinary is the evidence that adult talk in these early one-sided conversations is timed to leave spaces for the pre-verbal child's reply, and these pauses are the same length as normal adult-to-adult dialogue pauses (Stern, 1977). After such pauses, adults carry on the conversations as if they had received a reasonable response. By the end of their first year many infants are actually slotting their own contributions into these dialogue spaces created for them, and adults gradually 'up the demand' for more frequent, longer and more language-like contributions to these conversations and games.

Bruner (1975; 1983) described in some detail the game-like formats and rituals that prepare babies for language and social exchanges. Games (such as 'peep-bo'; naming parts of the body, toys, pets and objects; playful requests for information; and 'please' and 'thank you' routines with objects) establish the uses of language in meaningful contexts. Babies and adults do important things together in very predictable ways – routines such as feeding, dressing, bathing, playing and going on outings are marked by distinctive language. The important lesson for students of child development and language, as well as for pre-verbal infants, is that learning to do things with other people is the basis of learning to 'do things with words' (Austin, 1962). The research on the pre-verbal months suggests that babies from the start (supported by their adult partners) learn what words do in their world, understand what people are like, and what speakers mean or intend, in particular social contexts. Such learning is an essential part of what it means to be involved in human social interactions – the best metaphor we have for early language acquisition is that of a human conversation. We should take seriously the full force of the metaphor and not attribute all the intentions and activities to the adult partner.

Summary

- A lengthy period of very sensitive listening precedes the emergence of speech in infancy: infants appear to be tuned to human voices and behaviour at birth.

- A similarly sensitive and significant fascination with eyes and faces starts from birth. Newborn infants have a range of varied facial expressions and arm movements that attract and motivate adult interactions.

- Mutual eye gazing and patterns of inviting and ending eye contact are soon established by infants and carers. These sequences may have significance for the later turn-taking patterns of conversations when eye signals still remain important.

- Mutual communication, or intersubjectivity, is established between infants and carers in the first weeks of life and is part of a process of regarding the infant as an intelligent, playful and intentional human communicator from the start.

- The games, teasing and rituals played by infants and their carers establish a basis for a wide range of linguistic interactions and may help infants to develop insights about other people's minds and sensitivity to their emotional states.

Learning and teaching suggestions

- Keep a simple diary record of a baby's favourite sounds, first words and early word combinations. Note the baby's age (days, weeks, months), the context or event, approximately what the sounds or words sounded like to you and what you think might have been the meaning. If you are caring for children professionally, always share these word diaries with their families.

- Use group talking times (circle times or review sessions) with older children to raise language issues quite specifically; for example, ask them how they think they learnt to speak. Or ask them if their parents, carers and siblings remember the interesting things they said when they were babies. Gradually build up a collection of stories about 'How we learnt to talk'.

Understanding: sounds and meanings

All children begin by learning the sounds of their language(s) in playful communications with their carers. The meaningful (or semantic) aspect of early sounds has been demonstrated by long-term studies of some individual children who learnt how to mean by using a range of special sounds before recognizable words emerged (Halliday, 1975).

- *In the first two months* (bearing in mind that any of these ages are highly variable), noises that are mainly of the discomfort or physical-reflexes type predominate. However, they may have some influence on phonological developments in that they exercise the organs of speech production.
- *Between two and four months* the pleasure sounds develop (these are the rather musical and lower-pitched cooing and laughing responses that delight caring adults). The child's growing ability to experiment with moving the tongue and lips results in the 'ga-ga' and 'goo-goo' noises typical of this stage.
- *By about six months* the infant will have started to produce a greater variety of playful sounds consistently rather than accidentally. This may include many 'fun' noises, such as blowing bubbles or exploding air and moisture through the pursed lips in a 'raspberry'. At this point we should note the effect that all this playful experimentation with sounds is having on the adults around the child. Cooing, laughing and other vocal play is highly emotive for the adult carers: suddenly the baby seems to be a real personality with a potential for fun and humour. This often leads to a great upsurge in the number of games played between adult and child, including games that involve focusing joint attention on objects and toys. The hiding, seeking and slightly scary tactics of peekaboo, or of suddenly putting the adult face very close to the baby's face, may now occur. These strange practices can be thought of as ways of establishing patterns of expectations, coordinating mutual gaze and attention, and generally stimulating and getting in touch with another mind and personality.
- *Around six months* the distinctive development of babbling emerges. Babbling is the regular and rhythmic repetition of a small set of sounds, such as 'babababa'. It is at this stage that we can identify the input and effects of the dominant language used with the child because both the rhythms and the

sounds occurring in babbling reflect those used most frequently in the language. This stimulates a very special kind of response from the adults around because, in the case of a potentially English-speaking baby, such pleasing sequences as 'mamamama' and 'dadadada' are recognized as real and important words. These sounds are often taken up and repeated by adults and older children so that, again, we have mature speakers imitating babies. Such pleasurable and playful reinforcement will certainly be a factor in the young infant's earliest collection of rhythmic words, such as 'baba', 'mama', 'dada', 'wow wow' and 'nana'.

Around this period there are also signs that the infant is actually bringing about changes in the ways in which caring adults talk. As well as copying the child's word-like babbles, caregivers often exaggerate their own intonation patterns, facial expressions and gestures. The actual speech style of carers talking to babies usually includes lots of repetition and questions, as well as simplified clauses and vocabulary, including some baby-talk words. What seems to be going on here is a useful amount of word repetition – a rich demonstration of non-verbal communicative skills, examples of the different intonation patterns used in questions and statements, and a modelling of the highly expressive style of affectionate talk within a close human relationship. This register probably ensures mutual understanding, keeping two minds focused on the same topic.

- *Between 9 and 18 months* the development of sounds is rapid, and a great variety of tone and rhythm – as well as the tunes of the particular languages around the child – are noticeable. But most importantly, the signs of real language development are emerging because it seems clear at this stage that the infant intends to communicate meanings when uttering sounds. It is not just a matter of the child repeating the sounds and words adults appear to like – the child begins to use certain personal sounds systematically to express greetings, needs, requests, observations, pleasure and dislike. Some linguists would describe these as proto-words (Crystal, 2005; Halliday, 1975) because they are consistent, systematic and meaningful.

  Most babies can also accompany their own system of meaningful sounds with hand and finger pointing. They also demonstrate their sensitivity to the turn-taking patterns of conversations by looking at speakers who happen to be holding the floor. They can respond to simple verbal instructions and gestures, such as waving 'bye-bye', clapping their hands and attempting to say family names and basic family words.

- *Around 12–18 months* single words begin to appear and are often inaccurately described as 'lisping' or 'babyish' in pronunciation. This simplified pronunciation is a reflection of the child's difficulties in using and controlling the very precise movements of tongue, lips and palate required in speech. But these simplifications are well-focused strategies for coping with sound combinations in words, and they appear to be highly systematic. For example, infants may reduplicate, or repeat, an initial consonant so that the articulation of all the consonant sounds is restricted to one area of the mouth – as in 'bubber' (butter), 'goggy' or 'doddy' (doggy) and 'Dynan' for 'Dylan'.

The beginning sounds of new words seem to be very clear to the infant and result in such versions as, 'du' (duck) and 'be' (bed). Similarly, distinctive final parts of words may be pronounced first, as in 'ren' (Karen), 'tali' (Natalie) and 'tias' (Mattias). Complicated clusters of initial consonants are often reduced to simplify their articulation, as in 'poon' (spoon). Some children find words that start with an open vowel difficult and appear to need an extra consonant at the beginning in order to ease the production of the word, for instance, 'mapple' (apple).

Summary

- The very first sounds, cries and babbles exercise and develop the capacities of the speech organs, and the child's control over them.
- In their first months infants practise and perfect the habitual and significant sounds of the particular languages to which they are exposed.
- The roots of pleasurable games with persons and objects, and of language play for its own sake, are located in these early months. The production of sounds is rhythmic and musical and also involves whole-body movements such as bouncing, as well as hand and arm waving, leg kicking and head nodding.
- From the start infants begin to use their voices to control others and to get them to do things.
- Many infants appear to use a set of personally evolved sounds to express their needs and meanings systematically.

Functions: first words

The emergence of first words introduces the crucial issue of grammaticality (or syntax) in early language. The first words are usually one- and two-syllabled attempts at some meaningful names and items frequently encountered by the child in the daily routines of home. Personal gestures and intonation patterns, as well as the actual situation, are important guides to a full understanding of the child's meaning when using single words. Some of these single words appear to have the import of full sentences, and linguists refer to them as *holophrases*. These particular single-word utterances are not being used by the child simply as labels and naming devices – they actually function as commentaries and instructions. For example, 'cup' may mean

Where is my cup?
I've dropped my cup.
I want a drink.

There's a cup in that picture like mine.

Similarly, 'down' may be said to indicate

I want to go downstairs.
I want to get out of the high-chair.
You've dropped something on the floor.

Only the total and unique context in which the child uses these words can fully explain the intended meanings.

This fact highlights the particular social and cultural setting early language encodes for the child. The single-word utterance 'down' was used by a baby girl to comment on the family cat's dramatic leap down from the top of the tall refrigerator to the kitchen floor. Behind this child's simple observation is a rich background of talk and shared experiences in the family, some of it centred on the cat's preference for sitting on top of the very high refrigerator and jumping straight down to the floor when his supper bowl was put out! The real value of records of children's first words is not in the counting or scoring aspect, but in the remarkable insights they provide into the children's perceptions of their families and communities.

Linguists, as well as parents and other caring adults, become very excited about young children's first two-word utterances or word combinations. Again, in terms of exact meanings, they are open to many complex interpretations that can only be clarified by knowledge of the child and knowledge of the situation. The research literature contains many examples, such as 'allgone milk', 'no bed', 'more book', that are significant demonstrations of young children's originality as they set about learning languages. In fact, these examples are evidence of early grammars: they are combinations of words that express relationships and actions. For the first time the world is being organized by the child in terms of linguistic categories, such as actors, actions, objects, negation, possession, absence and so forth. A grammar of early utterances could be described as one that enables young speakers to do at least two very important things with words and simple word combinations:

- Early grammatical utterances can be used to interact with other people and get things done.
- They are a means of commenting on the world or a particular state of affairs.

These two major functions should not be underestimated, as they cover most of our adult uses of language. They are also the basis of a specific view of language and learning that emphasizes the significant interplay of an individual's active participation in the world with a more evaluating and spectator-like stance (Britton, 1992).

This dual stance that early language use begins to make possible was pithily summarized by Halliday as the possibility of being both an observer and an intruder (Halliday, 1975: 29–30). The child starts by being in only one role at any one time, through the use of simple utterances, but the gradual development of an adult grammar enables both functions to exist together. We can see and hear this possibility when the 5-year-old remarks, 'That's a nice red bike, I want one like that.'

The acquisition of an adult grammar and wider ranges of vocabulary makes rapid progress in the years from 2 to 4. Children's three- and four-word sentences produce a great variety of highly creative and unusual combinations. Names, questions and commentaries simply flow from the young speaker, as do all the what, why, how, where and who queries. The rather cryptic or 'telegraphic' style of speech lessens as young children begin to express connections, such as cause and effect and narrative sequence, with the linguistic items 'and', 'because', 'so', 'if' and 'when'. The years from 2 to 4 seem to be a peak period for young children's original and obviously unimitated language learning strategies. All the famous errors of overgeneralization of irregular plurals and past tenses belong to this stage in language development and indicate that young children are certainly not copying adults.

However, creativity in early language acquisition is not just a matter of 'wented', 'feets' and 'mouses'. Many children learning a range of world languages invent new usages by turning nouns into verbs, producing such forms as 'lawning' (mowing the lawn) and 'I seat belted myself' (Clark, 1982: 390, 402). These creations from 3- and 4-year-olds indicate considerable sensitivity to the existence of nouns that function as verbs in the standard adult language, as in 'brush' and the regular verb 'to brush'. Once again it is clear that 'lawning' and 'seat belted' are unlikely to have been copied from adult usage. Some children also invent complex new lexical items which are personal constructions based on known words and familiar contexts.

Example

At the age of 3, my younger daughter produced the memorable 'bed-night sweeties' which has remained in family parlance ever since! It seems to have evolved out of our general practice of attempting to keep the eating of sweets limited to the period between the end of the evening meal and bedtime, but it had obviously become part of the whole range of 'goodnight' rituals and associations.

This personal example illustrates the areas of significant private connections and family and cultural practices that children's early words and utterances encode. These are known as *semantic fields* because they indicate the major groups of meanings around which children's first language developments and experiments cluster. Much of this language is about the 'here-and-now' world of significant people, actions, food, the body, clothes, animals, vehicles, toys, games, household objects and social conventions. Other important categories are location, the 'up', 'down' and 'under' of toddlers' talk, adjectives and those terms that point things out ('look', 'see'), known to linguists as *deictics*. These semantic fields are of great social and cultural significance because they high-light the traditions, attitudes, rituals and beliefs of the community in which the young speaker is developing.

Summary

- First words can only be fully understood within the contexts in which they are uttered. Some of them are not just labels but stand for sentence-like commentaries or instructions.
- Two-word combinations are examples of early grammatical lan-guage: the words are put together in order to express the child's perceptions of actions and relationships.
- Early grammatical combinations enable young children to do two important things: to interact with other people and to get things done, and to comment on a state of affairs in the environment.
- In the years from 2 to 4 there is ample evidence of children's unique and unimitated language-learning strategies. Children evolve grammatical rules that produce some errors of overgeneralization in plurals and tenses. They also invent verbs and nouns by analogy with conventional forms.

Learning and teaching suggestions

- Set up baby-care provision in your indoor and outdoor areas and try to record (preferably on video) the children's talk to their 'babies'. Make obser-vation notes on their ability to modify their language: note any evidence of a baby-talk register, or dialect and language switching. Try to observe body language, eye contact and facial expressions. Add notes on these skills to the children's individual records and assessments.
- Show the children some films of young babies socializing and beginning to communicate and talk (available from educational film makers and govern-ment early years initiatives). Talk about what is happening and what carers and babies do together. Relate these matters to the children's own under-standing of what they use language for and what it does for them.

⚬➾ Key terms

Behaviourism: the belief that all behaviours are learnt, even such complex and sophisticated behaviours as language.

Cognitive: emphasizing the crucial role of general intellectual abilities in all learn-ing and considering language acquisition as part of cognitive development.

Nativist: the belief that humans are programmed to learn language due to innate and universal features of the mind.

Social interactionist: emphasizing the social purposes for language and the impetus it gives the child to learn language to get things done and participate in a social group.

Further reading

Aitchison, J. (2008) *The Articulate Mammal: An Introduction to Psycholinguistics.* 5th edn. London: Routledge.

Doherty, M.J. (2009) *Theory of Mind: How Children Understand Others' Thoughts and Feelings.* Hove: Psychology Press.

Karmiloff, K. and Karmiloff-Smith, A. (2001) *Pathways to Language: From Fetus to Adolescent.* Cambridge, MA, and London: Harvard University Press.

Nutbrown, C. and Page, J. (2008) *Working with Babies and Children. From Birth to Three.* London: Sage.

Pinker, S. (2002) *The Blank Slate.* London: Penguin Books.

Saxe, R. and Baron-Cohen, S. (eds) (2007) *Theory of Mind.* Hove: Psychology Press.

Siren Films (2008) *The Wonder Year.* www.sirenfilms.co.uk

Siren Films (2009) *Firm Foundations for Literacy 0–5.* www.sirenfilms.co.uk

CHAPTER 4

PSYCHOLINGUISTICS: LANGUAGE AND THINKING

This chapter includes:

- the relationship between language and thinking
- brain development in infancy
- words and concepts.

Important perspectives

The relationship debate

The discussion of early language acquisition in Chapter 3 shows that there is a considerable degree of interconnectedness between children's developing language and their thinking. There has always been some debate about which develops first – thought or language – and the exact nature and degree of interdependence between them. This chapter outlines four major approaches to these difficult issues. However, this relationship debate should not be seen as another potential conflict between opposing views, nor is it possible to identify any correct and undisputed answers. These differing perspectives on language and thought have provided useful insights and added to the state of knowledge about them.

Differing views on the probable relationships between language and thinking have also had a direct bearing on their exponents' preferred explanations of early language acquisition. Therefore, the following discussion will still be concerned with early language as well as cognitive theories. Any account of language and thinking must offer possible theories about how they begin and develop in infancy and early childhood.

Linguistic determinism

In the early decades of the twentieth century, language was seen as controlling and determining the patterns of habitual thought and behaviour. An American linguist, Benjamin Lee Whorf, was mainly responsible for this claim, although it is also associated with aspects of the work of Whorf's mentor, Edward Sapir. Their theory, the Sapir–Whorf hypothesis, suggests that a particular language will dominate and shape its users' perceptions of reality, providing their total world view. Whorf's fieldwork among the declining South and North American Indian communities revealed the inextricable links between a culture and its language, as well as the ways in which the vocabulary of a language charted the significant and habitual features of the life of the language community.

These *semantic fields*, which are basically groups of words about related areas of meaning, were not the only determining features. The actual grammatical patterns, or syntax, for referring to time or to actions were very different from European forms. These unusual features of some remote languages led Whorf to conclude that language must structure thought – it determines the ways of thinking and the responses of members of a language community. This view is usually called *linguistic determinism* and it has a further theroetical implication, known as *linguistic relativity*. This claims that for a variety of geographical, climatic, social and cultural reasons, the categories of each language are unique.

The major problem with this kind of hypothesis is that it views infancy and early childhood as being subject to a process of socialization into a tightly defined world-picture, a closed system of restricted thinking. We are then left with a set of difficulties and alternatives this approach does not address. What of the possibility of independent thought existing before language, or of types of thought without language? What of the influence on thought of our unique individual experiences with objects and people? What of the successful efforts people make to communicate and see the points of view of people from other cultural and linguistic traditions? What of the position of bilinguals? Their languages may well give them a hold on two cultural worlds but this can be more of an enrichment than a problem. Are they really muddled and inadequate thinkers and culturally stateless persons? Finally, what of the very real evidence that good translations between languages are possible and do enrich our lives?

In fact, we know that all these ways of escaping the restrictions of one language are possible. They require conscious effort, goodwill and more elaborated uses of language. We may well have to resort to several words or phrases when one will do in another language. This is necessary because different languages put into words the important and the obvious in the life and experiences of their particular language community.

Babies and young children are initiated into the language uses and the ways of thinking and living of their communities. However, this is a framework, a trellis for supporting their habitual ways of thinking about experiences and the world, not a linguistic straitjacket. A weaker version of the Sapir–Whorf hypothesis has been used by some sociologists and educators to suggest that many children's habitual ways of using language may have a limiting effect on their thinking and their progress in formal education. While some children are readily 'at home' with the language habits and usages of teachers and the linguistic demands of the curriculum, many others may be initially confused and disadvantaged. These issues will be returned to in subsequent chapters.

Piagetian views

There is a totally opposite position to that of linguistic determinism, one that argues that thought exists before language and provides the mental structures from which language develops. The researcher responsible for this hypothesis, Jean Piaget, was a biologist by training, but his life's work was the study of the origins of thinking processes in young children. A central feature of his approach is the emphasis it places on the learning achieved by infants in the first 18 months or so of life. This is the period before the main onset of verbal language in many children but, from a Piagetian standpoint, it is the cognitive achievements of these early months that make language possible.

Action, or doing things to the environment, is the way in which the child learns. Activity creates mental structures or *schemas* that can be used again and modified in further experiences and actions. Knowledge is seen as rather like a store of successful encounters with the environment. For the pre-verbal infant, these encounters become sets of schemas or mental representations of successful actions, such as reaching and grasping a toy, putting a range of objects in the mouth, shaking a rattle and opening a container. In all these thinking and problem-solving behaviours, the important features are the active doing (the motor element) and the seeing, touching, tasting and listening (the sensory element). Hence, this first and most significant of Piaget's stages of development is known as the *sensorimotor period*.

The theory allows for new developments in the child's thinking by stressing the need to restructure and modify schemas in the face of unpredictable and novel experiences. For instance, some toys will not be easily grasped, some objects will not fit in the mouth or taste tolerable, and even containers will have a variety of lids and fitting devices. The necessary changes and modifications of the infant's previously learnt ways of acting on these things are described as a process of *accommodation*. The complementary aspect of this learning process is knowing or recognizing a toy or object in terms of what can be done with it, and this is generally described as *assimilation*.

Piaget's approach emphasizes the ways in which child thinking differs significantly from adult thinking. In particular, the Piagetian concept of child *egocentrism* reflects his view that all thinking originates in personal actions on the environment. In the early years, thinking is closely shaped by the child's actual perceptions and unique perspectives on events and objects. This appears to be very much a matter of physical perceptions and personal bodycentredness – a case of what can be done with and to objects and materials. It is unfortunate that the term egocentrism is often confused with the psychological and moral notions of egocentric as self-centred and self-absorbed behaviour.

Early thinking does appear to be dominated by perception and the very young child's inability to give consideration to more than one physical feature of a situation at a time, or allow for the differing perspectives, physical as well as mental, that others may have on the same situation. Early language is seen as dominated by *egocentric speech*, a kind of personal monologue-cum-running commentary on actions and perceptions. Language is not thought to be truly socialized and directed out towards others until about 7 years of age.

The order and progression of the stages of thinking in the original Piagetian theory reflect a belief in 'readiness' as an important element in development. All new stages (language being just one) must wait for the appropriate mental structures to develop and to mature. Adult verbal instructions to children will have little effect on these developments. However, the theory can be rightly criticized for underestimating the most significant feature of a child's environment – other human beings.

To some extent, Piaget's theory minimized the significance of adults and other children in an infant's early language and thinking development, particularly the crucial part played by the adult–infant interactions discussed in Chapter 3. Furthermore, a theory that minimizes the role of adult instructions and guidance in advance of the child's mental readiness could be in danger of making early education irrelevant! This potential weakness has been known to show up in the misguided policies of some early years settings, schools and individual practitioners, who thought they were putting Piaget into practice by preparing rich environments of materials, objects and experiences for young children, and then stepping back. They thus left the children virtually alone to explore, solve problems and discover concepts for themselves. This is a travesty of the work of a great and original thinker, who was not a professional educator but a scientist who had no intention of setting out programmes for teachers. The work of Piaget has been reappraised over the years and still influences theorists and practitioners (Athey, 2007; Bruce, 2010).

Piaget's legacy: schemas and dispositions

Modern early years researchers and practitioners have developed new insights into how young children learn by extending Piaget's claim that early thinking is distinctive and highly active.

Schema theories identify very regular patterns of behaviour, or thinking in action. Young children can be observed hiding toys and objects in bags and boxes, or tying up everything with string and ribbons, or moving toys and anything else from one area to another. These schemas are indications of children's personal ways of exploring the world, experimenting with materials and phenomena, and thinking about them (see the work of Nutbrown, 2006; Whalley and the Pen Green Centre Team, 2007).

Dispositions are the unique or characteristic attitudes and responses of individual children to life and experience. They are probably inherited and may be nurtured rather than taught, but they include such useful learning styles as persistence, cooperation and curiosity (Figure 4.1). Many educators now plan their work with young children in order to support such dispositions and include them in their record-keeping and assessment procedures (Carr, 2001).

Figure 4.1 Curiosity – 4-year-olds discover their reflections in mirror tiles on the floor

Learning and teaching suggestion

- Observe young children's play and interests closely and pick up on and record any schemas. Also, chart the emergence of dispositions over time. Video recording is particularly helpful as it allows for lots of re-viewing, discussion and reflection. Practitioners should ask parents and other carers not just to give their permission for this, but to participate in the observing and recording. You might be able to send simple video cameras home.

Perspectives from Bruner and Vygotsky

Many psychologists, linguists and educators whose early work was inspired by Piaget went on to link his demonstrations of the ways in which child thought appears to be very different from adult thinking, with accounts of the social and cultural foundations of human thinking, learning and language. Two influential researchers, Lev Vygotsky and Jerome Bruner, have made major contributions to the language and thought debate.

Jerome Bruner

Bruner's early work is often linked with Piaget's studies of the early stages of children's thinking, particularly as Bruner also describes a period in the first 18 months when thinking and learning are the result of physical actions on the environment.

- This *enactive* phase of representing experience is seen as the first of a series of thinking strategies that, although they evolve and undergo many reformulations, are still the basis of all later thinking, even in adulthood.
- *Enactive*, or *action-based thinking*, is soon enriched by *iconic* thinking that creates internalized images or 'pictures in the head' of experiences and encounters with the environment.
- The development of language then leads to a capacity for *symbolic thinking*. This is not just another stage in Bruner's theory, *symbolic thought* is a radical reorganization and transformation of children's thinking and behaviour.
- The transforming power of language as a tool for thinking is one of two distinctive aspects of Bruner's view of language and thought.
- The other is the immense significance of the human social and cultural environments into which children are born. The activities of older people who care for children, participate in language-like games and real conversations with them, and organize small and manageable chunks of social and cultural experience for them to engage with, actually create a scaffold for easy access to the language and culture of the community.

In partnership with adults, infants and small children are apprentices to life, language and learning. Children work alongside 'experts' who already know the craft or art of being human, but they gradually take over more and more bits of the ways and skills they see demonstrated daily. Bruner does not see the thinking processes of adults as fundamentally different from those of infants, mainly because what they have in common is the tool of language that distinguishes all human thought and culture. Language and socialization put a range of strategies for coping at the disposal of both children and adults but, of course, adult experience of language and culture is more extensive, varied and complex.

Thinking symbolically would perhaps best characterize Bruner's view of human thinking and it is language, more than any other system of symbols, that provides the richest range of concepts and distinctions for this. Language in its cultural setting frees child and adult thought from the narrow constraints of the here and now. We can use words instead of always having to take action, and these linguistic rehearsals and substitutes create the worlds of the mind and the imagination.

Lev Vygotsky

The contribution of Vygotsky to this debate can be seen as an inspired compromise between the views of Whorf and Piaget, leading to some radically new theories. He saw that there were powerful but independent mental and linguistic elements in human thinking and he also claimed that social experiences in early childhood were crucial to the formation of thought.

Vygotsky: major themes

- *A revolutionary methodology*: he looked at the genetic roots of language and thinking in the human species by first considering these features, or their origins, in our nearest anthropoid cousins, the great apes. From these genetic studies he developed daring and perceptive ideas that transformed the approaches of traditional developmental psychology, which studied the origins of language and thinking in the individual child.

- *Thinking is social*: the higher mental processes in the individual (for example, thinking with symbols, such as words and concepts) actually originate in social relationships. Language and other symbolic systems, such as mathematics, writing and art, are psychological tools for thinking developed by cultures.

- *Mental processes are mediated through signs*: the theme of mediation is central to this view of language. Mental processes can only be understood through the psychological tools, the linguistic, mathematical or cultural signs, that mediate them. We can only really understand children's thoughts by a process of trying to understand their gestures, pictures and words. In the case of their words and language, this

(Continued)

(Continued)

involves trying to appreciate the cultural meanings of their words, the unique contexts in which they are being used, the range of previous experiences and motivations that may lie behind them and, even, the style of the utterances and all the non-verbal messages that always accompany words. Just as adults mediate between the child and the language and culture, so language, as a system, mediates between the individual and the continual impact of random sensory stimuli.

• *Education mediates between spontaneous and scientific concepts*: there is also a need for mediation between the spontaneous concepts we discover by exploring the physical environment, for example, 'hot' or 'wet', and the scientific or non-spontaneous concepts we must learn with help. The latter concepts are created by cultures in the process of living, coping and thinking, and their preservation is too important to be left to chance: they are taught (or mediated) to the next generation by some form of education. We can include in this 'scientific' category, literacy, as well as scientific, mathematical, technical and aesthetic concepts.

Vygotsky's research and thinking were done in the 1920s and early 1930s, and first published in 1934 – the year of his death. He has been a powerful influence on many later psychologists, linguists and educators, and the implications of his theories are still being explored. His study of the failed attempts to teach language to apes in the early twentieth century convinced him that in the species, as well as in the individual child, thought and speech have different roots. However, at about the age of 2 in individual human development, the separate processes combine.

The earliest thinking in apes and human infants is action based and concerned with purposeful problem-solving: reaching for food or toys and opening containers are typical examples. The earliest 'speech' is sound produced by air leaving the lungs and passing through the throat, nose and mouth. This provides a very powerful emotional release, as in cries, screams and grunts of pleasure. But this 'speech' also has a definite social function – it keeps the individual in close contact with others and attracts attention and help.

In the human infant, when a relatively high level of development has been reached in both pre-verbal thinking and pre-intellectual speech, the two processes begin to join together to create a new kind of mental function, *verbal thinking*. This spontaneous merging is unique to the human species and its onset is marked by new language activities in the individual child. Thoughts can be verbalized and speech begins to express rational ideas and requests. This is not an overnight achievement and verbalizing our thoughts and organizing rational speech and writing are the demanding preoccupations of a lifetime.

Vygotsky also noted that the fusion of thought and speech is partial – some areas of thinking and of speech remain unaffected. Thus, we still appear to be capable of outbursts of non-rational speech (Pinker, 2007), under emotional stress (as in swearing) or in mindless chanting and rote recitations. We also retain some powerful traces of physical, action-based thinking, particularly in skilled tool use, motor habits (moving up and down a familiar staircase) and in such body memories as retaining the ability to swim or ride a bicycle after years of not doing so.

The onset of verbal thinking in infancy is marked by two unmistakable symptoms: the child has a sudden curiosity about words and names for everything, and there is a correspondingly rapid increase in the child's vocabulary. These symptoms have already been outlined in the previous chapter, but Vygotsky links this dramatic change in the direction of human thought and language with another puzzling aspect of early language. What is the function and the fate of all that talking to themselves out loud that typifies much of the language activity of small children from around 2 to 5 years of age? Piaget had already observed and identified this verbal accompaniment to the child's activities, describing it as egocentric speech (Piaget, 1926). His initial view was that it simply died away as the child matured and developed the ability to take the perspectives of others into account and produce appropriately socialized speech.

Vygotsky disagreed with this explanation and produced a rather different account of the evolution of egocentric speech, claiming that as the child's speech was, in any case, social in its origins, egocentric speech was not likely to be a symptom of immature egocentrism that disappeared as the child became socialized in speech and behaviour. On the contrary, egocentric speech is probably the developmental link between overt language and inner speech or verbal thinking. We all use this continually 'in our heads' as a means of planning, organizing and rehearsing our intellectual, linguistic, social and practical endeavours. Vygotsky noted that the young child's egocentric speech was already well suited to planning and organizing the child's activities and showed a tendency to become incomprehensible to others. The following example of a 3-year-old attempting to count eight items indicates some of these features.

> 'One, two, three, four, eight, ten, eleben. No try dat again. One, two, three, four, five, ten, eleben. No, try dat again. One! two! three-e-four-five, ten eleben – One! two, three, four, five, six, seven, eleben, whew!' (Gardner, 1980: 32).

The developmental pattern is, first, social speech, then egocentric speech that appears to branch off, turning inward to become inner speech and continuing to develop as a means of verbal thought. Of course, normal overt social speech also continues to develop, becoming even more responsive to others, as well as capable of expressing more and more of the thinking processes of the individual.

Vygotsky's approach puts its main emphasis on the social nature of the speech that is gradually internalized to become a means of higher thinking. 'The child's intellectual growth is contingent on his mastering the social means of thought, that is, language' (Vygotsky, 1986: 94). From the educational point of view, this not only stresses the central significance of human language and culture in the processes of thinking, but also highlights the impact of the shared and cooperative ways in which language is first acquired. In the light of this influential approach, the importance of communication and talk with key persons and carers in the early years is huge.

Learning and teaching implications

The way in which early language is learnt in partnership with another led Vygotsky to consider some of the implications for learning and teaching. Small children start by being controlled by others but internalize the language adults use, along with the emotional quality of the relationships, thus acquiring a means of self-control. The 3-year-old quoted above, repeated the phrase, 'No, try dat again' and this is likely to have been learned from a tutoring and caring adult. It seems to act as an attention-focusing device and a warm counsel of encouragement.

Vygotsky pinpoints this strategy and makes it relevant, not only for early language and thinking, but also for all learning and teaching encounters: 'what the child can do in cooperation today he can do alone tomorrow' (Vygotsky, 1986: 188). This highlights the obvious fact that words and concepts give children access to their languages and their cultures and begin to transform their thinking (Figure 4.2).

Figure 4.2   **Words and concepts transform thinking: using words and pictures to sort data and choose a dog! (Reception)**

Learning and teaching suggestion

- Listen to what young children say and keep notes of any puzzling comments so that you can reflect on them and attempt to follow the patterns of individual children's thinking.

Brainy babies

Neuroscience and brainy babies

Contemporary research using brain-imaging technology is now able, quite literally, to look at the very earliest stages in babies' thinking as they occur. The study of the development of babies' brains is at the forefront of scientific research. Neuroscience, as it is called, indicates that the first year of life is of huge significance in the development of human thinking.

At birth the brain is extremely 'plastic', or adaptable, and rich in potential. However, the millions of brain cells, or neurons, are not connected by the all-important neural pathways, or synapses, that make complex thinking possible. This crucial linking up happens in the first year or so of life and is triggered by daily experiences of being handled, moved about, talked to, played with and generally stimulated. Huge numbers of synaptic connections are made in the first three years, far more than are found in adult brains. It is known that connections which are not used frequently are 'pruned'. This pattern of constantly creating and pruning connections continues until the onset of early adolescence (around 10 years of age). The slowing down of this process of constant rewiring results in fewer but more efficient and frequently used neural pathways for thought, language and cultural influences.

We might say that babies almost literally create their brains in partnership with their carers. Some research claims that 'the quality of the relationship between parent and child influences both the biochemistry and the structure of the brain' (Gerhardt, 2004: 211). Pleasurable interactions between parent and baby actually build up that area of the brain (prefrontal cortex) concerned with self-regulation and social interactions (ibid: 39).

The stimulation needed for the growth of brain connections between cells is ordinary sensory and social experiences in families and small groups. This is nothing to do with a mad world of hot-housing babies but everything to do with affectionate good 'parenting' by a few consistent carers, plus exposure to many sensory experiences such as touching, holding, tasting, listening, seeing, moving and changing positions.

Neuroscience itself is rapidly developing and changing and any implications claimed for early care and education must be treated with caution. For instance, while it is obvious that deprived environments are never good for the brain, it could also be the case that deliberately and artificially enriched environments may not be necessary (Blakemore and Frith, 2005). Perhaps practitioners and families should be wary of the many well-publicized programmes for babies that offer exercises for the brain, or promise Einstein-like powers! What we can say with some confidence is that,

- the first year of life is proving to be ever more significant in human development
- babies are active thinkers and in process of developing their own brains
- sensory stimulation and pleasurable social interactions with carers trigger the growth of synaptic links, the all-important connections in the brain.

Summary

- There are differing views about the nature of language and thought, and the kind and degree of relationship between them. These various approaches also lead to different accounts of early language acquisition.

- The Sapir–Whorf hypothesis focuses on the differences between languages and claims that particular languages determine their speakers' ways of thinking. The particular categories and concepts of a language are considered to be unique to that language.

- The view of Piaget is that thought develops first from sensorimotor activities and creates the mental structures crucial for language development. The ability to use language in abstract and symbolic ways develops in early adolescence with formal operations.

- Bruner acknowledges the significance of early pre-verbal thinking but he stresses the role of adults in organizing language and cultural experiences for the child. Language as a system reorganizes and transforms human thinking – it is the tool for symbolic thought.

- Vygotsky claimed that thought and speech have different genetic roots and growth but they join together, at around the age of 2, to create verbal thought. The primary function of speech is social but from this there develops, in infancy, egocentric speech for planning and self-organization. This turns inward to become inner speech and verbal thinking. Vygotsky stresses the importance for thinking of the child's dialogues and activities with adults: the internalization of these dialogues brings the tool of language to bear on the structures of thought.

- Neuroscience and modern technologies reveal the way in which the brain develops and builds neural connections in response to pleasurable social interactions and sensory stimulation in the first year of life.

Learning and teaching suggestions

- Spend time just looking out of a window with babies and young children and talk with them about what they can see.
- Devise a range of stimulating experiences for babies and toddlers: suspend bold mobiles (black and white as well as coloured) over cots and changing mats; provide simple 'treasure baskets' (Goldschmied and Jackson, 2004) filled with everyday objects (wooden and metal spoons, fir cones, sponges, balls, lids); play games like 'peep-bo' and finger rhymes like 'Walking round the garden … '; listen to music, provide bell bracelets and anklets, rain-makers and castanets, do lots of clapping, dancing and singing.

Words and concepts

The nature of words and concepts has been taken for granted throughout this discussion and it is time to pull together some assumptions about the early emergence of words, the rapid growth in young children's vocabulary and the ways in which children's words reflect their social and cultural experiences and their own thinking.

- The verbal and social welcome given to newborn babies reflects adults' belief that sharing meanings and social communication with newborns is possible. Adults continue to attribute these social motives and abilities to all the early responses of babies (burps, hiccups, cries, gurgles) and to their later sounds and words.
- From the start of their relationship, adult and infant take part in mutual ques-tion-and-answer routines. This implies a practical belief that these language games have meaning and that questions are potentially capable of being answered by infants.
- Bruner (1983: 86) has also pointed out that most carers do work on the assumption that no one is entirely ignorant, not even an infant, and no adult is all-knowing either.

These fascinating behaviours highlight the important fact that meaning is far more extensive and complex than individual words: areas of meaning have to be constantly sorted out, negotiated and clarified. The fact that at some time we have all had the experience of struggling to put our meanings into words for an important letter, essay or argument indicates this. Such struggles with words and meanings are a daily feature of children's gradual acquisition of words and con-cepts in infancy and in the early years of schooling. Perhaps we are not too aware of this because the struggle is often shared with an older language user and is a source of pleasure and delight for both partners.

> ## Example
> It is breakfast and 3-year-old Mattias drains his mug of milk and asks for 'More, mummy'. His mother inadvertently overfills the mug and as he struggles to hold it and drink he says 'My milk's too big'.

The business of establishing mutual reference, what it is we are both pointing to, referring to or discussing, is started in the infant's earliest weeks and months. At this stage, as in the later labelling-of-the-environment stage, mutual negotiations and feedback are important and effort goes into getting it as right as is humanly possible. Bruner's (1983) analysis of a possible developmental pattern for establishing early reference focused on carers' games with babies and the progress from simple eye contacts to shared commentaries on interesting objects, people and events. Often a great number of 'where is it?' and 'what is it?' games and rituals develop around this stage and they further reinforce the infant's ability to communicate, refer to things and share meanings with adults and older children. Similarly, book and picture reading, involving shared pointing and naming, support and strengthen the child's early awareness of words as labels that mark out and refer to areas of meaning.

Labelling is an important feature of early language and thinking, and adults and older children tend to name a whole object for a baby. They will say, 'it's a horse', rather than 'it's a grey hair on the left fetlock of a Suffolk Punch stallion'. The establishment of such big basic generic categories like 'horse' enables beginners to get a grip on the language. Broad classifications are a good start. Subsets and other distinctions are organized and refined over time, by general experience as well as formal education.

Pairing objects and names in this way demonstrates a fundamental feature of a linguistic system. There is a conventional, or culturally agreed, relationship between *the sign* (picture, word), *the phonetic pattern* (sound) 'horse' and *the signified*, the actual living creature in front of us, or its pictorial representation. Playing linguistic games with experienced speakers eases children into the ways in which their communities name the world. A great deal of object naming occurs in early infancy, not just when looking at picture books, magazines and photos, but when participating in daily routines, games of I-spy, peekaboo and body labelling ('where's your nose?') and even when focusing on some television images. In the early years, conversations with attentive adults help children to sort out their understandings of words and concepts and the mysteries of the world.

> ## Example
> In an early years centre, a boy who is not quite 3 is fascinated by the beautiful crescent-shaped shell necklace worn by Donna, his key person. He is a Farsi speaker at home and English is his second language. He points at the necklace, 'Look moon.' He then points upwards, 'How did you get it from up there?'

Vygotsky's research into concept formation and Piaget's and Bruner's into the development of early representation indicate that in the first 18 months or so infants move gradually from acting on their environments and solving problems 'with their bodies', to acting and problem-solving 'in their heads'. The words children acquire are powerful tools for identifying, sorting, classifying and reorganizing information and experience.

Words refer to actual things, states and events in the world, but they are the evidence of underlying concepts or classifications in the minds of speakers. Concepts are general categories and they make symbolic thinking possible. Symbolic thinking is thinking freed from dependence on physical perceptions and present actions: all the action and manipulation is in the head. It is these concepts, or general linguistic categories, that become increasingly significant in children's thinking strategies and are dominant in mature adult thinking. But concepts have their origins in perceptions, actions and the shared learning of language in communities.

Concepts are built up slowly in individual development. They are the collaborative and shared creations of the linguistic community but they are taken over by individuals and coloured by personal feelings and associations. The fact that concepts develop over time and by a process of negotiation and modification in individual language learning is demonstrated by small children's many over- and under-extensions of words in use. At this stage every man in the street may be called 'daddy' (over-extension) and 'bottle' can only be the feeding bottle belonging to this particular baby (under-extension).

Thinking with concepts is a flexible and powerful system because it enables us to generalize and group together instances of 'the same'. With this grouping potential we are also able to differentiate and classify those events and things that are 'not' instances. Linguistic concepts reflect an infinite range of possible hierarchies and categories: many of these mirror habitual ways of thinking in particular cultural traditions. Concepts are a flexible range of options that help us to impose some order and pattern on the complexity and diversity of raw experience. This infinitely adaptable tool for thinking and organizing knowledge is created in the process of learning a language. A concept may start its slow growth from a picture-book label, a simple toy or the experience of being held up by an adult to look out of the window. The development of concepts is affected by personal life experiences, cultural traditions and the subtle processes by which any new information, new experiences and new words are matched to, and integrated with, the already experienced, named and known. The range of language modes – listening and talking, writing and reading – as well as quiet reflection and the shared life of homes and the wider community, are all influences on individual conceptual thinking.

Summary

- Meaning and reference are first established in the games and inter- actions that are the start of joint attention between adults and their infants.
- Labelling objects, actions, events and ideas begins in earliest infancy and helps to isolate words as specific areas of meaning. First labels are usually general names for things but they demon- strate the language community's ways of classifying the world.
- Words refer to actual experiences and things in the world but they also stand for concepts or classifications in the minds of speakers.
- Concepts are generalized categories: they classify similarities, dif- ferences and hierarchies (or families) of connected ideas, objects and happenings.
- Thinking with concepts develops with language use and is a life- long process of learning to handle new experiences and information by modifying and reorganizing the already known and familiar.

Learning and teaching suggestions

- Look at picture books and name people, animals and objects; make some of the appropriate noises and talk about what might be going on.
- Introduce simplified games of 'I-Spy' to young talkers, but use colours as the clues before gradually going on to initial 'sounds' and letters.

⊶ Key terms

Dispositions: stable attitudes, or patterns of responses found in individual approaches to learning and participating – curiosity or persistence, for example.
Linguistic determinism: the claim that an individual's thinking and world view is tightly shaped by the language of their specific speech community.
Neuroscience: the study of how the brain develops and changes.
Schemas: patterns of behaviour into which experiences are assimilated and coor- dinated – distinctive ways of thinking and learning.

📖 Further reading

Aitchison, J. (2003) *Words in the Mind: An Introduction to the Mental Lexicon*. 3rd edn. Oxford: Blackwell.

Athey, C. (2007) *Extending Thought in Young Children: a Parent–Teacher Partnership*. 2nd edn. London: Paul Chapman Publishing.

Blakemore, S.-J. and Frith, U. (2005) *The Learning Brain: Lessons for Education*. Oxford: Blackwell.

Fabian, H. and Mould, C. (eds) (2009) *Development and Learning for Very Young Children*. London: Sage Publications.

Gerhardt, S. (2004) *Why Love Matters: How Affection Shapes a Baby's Brain*. Hove: Routledge.

Goldschmied, E. and Jackson, S. (2004) *People Under Three: Young Children in Day Care*. 2nd edn. London: Routledge.

Gopnik, A., Meltzoff, A. and Kuhl, P. (1999) *How Babies Think: The Science of Childhood*. London: Weidenfeld and Nicolson.

Goswami, U. (2008) *Cognitive Development: The Learning Brain*. Hove: Psychology Press.

Meadows, S. (2006) *The Child as Thinker: The Development and Acquisition of Cognition in Childhood*. 2nd edn. London: Routledge.

Nutbrown, C. (2006) *Threads of Thinking: Young Children Learning and the Role of Early Education*. 3rd edn. London: Sage.

Pinker, S. (2007) *The Stuff of Thought. Language as a Window into Human Nature*. London: Penguin Books.

Vygotsky, L.S. (1986) *Thought and Language*. Revd and ed. by A. Kozulin. Cambridge, MA: MIT Press.

CHAPTER 5

THE EARLY YEARS PRACTITIONER AND KNOWLEDGE ABOUT LANGUAGE

This chapter includes:

- practitioner knowledge about language
- aspects of language study in early years settings
- aspects of language in social settings
- aspects of language, thinking and learning in the early years.

Theory into practice

A curriculum is always a selection from the available knowledge and experiential resources of a culture and even a nationally imposed curriculum only stipulates broad areas of consensus. There are still many choices to be made, from linguistics as well as myriad other activities and disciplines. Choices and value judgements are unavoidable. At every point in the day, early years practitioners are saying and implying, 'this rather than that'. It is surely better for these choices to be informed rather than haphazard, to be explicit rather than hidden, or even irrational. Practitioners have to make sense of language knowledge, not just for 'these children', but for these children in this place, at this time and in relation to these families and these communities. Professional involvement in children's homes and communities is an acknowledgement of children's great potential for language and learning and the role of their families as educators. Early years settings and schools cannot hope to be just like homes and families but they may, as institutions staffed by caring and knowledgeable practitioners, learn how to minimize their drawbacks and develop good human learning practices.

The choices made by practitioners must be informed and this is where the usefulness of a body of knowledge such as linguistics can be assessed. So, of what use to early childhood educators and young learners is the material in the previous chapters? This question is one we all have to answer for ourselves: statutory requirements, lists of easy answers and model lesson plans are not really helpful. After all, they lack the crucial contextual knowledge of situations, families, individuals and pedagogy which only the professional practitioner can bring together.

In the context of this book, informed choices guiding the move from theory into practice will necessitate

- some understanding of the development of the modern study of linguistics with its strong emphasis on communication and spoken language, including an awareness of linguists' accounts of how language works as a system (Chapter 1)
- awareness of how languages are understood, learned and used in particular social settings (Chapters 2, 3 and 4)
- practitioners knowing how to stimulate and nurture young children's conscious knowledge about, and delight in, their own languages.

The following sections are pointers towards educationally worthwhile practices that might be developed from some of the things families, children and practitioners know about language as a system, language in social settings and language in thinking and learning.

Knowledge about language

A kind of 'national view of language' is now enshrined in the separate curriculum frameworks for England, Wales, Scotland and Northern Ireland. But, one of the great dangers of formalizing in legislation what counts as knowledge about language is the creation of an orthodoxy, a kind of official view of language. This will tend to underestimate the inexperienced and very young users of a particular language, as well as any other people who are in the process of learning the language. An established national view of language (or of anything else) is always in danger of becoming petrified and unchangeable. The irony of this is that languages are always changing in subtle and complex ways in order to meet the evolving needs and circumstances of their speakers.

Language knowledge for early years practitioners should, at the very least, include familiarity with some of the detailed, long-term studies that reveal the richness and intellectual power of young children's language development in secure and familiar domestic settings (Campbell, 1999; Heath, 1983; Tizard and Hughes, 2002; Whitehead, 2002; 2007). The grammatical, cognitive and social perspectives outlined in the first part of this book suggest that early years practitioners and families should know that:

- all children are active linguists
- all languages are complex grammatical systems
- all natural languages are, or have been, spoken
- language and thinking are inextricably linked.

This knowledge should be an expansion and enrichment of practitioners' insights, not a requirement to narrow our concerns to a tight set of goals for communication, language and literacy. Language in use for living and learning should still be at the heart of the language curriculum and this should inform all the thinking and professional practices of practitioners.

Early years practitioners may be helped by holding on to some important curriculum principles for language planning.

- Babies and very young children entering group care and education settings are in the process of accomplishing their greatest intellectual and social feat of learning: they are, with very rare exceptions, learning to produce and understand a language, or two!
- Our professional practices depend on making informed choices based on our knowledge and experience of children, society and the curriculum. But these choices are only provisional and should always be subject to professional criticism and reappraisal.
- Worthwhile care and education in the early years should be dominated by the children's need to discover, organize, make sense of and enquire about their worlds. These essential cognitive activities will be developed by play and symbolic representation which enable children (and adults) to repeat, hold on to and reflect on ideas, feelings and events.
- This 'holding' is possible because symbols that stand for ideas and experiences of all kinds are created through playing, gesturing, making marks, drawing, building, labelling, naming, story-telling and writing. Symbols reflect not just the personal lives and interests of individuals, but the social and cultural practices of communities.

The most significant aspect of knowledge about language for the early years practitioner is the insight that language is about human potential.

This positive approach can be found in the Early Years Foundation Stage (DCSF, 2008) guidance for England and in the documentation for the early years in Wales, Scotland and Northern Ireland. All this legislation appears to acknowledge the importance of play and communication as the essential precursors to children's language and literacy development.

Language study in early years settings

The study of language may seem to be rather abstract and remote from the concerns of very young children, and not likely to touch their lives. But this view does not stand up to serious examination.

- Very young children are, as I have claimed above, active linguists. They are born communicators, eavesdroppers, language learners, speakers and listeners; many are happily bilingual and they are all somewhere on the way to becoming writers and readers. There is nothing remote about their degree of involvement in language matters: much of what researchers know about linguistics is based on studies of child language acquisition and development.
- The professionals who work with young children are actually making linguistic decisions throughout the day and these need to be educationally as well as linguistically 'good' reasons for intervention. The practitioner should judge 'worthwhile' activities and decisions as being of value primarily for the children. These judgements should lead to choosing, resourcing and supporting activities and areas of knowledge (including language) that are believed to be intrinsically valuable and interesting to the children, that extend what they know and can do already, that enrich their thinking and imagining, and that increase their self-control, well-being and independence.
- Potential language study has gone on in early years settings and homes for a long time, but we have just called it by different names:

> talking; listening; interacting; playing and role play; mime; action songs and rhymes; singing; poetry; nursery and nonsense rhymes; mark-making; drawing; emergent writing; story-telling; story-reading; shared reading; looking at books; making labels, lists, books, notices, greetings, directions and instructions; using letter magnets, computers and printing sets; shared writing.

This rich panorama of language study can be brought into sharper focus if we concentrate on four significant aspects of the language curriculum:

- playing with language
- telling stories and sharing books
- writing
- using 'words about language'.

Playing with language

Playing with language starts with sound and it starts in the cradle. Sound is the very stuff of language and it is exploited and mucked about whenever and wherever babies (and carers) blow 'raspberries', gurgle, squeal and babble for the sheer delight of doing it. Infants continue to play this kind of language game when they are alone at night, well into the second and third year of life (Nelson, 1989; Weir, 1962). Researchers have recorded highly patterned rhyming and alliterative sequences by young children which indicate a very early delight in practising and playing with language:

> bink
>
> let bobo bink
>
> bink ben bink
>
> blue kink. (Weir, 1962: 105)

This recording of Anthony at 2 years 6 months was made in the 1950s, but modern research studies now highlight the significance of alliteration and rhyme for children's early success in learning to read and understand the writing system (Bryant and Bradley, 1985; Goswami and Bryant, 1990; Bruce and Spratt, 2008). These issues are explored further in Chapter 7 but the implications are already becoming clear. We should avoid reliance on such oddities as 'sound of the week' and phonic lists with very young children, mainly because people talking and playing with language are the real source of phonological knowledge – not arbitrary lists! Children in early years settings need opportunities to babble and chatter as well as experiencing a rich diet of songs, rhymes, poetry, nonsense verse, word games and commercial and home-made alphabets.

> ## Example
> Four- and 5-year-old children in a language-rich Reception class frequently produce detailed pictures and rhyming captions that reflect a mixture of environmental studies and a lot of playful imagination: 'My mole is dancing in a hole in the South Pole.'
>
> (St John's Infant School, Norfolk)

Play with language can be mildly naughty when rude noises and silly words emerge from phonological and alphabetical experiments, but this subversive aspect of language play is not only motivating for the young linguist, it is intellectually stimulating. For it is not only sounds and words that are played around with; right from the start ideas are turned upside down (Figure 5.1).

In the 1920s Chukovsky (1963: 94) wrote of the 'topsy-turvies' which constitute children's first jokes and the humour of ancient folk tales and nursery rhymes. This is the world of cottages running away on chicken legs, adults going to sea in a sieve, cold porridge burning the mouth and cows jumping over the moon! The examples spring endlessly to mind, but it is worth thinking of them as test cases of reality in a culture, and as soon as little children get to know what is what, they exploit it relentlessly. It is as if knowing something means knowing its opposite and its 'non-instances'.

Figure 5.1   **Playing with ideas: what if trees were like people and people were trees? (Niamh, Reception)**

Example

My then 5-year-old grandson indicated his awareness of the cultural assumption that children must learn to count: 'I can count up to one hundred. One, two, miss a few, ninety-nine, a hundred.'

The power of such subversion is that it not only gets round the problem, it amuses adults and deflects criticism, but it also snatches back some self-esteem. This is crucial for the young and vulnerable who are never quite old enough, big enough or knowledgeable enough, hence the significance of all those characters in stories, folk tales and nursery rhymes who are sillier than any living child.

More about play

- Babies start with sensory explorations of movement, space and texture, but sounds, particularly voices, rhythmic and repeated language patterns, eye contact and facial expressions, are laying the foundations of language. Pleasure and delight in the expectation that things can happen again and again develop rapidly and are extended by 'peekaboo' games, bouncing rhymes, mobiles, balls, moving toys and splashing water.

- Toddlers talk to toys, special blankets and, increasingly, to themselves. They are creating imaginary, or pretend, scenarios and stories and organizing their own thinking. They love to hide away in boxes, under tables or in outdoor dens, and await discovery. They also like to 'lift the flaps' in books and predict and discover what is going on.

- Socio-dramatic play is a feature of the early years as children investigate being like someone else, perhaps a story or television character, an animal, a parent, minder, teacher or doctor. This pretend involves talking as well as behaving and dressing like the character. Adults can provide relevant literacy materials in pretend homes, clinics, garages, hairdressers and construction sites.

- Play is the key, and the child creates the rules, makes the decisions and is in control. Adults may be invited or welcomed into the play and can then model some appropriate language and literacy practices, writing a shopping list, for example, or checking some information on the computer.

Telling stories and sharing books

Early encounters with stories and books support language study by introducing children to distinctive language and narrative patterns, such as beginnings, threats, challenges, solutions and endings. These kinds of events are marked by ritual openings, as in 'once upon a time', stylized descriptions such as 'rose red', and formal endings where all issues are resolved by the language of 'happy ever afters'. This is not a bit like the everyday spoken English heard and used on buses and in supermarkets, schools, playgroups and clinics, because this is the language of literary genres. However, it is far from unimportant because it provides a first bridge to written Standard English (SE): just hearing all kinds of stories and poetry read aloud enables children to become familiar with the distinctive patterns of written language. This implication holds good for the language of non-fiction information texts and we should give much more time to reading these texts aloud with children than we generally do. Many picture books are full of information (*ABC UK*, Dunn and Bate, 2008; *Egg Drop*, Grey, 2002; *Harry and the Dinosaurs Go to School*, Whybrow and Reynolds, 2006). Picture books can also introduce children to aspects of language such as alliteration (*Who's a Clever Baby Then?* McKee, 1988), or the clues to words given by end rhymes (*Each Peach Pear Plum*, Ahlberg and Ahlberg, 1977b; *The Jolly Postman*, Ahlberg and Ahlberg, 1986), and some explore dialects of English and the delights of rare and beautiful words (*The Mousehole Cat*, Barber and Bayley, 1990; *Flossie and the Fox*, McKissack and Isadora, 1986). There are even deceptively simple picture books (still in print after decades) which play with the nature and functions of adjectives and nouns, as well as colours – so why do we need 'colour tables' (*But Where Is the Green Parrot?* Zacharias and Zacharias, 1965; *Mr Rabbit and the Lovely Present*, Zolotow and Sendak, 1968)?

If we add to these experiences with books, games with print sets, magnetic letters, computer keyboards and important words and sentences written on strips of paper, we are helping children to explore the creative, or combinatorial, power of language. We are also teaching the first lesson of literacy: speech and writing are different. Talk is experienced as a stream of sound, but if it is to become writing it must be broken down into words and, eventually, smaller sound elements.

Writing

The fundamental focus of all literacy work must be to establish the understanding that writing conveys meaningful messages: messages that are informative, important and often pleasurable. Very young children use some powerful strategies in order to understand writing and these will be discussed in Chapter 8, but certain elements are worth noting here in the context of language study.

- There is the very effective strategy which we might call '*watch the others*' and this includes watching not just adults, older children and peers, but looking at television, posters, street signs, shops, vehicles, junk mail and public buildings.
- There is the '*use your name*' ploy which gives every child a useful tool for breaking into the writing system. Names matter, they place you in the world and are frequently heard and seen in many contexts, but, most importantly of all for the beginning writer and reader, they are a known combination of meaningful sounds and symbols. Names give children daily demonstrations of how the alphabetic system works and initial letters and sounds are of great significance for this: 'That's D for Daniel', said Daniel, pointing to a museum dinosaur poster.
- '*Exploit what you know*' enables very young infants to get started on written communications as they use powerful cultural symbols like 'x' for kisses on letters, or various marks and even letters from their names on messages. The emerging principle seems to be one of 'use what you do know and have a

pretend go at the unknown bits'. This can develop into a full-blown emergent literacy strategy of using alphabetic knowledge, as well as exploiting those letter names which sound like words and syllables in frequent use: RUDF (are you deaf?) (Bissex, 1980: 3).

These inventive strategies and processes will take young children a long way along the road to understanding the alphabetic system. Children can be supported by provision which includes writing in play areas, indoors and outside (Figure 5.2); collecting advertising copy, newspapers, magazines and leaflets; and having opportunities to hear, see, discuss and create play scripts, television news bulletins, weather forecasts, emails, text messages, and so on.

Figure 5.2 **Writing in play areas (3 years)**

Using words about language

The use of 'words about language' is known to professional linguists as 'metalinguistics' and is an important component of serious language study at any level. For very young children and their practitioners it is a matter of being confident about understanding and using some special vocabulary for genuine purposes. This involves the regular use of such terms as 'word', 'letter', 'sound', 'upper case', 'lower case' and, even, 'sentence'. Such practices as reading large-format books with groups of children, making notices and leaving messages, creating pieces of shared writing and making books together, naturally require the use of even more specialized 'language about language': for example, 'cover', 'title', 'author', 'illustrator', 'publisher', 'printer', 'page', 'endpaper' and 'chapter'.

This approach is not only meaningful and pleasurable for children and adults, it is a sensible way of ensuring that children develop an interest in words and the language of particular written forms (genres) and social settings. Giving children opportunities to consider the characteristics of different kinds of texts, such as lists, recipes or poems, helps to extend their spoken and written vocabulary and their interest in how language works.

Language study need not be narrow, dull and limiting; it should be about playing with sounds and meanings and loving language. It is going on all the time and the children are keen to show us the way, as I discovered on a visit to a Year 1 class when two 6-year-olds set about subverting a particularly dreary science lesson on the naming of the parts of a tree.

> 'This is the bark,' said the teacher.
>
> 'Woof, woof,' said a little voice.
>
> 'And this is the trunk.'
>
> 'Elephants have trunks,' piped up another little linguist.

Language in social settings

Children are born into language-using communities and they gradually learn to communicate and share the language or languages of their particular social worlds. Earlier chapters have emphasized the high degree of linguistic variety within and between language communities, as well as the range of language choices individual speakers operate. The wealth of research material on infant and caregiver behaviours tends to be predominantly biased towards American and European cultures, and towards the child-rearing practices of mainstream, school-orientated or middle-class groups. We still have only a partial picture of the early stages of language learning, and many children in our early years settings and schools will have experienced cultural practices that are different and unknown to their practitioners.

There are many ways of welcoming babies into the world, nurturing them and supporting their learning of the particular languages and communicative traditions of their groups and societies. Attempts to understand and to record these other ways have begun to influence linguists, psychologists and educators. These approaches are generally described as 'ethnographic' and the most widely known studies are those that have investigated how young children experience and respond to forms of literacy and early schooling in cultures that are not traditionally schooling and book orientated. Ethnographic studies are a branch of anthropology and focus on all aspects of the social life of a distinctive group. Ethnographers go to great lengths to make themselves part of the social worlds they study, accepting their norms and styles, and avoiding, as far as possible, the use of intrusive and alien technologies and styles of interaction.

The result is many long-term studies closely based on daily life in homes, family groups, nurseries and schools (see, for example, Barratt-Pugh and Rohl, 2000; Brooker, 2002; 2008; Heath, 1983; Marsh and Hallett, 2008; Serpell et al., 2005; Whalley and Pen Green Centre Team, 2007). This work focuses on such issues as who the main caregivers of babies are in the early months and years of language acquisition and what the characteristic features of their interactions and relationships are, as well as raising questions about the degree of sensitive understanding these young children encounter on entering group settings. The answers to these questions are tentative, but can be added to our own cultural assumptions about language learning.

The human infant is highly valued and cared for with some deep affection and, although not always mothered by only one adult, is the special responsibility of certain adults and groups of older children. The main aim of these carers seems to include 'teaching' the infant the ways and the language of the community. This is not necessarily done by looking at picture books or playing games of peekaboo and 'what's this?'. Instead, there may be instructions in religious stories, rituals and eating habits, or the involvement of the infant in the games, songs and language play of older children (Heath, 1983). Behind all these teaching activities in many cultures is a strong desire to help young children join the community as full speaking members as soon as possible. To this end, interactions with very young children are generally tolerant of their inadequacies, supportive of lots of language practice, full of praise and pride in the children's progress and, sometimes (but not always), simplified in the range of linguistic forms used:

> Mother: I got washing to do, ironing to do, hoovering …
>
> Child: Yes?
>
> Mother: Well, it all takes time.
>
> Child: And then you're finished?
>
> Mother: Yes.
>
> Child: I don't want you to do hoovering and washing.
>
> Mother: I'm sorry, but I've got to. (Tizard and Hughes, 2002: 75)

Donna, the child, was learning not just some language patterns but the realities of working life and priorities for women and children of a specific social class in inner London. In communities and societies everywhere, children learn their languages as part and parcel of their learning about roles and functions individuals perform in the community. They learn when to speak and when to stay silent, when to be deferential and when to assert their rights as speakers. The complexity of these judgements makes them part of the inside knowledge of a group.

Educators who are on the fringes of many communities must, like ethnographers, try to observe, understand and acknowledge without imposing their inappropriate judgements. If early years practitioners can learn to listen to their children and their families without prejudice, they too may learn to move more easily and confidently between language worlds and cultures. This is, after all, what schooling demands of many of these young children. Cultural variety also involves diverse kinds of voice intonation and pitch patterns, and markedly different ranges of body language. Such differences put considerable responsibility on the practitioner to be knowledgeable, observant and less easily offended than the average person.

So many different 'ways with words' (Heath, 1983) should shake us out of our Western research complacency but not obscure the fact that all children learn to speak in broadly similar stages and rates. Children learn to insert themselves and their needs into the ongoing concerns of the group and they learn to involve other people in doing things for them. Researchers are now aware that this is achieved in secure and intimate first relationships which allow infants to be playful, bold and teasing (Reddy, 1991; Trevarthen, 1993; 2002). The role of older and more experienced members of the community remains very significant in all children's learning and language acquisition. This role may be performed differently, according to the values and beliefs of the group, but it is geared to the child's well-being and eventual full participation in the community:

> They gotta know what works and what don't, you sit in a chair, but if you hafta, you can sit on other things too – stool, a trunk, a step, a bucket. Whatcha call it ain't so important as whatcha do with it. That's what things 'n people are for, ain't it? (Heath, 1983: 112)

One other common factor emerges from studies of learning to speak in many cultures: the central role of oral narratives. Children learn much of their language and their culture by listening to the telling of anecdotes, legends, gossip, stories, jokes, dreams and memories, and they are often encouraged to make their own story contributions, or praised for seizing the story-telling initiative (see Chapter 6).

Multilingualism in early years settings

Many children in early years settings are already bilingual or at some stage in the process of acquiring their second language, usually that of the group settings, schools and wider society. The reality of life in many multilingual families may be one language with parents; another for grandparents; another for religious observances and instruction; another for neighbours, shops and schools. This degree of linguistic variety is quite usual for many young children

(Brooker, 2002; Drury, 2007; Gregory, 2008) and sometimes leads to situations in which these children become the essential mediators, advisers and links between their families and the mainstream public world (Gregory et al., 2004).

Bilingualism is an asset which increases children's linguistic awareness, cultural sensitivity and cognitive functioning. Similarly, teaching and caring for young bilinguals can offer practitioners the same benefits, but only if they are open to challenging new ideas. Young bilinguals are already operating with at least two potent symbolic systems for handling thought and experience, and their language learning in group settings is best supported by miming, signing and a variety of representational forms, such as pictures, stories, puppets, modelling and building, music and visits in the wider community.

Faced with children's linguistic creativity and diversity, monolingual practitioners must first acknowledge the greater linguistic skills, experience and potential of their pupils. A start can then be made on using other languages in early years settings and schools for important functions and the prestigious curriculum areas. Dual language signs on cloakrooms and offices are useful, but restricting some languages to very basic functions signals their possible exclusion from education, achievement and success in the wider dominant culture. To exclude a language is to exclude its speakers. Even the well-intentioned arrangement of two languages in dual language textbooks and other materials needs careful thought: unintended hidden messages about status and values should be anticipated and avoided. A few authors and publishers have begun to change the practice of printing English first, with other languages underneath, and there is a modest amount of worthwhile children's literature and reference texts in several languages – but still not enough. However, practitioners can get help in finding what publications are available by subscribing to a children's books journal such as *Books for Keeps*.

We can make our own bilingual texts in our settings, as well as games and other materials, including, most importantly, the contributions and involvement of the children's families. Technologies such as computers and publishing software, ring-binding and laminating machines, photocopiers, digital cameras and so on, support and extend the professional skills of the practitioners and families, as well as the children.

None of us has the linguistic skills and cultural experiences to meet the language needs and strengths of all the bilingual children in our settings. Recruiting some bilingual staff, as well as inviting the participation of parents, grandparents, older siblings and other members of the local linguistic groups, can provide a rich human resource of multi-language tutors and literacy materials (Kenner, 2000). This open-door policy can also teach us a great deal about the home and community-based language and literacy experiences of the children and the expectations their families have of schools, nurseries, children's centres and other early years settings (Brooker, 2002; Gregory, 2008).

If learning a new language is about 'making sense of a new world' (Gregory, 2008), we should all make a start on an effective policy for bilingualism by learning as much as possible about the spoken and written forms and traditions of the languages used in our early years settings and communities. We should always be very positive about the languages of the children in our settings: encouraging play, talk and singing between speakers of languages we do not ourselves understand and use, as well as supporting these children as they take on the roles of interpreters. We can encourage older, or more confident, bilingual children, as well as parents and other family members, to be support tutors for us and the children. This human network will enable us to make a start on teaching and learning the songs, dances, rhymes, legends and stories of other cultures – sometimes in translation and always in the original forms.

Story-telling supported by gestures, dramatic expressions, pictures and other props or guides to meaning, and poetry and song with their rhythmic musical messages, can be accessible human experiences across many languages in the early years setting. Children, parents and practitioners can write and print bilingual texts about the children's lives and learning, and collect examples of the different scripts in use in the community. This could be extended to the writing of letters, notes and information about the group setting so that genuine and mutually helpful multi-language material emerges out of real needs and is formulated for real audiences. Such collaborations may help us to understand other languages, appreciate the complexities of bilingual choices and of translations between languages, and even help us to understand other people a little better.

Standard English (SE)

- All dialects, not just Standard English, have distinctive vocabulary, plus rules and conventions of grammar, spelling and punctuation (see Trudgill, 2003).

- Standard English has acquired its considerable social prestige just because it is the required 'standard' and is used in all serious and influential communications, professions, the media, and centres of power and authority.

- The use of Standard English should not be linked to the use of Received Pronunciation (RP). Changing our accents is a complex matter of phonological adjustments and psychological motivation. Children begin their speaking lives sounding like the people around them and they go on to develop their accents in ways that reflect the various significant groups they attach themselves to, including peer groups in early years settings, schools, clubs and streets. We all change our accents if we wish to sound like and be accepted by particular groups, so that many of us end up being flexible users of several ranges of English accent.

- Simple communication devices such as pretend telephones and answering machines, radios, televisions and video recorders, installed in the role-play homes, clinics, offices and cafés we set up in the outside and inside areas of our settings, can stimulate impressive language switching and playful experiments with standard dialect and even RP.

- We should learn to make the most of the great range of possibilities for language switching, new communication styles and new vocabulary found in stories and literature. The challenge of dramatizing a story is, how do you talk, gesture and walk like a queen, a shopkeeper, a fairy godmother, a pop star, a cunning monkey or a hungry monster? Making and using puppets provides another way of changing and exploring all the possibilities of language in use. While a child is hidden behind the persona of a puppet many emotional, cognitive and linguistic risks can be taken: rude challenges to powerful adults and expressions of terrible violence are all safely licensed.

- Young children are at the start of their language awareness journey, and the best thing that can happen to them is to spend part of their day with lively, sensitive and caring people who use SE dialect. Such experiences may leave open for most children the possibility of using SE themselves when they need it and judge it to be useful for a range of purposes.

Language, thinking and learning

The discussions in the first part of this book have returned frequently to the significance of some kind of adult–child partnership in early learning in general and in language learning in particular. It has been claimed that early language acquisition can be likened to getting involved in meaningful and mutually satisfying conversations with people we care about and respect. This model of how we are helped to achieve our greatest feat of human learning – the understanding and production of meaningful and appropriate language – might well serve as a model for caring, communicating, learning and teaching in the early years. Planning, introducing and developing a curriculum for the early years should be guided by the principle that *young children need to be involved in doing things with people and with words*.

Vygotsky (1978) claimed that adults make a special contribution to children's learning and development. He described this (ibid.: 85) as 'a new and exceptionally important concept': the zone of proximal development. The significance of this idea is that instead of gearing teaching and learning to what is apparently a child's present level of development and competence, good caring, parenting and teaching always aim for potential by taking young learners, with adult support, just beyond their present achievements. *The zone of proximal development is the key area of the child's maturing and emerging abilities.* This is where, with adult support, a child's language and thinking are most fruitfully developed. This theory, which focuses on adult assistance and support in child learning, is an explanation of 'how the more competent assist the young and less competent to reach that higher ground from which to reflect more abstractly about the nature of things' (Bruner, 1986: 73). It is a description of good educational and child-rearing practices in many cultures, homes, early years settings and schools. It must also be the crucial factor in the remarkable success of projects that encourage families to enjoy reading, writing and mathematical activities at home with their children. Long-term research projects also highlight the significant contribution to children's thinking and learning made by professional educators who involve young children in one-to-one conversations that are a form of 'sustained shared thinking' (Siraj-Blatchford et al., 2002).

The studies of language acquisition discussed in Chapter 3 reveal general features that could inspire our thinking and planning for language learning and development in early years group settings and classrooms. One set of factors is the richness and complexity of the social, cultural and linguistic input to which babies and infants are exposed. In the world outside schools and institutions there is little evidence of controlled and restricted language models, of limited access to adults or rather narrow and safe notions of what is sensible and suitable for children to see and do in terms of daily life and work. This may account for the intriguing fact that children often display greater ingenuity and determination in their linguistic and general learning outside classrooms than in them. In streets, homes and markets small children make choices, switch languages and dialects, argue, build, repair, feed animals, help smaller infants, make messes and mistakes and even clear them up. This is not an argument for unregulated child exploitation and labour, but a reminder that children are people and already on the way to being well versed in the values and preoccupations of their cultures.

Perhaps something of this richness of human experience could be allowed to permeate and make human sense of the curriculum in the early years (Figure 5.3). It can be seen as a warning about the impoverishment of learning that occurs if we present children with very limited models of language in use and rather artificial examples of written language designed especially for beginning readers and writers. Research and observations suggest that children can only begin to develop their full linguistic and cognitive potential in response to language and situations that make real demands on them and extend some of their own interests and present understandings. This has implications that need to be fully worked out in language, literacy and literature policies in the early years of schooling (see Part II).

In our understandable anxiety to get children going on the subjects of the curriculum and to develop their language, now that we have goals to reach and assessments to prepare for, we may be in danger of forgetting the very lengthy periods of watching and listening that precede language production in first- and second-language learning in infancy. We should also keep in mind the prior establishment of interpersonal understanding that characterizes the emergence of language, as well as remembering that the earliest utterances are functional (see Chapter 3). Early years practitioners can plan for and establish the kinds of environments and interpersonal relationships that sustain and maximize children's chances of watching, listening, interacting, talking, playing and experimenting with language and with people. Young children themselves will be motivated by their desire to be involved in the social life around them, to understand what is going on and, of course, to get the affection, help and good things which language can deliver.

Figure 5.3   Making human sense of the curriculum – following a recipe with words and pictures (Reception)

Possible problems

Any number of physical, cognitive and/or emotional problems in infancy and early childhood can make an adverse impact on children's communication and language development. It is also clear that difficulties and delays in language development can cause social and emotional problems that have a negative effect on children's educational progress.

Children with degrees of language delay, communication difficulties and problems with speech production will inevitably experience some frustration and emotional disturbance. Early years practitioners will need to support these children with ample opportunities for play and social contacts, energetic activity and signing, gesturing, mark-making, drawing, painting and modelling. Young children on the autism disorder spectrum need lots of visual clues and indicators, frequent eye contact and close personal communication, as well as helpful early warnings and reassurances about changes of activity, location and people. They will also need specific help in order to understand and interpret the facial expressions and body language of other children and adults. The bold, expressive illustrations of faces and emotions in children's picture books can be a great help to some high functioning children on the autistic spectrum.

Example

Nine-year-old Robert was seen by his mother grimacing dramatically in front of a large bedroom mirror. When she asked what he was doing, he replied, 'I'm practising my faces.' Apparently, Robert, who is high functioning autistic, had been involved in experimental tutoring using books with illustrations similar to those in 'Thomas the Tank Engine' (Awdry, 1997) books.

Any impairment to a child's sight or hearing will have some effect on levels of frustration, emotional well-being and understanding. Practitioners must ensure that alternative modes of communication are enriched. Children with impaired hearing will be particularly dependent on facial expressions, lip movements, gestures and body language, signing systems and picture clues. Children who have visual impairments will need access to tactile, sensory communications through touch, smell and hearing, so a rich oral curriculum of talk, rhyme, song and music is essential.

Restricted and limited language use in children suggests, leaving aside sensory, cognitive and physical impairments, restricted and limited lives that may be very low on ordinary talk, care, domestic routines and general involvement with more experienced and competent adults. Good early years provision and care in group settings can compensate for the rare cases of deprivation of these requirements by enriching and expanding ordinary human activities and language-learning practices.

'Good enough' language teachers like 'good enough' parents and carers (Winnicott, 1971: 13) mediate between young children and the wider world of language use, presenting infants with just enough novelty and challenge in secure and unthreatening situations. What constitutes 'just enough' novelty and challenge must be decided on the basis of the zone of proximal development indicated by children's spontaneous play, pretence, dispositions and interests.

Early years settings are increasingly responsible for infants under 3 years of age and a rich range of communication strategies for babies must be planned for and developed. It is important that we focus on the huge potential of these very young learners and understand that they are skilful communicators. Their needs may be summarized as:

- being in warm and loving relationships
- finding a voice in a variety of ways
- listening and responding to what is going on
- making meaning with a key person.

The notion of a relationship with a key person at home and in the care and education setting is essential for the young child's well-being and language development (Goldschmied and Jackson, 2004). Other researchers have also confirmed this approach (Elfer et al., 2003) for children who are cared for on a daily basis away from their parents and claim that it sets them up for life.

In early years settings there must continue to be a particular focus on the role of communication and spoken language for a wide range of functions and situations. The non-verbal interactions and the talk children use to sustain their play and pretending are crucial, as is their emerging interest in the language of books and other literary forms. But, first and foremost, early years settings should be organized to promote genuinely mutual contacts and conversations between children and adults, and between children and children. This may well involve reorganizing the space, the furniture and the routines, or bringing in adults from the community to talk with (not at) children and share with them cooking, dancing, singing, building, birdwatching and gardening. The interesting thing about these kinds of projects is that they involve so much essential talking, signing, negotiating, planning, estimating, sorting, ordering, predicting, writing and reading that attainment targets and goals for communication, language and literacy are achieved and surpassed in the course of worthwhile cooperative learning.

 Further reading

Britton, J.N. (1992) *Language and Learning*. Harmondsworth: Penguin.

Brock, A. and Rankin, C. (2008) *Communication, Language and Literacy from Birth to Five*. London: Sage.

Bruce, T. (ed.) (2010) *Early Childhood: A Guide for Students*. 2nd edn. London: Sage.

Clark, A. and Moss, P. (2001) *Listening to Young Children: The Mosaic Approach*. London: National Children's Bureau/Joseph Rowntree Foundation.

Department for Children, Schools and Families (DCSF) (2008) *The Early Years Foundation Stage: Setting the Standards for Learning, Development and Care for Children from Birth to Five*. Nottingham: DCSF Publications.

Makin, L. and Whitehead, M. (2004) *How to Develop Children's Early Literacy: A Guide for Professional Carers and Educators*. London: Paul Chapman Publishing.

Nyland, B., Ferris, J. and Dunn, L. (2008) 'Mindful hands, gestures as language: listening to children', *Early Years: An International Journal of Research and Development*, 28(1): 73–80.

Siraj-Blatchford, I. and Manni, L. (2008) '"Would you like to tidy up now?" An analysis of adult questioning in the English Foundation Stage', *Early Years: An International Journal of Research and Development*, 28(1): 5–22.

Whitehead, M. (2009) *Supporting Language and Literacy Development in the Early Years*. 2nd edn. Maidenhead: Open University Press.

Whitehead, M. (2007) *Developing Language and Literacy with Young Children*. 3rd edn. London: Paul Chapman Publishing.

PART II

LITERACY

CHAPTER 6

NARRATIVE AND STORYING

This chapter includes:

- the nature of narrative
- storying and making meanings
- developmental stories
- storying in early years settings.

Experiences of stories are highly significant in our lives and in the development of literacy. It is now usual to find that books on language, learning and early literacy include sections on the importance of children's experiences with stories. However, it is worth remembering that parents and early years practitioners have always tried to link the pleasures of telling stories and sharing books with their children's first attempts at reading. But understanding why encounters with stories have great significance for early literacy depends on more than good sense and cosy feelings about story-telling and books, important as they are. Professional practitioners' knowledge about the nature of stories must go deeper and include some insights into the nature of narrative.

Narrative

Narrative is the backbone of any story:

> I'll tell you a story
>
> About Jack a Nory
>
> And now my story's begun. (Traditional rhyme)

At its most elemental, narrative begins with the urge to tell about an event, person or feeling. Narrating may even be the oldest and most basic human language activity. 'Someone telling someone else that something happened' (Smith, 1981: 228) is the beginning of legends, chronicles, history, memoirs, biography and novels. Basic narrative is preoccupied with holding on to occurrences by telling about them and creating sequences of events ordered in time:

> Solomon Grundy,
>
> Born on a Monday,
>
> Christened on Tuesday,
>
> Married on Wednesday … (Traditional rhyme)

This remembering, retelling and ordering into a sequence hints at the ancient links between telling a tale and 'tallying' or counting and ordering any other sequence of events. Tellers are counters in the mathematical sense as well as in the story sense, giving their 'accounts' of life and events.

Professional students of narrative have speculated on the possible reasons that drive us all to tell endless stories about our daily lives, our families, our holidays, our childhoods and our probable futures. There are no undisputed answers to the speculations but narrating seems to be closely linked to the organization and recall of memory. The suggestion has been made that our narratives constitute a continuing proof of our existence, a sort of notch-cutting that bears witness to our lives (Le Guin, 1981: 194).

Another remarkable feature of narrative is the urge to evaluate or make judgements about persons and events. Narratives that are just concerned with telling a sequence of events in time order can become very tedious: we are only prepared to tolerate a sequence of 'and then … and then … and then … ' for a limited time. We are really waiting for clues to the teller's opinions, feelings and values. Indeed, it seems that this urge to tell a tale is really directed towards explaining, gossiping and speculating about human behaviour and the chances of life.

> Ding, dong, bell,
>
> Pussy's in the well.
>
> Who put her in?
>
> Little Johnny Green. (Traditional rhyme)

All this remembering, ordering, explaining and evaluating gives meaning and significance to the endless stream of sensations and events that we experience. What is very important and yet easily taken for granted in ordinary everyday narrating is the possibility of holding on to and repeating or representing for consideration what was in actuality a transient happening. Narrative is much concerned with going over sequences of events and giving them shape and pattern and, consequently, some kind of meaning or significance. This 're-presentation' of experiences in order to understand them better is a marked feature of human thinking, occurring in children's play, in art and across cultures. Representation, in this sense, is a central theme of the next *two* chapters on literature and early literacy. This present discussion introduces the fundamental insight that single fleeting events or feelings can be narrated or told any number of times and modified and shaped by the telling. We all feel the need to go over and over sequences of complex, joyful or terrible events in order to make them comprehensible or bearable. We have to live with our stories and we have to get them right. Everyday narrating is concerned with the extremes of celebrating and mourning, as well as with the middle ground where we sort out and construct our personal attitudes, beliefs and assumptions.

These strong claims for the importance of narrative in human experience, thought and culture are supported by psychologists and literary scholars. Literary scholars have claimed that narrative may be a primary act of mind, demonstrated in such cognitive activities as dreaming, remembering, planning, daydreaming and a whole range of language uses (Hardy, 1977: 12). We do not learn to be narrators simply by hearing stories and encountering books; on the contrary, we bring our own powerful and spontaneous narrative drive to bear on the stories of our cultures.

This view can be joined to another claim from research psychology, that human beings live more by fiction than by fact (Gregory, 1977: 394). The suggestion is that the endless narratives we are inclined to generate in our thinking are 'brain fictions' or hypotheses about the possible outcomes of courses of action and sequences of events – the scientist's hypothesis is a story which has great predictive power and flexibility. Narrative may be a crucial element in human evolution and intelligent adaptability, enabling the species to predict or make up stories about likely outcomes as well as remote possibilities. As we generate these scenarios we are evolving narratives of how we might react and cope.

Narrative form provides a way of holding on to experience and exploiting repetition to create a pattern suggestive of order, regularity and permanence:

> January brings the snow,
>
> Makes our feet and fingers glow.
>
> February brings the rain,
>
> Thaws the frozen lake again. (Sara Coleridge)[1]

But narrative also enables us to review the past and contemplate change and revolution: 'When Adam delved and Eve span,/Who was then the gentleman?' (John Ball).[2]

Narrative's traditional concern with implied and explicit values and judgements sharpens our awareness of the human voice or teller behind every story. The narrative invites at least our interest in the systems of values and the assumptions of the narrator, if not our whole-hearted approval. Sometimes we are given a conspiratorial nudge, or directly addressed as 'gentle listener' or 'dear reader' and invited to participate in the creation of the narrative spell. Young children readily join in the charm-like refrains that occur in traditional and modern tales, although they may be quite surprised if addressed directly by the authorial voice. This convention is learnt by exposure to the cultural forms of story-telling.

The issue of familiarity with conventions highlights the culturally diverse traditions of narrative. We need to cultivate greater sensitivity to the variety of narrative forms that have evolved. For instance, not all cultures have perceived time as linear and thrusting forwards into the future, as if carried on a railway track:

> To-morrow, and to-morrow, and to-morrow,
>
> Creeps in this petty pace from day to day,
>
> To the last syllable of recorded time; (William Shakespeare, *Macbeth*, V. v. 19)

Accordingly, not all cultural narratives and stories display a progression from a clear beginning, through a middle phase to a satisfactory ending where all the strands are neatly tied up. This familiar form has been created by literacy and young children need to be introduced to the pattern of the Western book-orientated tradition as an essential part of their emergence into literacy. However, this book-dominated kind of narrative need not be an alienating shock for children socialized into different traditions. Young children's urge to tell about events, to recall sequences of actions, to indulge in repeated tellings and to speculate about feelings and values must be nurtured as the only sound basis for literacy.

Learning and teaching suggestion

- In face-to-face play with the under-3s, tell little stories about their fingers and toes ('this little piggy went to market … '). Similar story games can apply to noses, chins, eyes and mouths!

Storying

'Storying' is a useful way to describe our continual creation of the basic and spontaneous narratives discussed in this chapter. The term is sometimes used as a way of distinguishing this personal narrative activity from the published or traditional stories current in a community. However, all storying and stories originate in a human need to make meaningful patterns and interpret experiences. Whole communities, as well as individuals, create these explanatory narratives.

Cultures making meanings

In the communities most of us know, dominated by print and the published book, it is not immediately obvious that cultures still create their meanings, histories and value systems through the explanatory narratives they generate and share. Modern publication tends to stress literacy as a matter of individual authorship and ownership, but the most formative cultural tales continue to be the anonymous and collective myths, legends and religious stories of the oral tradition. In these narratives, now fixed in print, we can still sense the active creation of cultural meanings as patterns of values and beliefs were thrashed out. The stress on the origins of the universe and human life; the concern with the relationships between the worlds of nature, gods and humanity; the issues of right and wrong behaviour and the ultimate meaning of life, are preserved in the myths and legends of all human groups. The usual narrative concern with values is strongly present in this early literature. Time and sequence are also crucial to communities: early storying was the main way of holding on to the chronicles of shared events, the history of a cultural group. The song-like recitation of events and eras, victories and disasters, was crucial to the creation of a sense of group experience and shared history – the origins of the word 'history' itself are linked as much with narrative as inquiry.

Traditional storying in oral cultures was not confined to mythical or epic events: folk tales were also shaped to explore the lives of humble people and to offer them advice, hope and consolation. The harsh facts and conditions of ordinary people's lives are still traceable in the prevalence in the tales of early deaths, restless ghosts, abandoned children, disastrous harvests, dying livestock and other catastrophes. However, comforts such as human love and fidelity, unexpected good luck, second chances and dreams of a better future are offered as solace and encouragement.

It would be a mistake to think that these traditional patterns of storying have now finished. Cultures and groups still need to tally the tales of their successes and failures and make of them a bearable record. Perhaps one can best see this in action in Western cultures when the media shape the public's responses to disasters and celebrations, as well as signalling the official view.

The significance of community narratives about street gangs, pop idols or football stars lies in the fact that they create symbols. Symbols generally represent something beyond themselves, by convention or association, and this is particularly important when the something else they stand for is difficult to grasp or as abstract and intangible as beliefs, attitudes, aspirations, emotions and ideas. Symbols make abstractions real, pictureable or tangible. Perhaps some obvious examples might be a wedding ring, a distinctive hairstyle or a degree-conferment ceremony.

The symbols created by the traditional and contemporary narratives of a culture are a kind of ready-made resource for the individual. They are taken over and used in the personal storying of all of us. They seem to become a special shorthand in the drawings, paintings and oral narratives of very small children: 'a big bad wolf'; 'the robber is going to shoot you'; 'some fierce dinosaurs'.

Complete stories as well as characters work in this symbolic way. Anansi, the spider man, represents for many of us human cunning, optimism and ingenuity. Robin Hood stands for the noble outlaw from a corrupt society, and similar characters are found in many diverse oral traditions. A Cinderella story occurs in numerous cultures and represents the eventual triumphant maturity of the poorest and most undervalued child. Or does it? Arguments about what these stories and characters symbolize only illustrate the power and the flexibility of the tales. We take them over and make of them what we will, or what we need.

Learning and teaching suggestions

- Create an environment in which telling and listening to stories have a very high priority. This requires planning for group talking and telling times; ample opportunities for individual child/adult confidences and chat; areas in the setting where children can talk in small informal groups (in gardens and outdoor spaces – sandpits, digging pits, climbing apparatus, trees, bushes, dens, playhouses/arbours; indoors – book corners, home-play areas, 'offices', 'clinics', 'garages', water trays, blockplay, clay tables, cooking areas).

- Think of how much quiet, intimate talk and narrating can go on in the course of changing nappies; feeding babies and helping toddlers with food; looking at a picture book; listening to a child reading a text; or tidying up and clearing away toys, tools and materials. Just try to boost the narrative potential of washing out paint pots and palettes or cleaning out the rabbit/hamster/goldfish!

Individuals making meanings

> If it's a story I'm telling, then I have control over the ending. Then there will be an ending, to the story, and real life will come after it. I can pick up where I left off. (Atwood, 1987: 49)

Patterns of group beliefs and values dominate cultural storying but a concern with controlling our own lives and preserving personal identity permeates individual storying. This is reflected in the constant need to go over events in our lives in an effort to make sense of our very existence and historical actuality:

> To begin my life with the beginning of my life, I record that I was born (as I have been informed and believe) on a Friday, at twelve o'clock at night. It was remarked that the clock began to strike, and I began to cry, simultaneously. (Charles Dickens, *David Copperfield*, 1850)

Much of individual storying is like this – entries in a mental diary or notches cut as reminders of our very existence, achievements and struggles. However, telling our own story is never totally concerned with self because it is always the story of becoming a person in a social world. Individual storying is, therefore, full of other people and the difficulties and pleasures of relationships.

Listing

Ways of evaluating and musing on the possibilities of life can vary with age and with culture. Lists of inventories of activities, preferences, achievements, people and places occur in records of very young children talking to themselves while alone in bed (Weir, 1962). Lists of known words, letters and numerals are also made by young children who are beginning to explore the nature of writing. This is not surprising as listing is a powerful method of tallying or taking a count of what we have done, seen, acquired, felt or learnt and occurs in many cultures and literatures. The Hebraic tradition (in the Old Testament), the Greek Homeric narratives and the stories of the American Indian tribes, list the achievements, personal qualities and property of their protagonists. A twentieth-century novel can still make dramatic use of listing with the names of many of the tunes featured in a piano-playing marathon (Burgess, 1987) and a contemporary picture book does the same with a repeated roll call of dinosaur names (Whybrow and Reynolds, 1999).

In listing we are not merely recording what we remember, we are preserving the world, the events and the passions that have made us what we are.

A fictional self

If we are to some extent what we know about ourselves, we are also a created fiction. As we tell a never-ending story about our life we create a fictional self around whom we weave adventures, feelings and expectations, anxious to improve on our heat-of-the-moment reactions by a continual editing process. This storying may be restricted to Western literate cultures (Scollon and Scollon, 1981) but the ability to place ourselves right in the centre of a story is a valuable start to becoming a reader and writer.

Once the self can be narrated about like a fictional character, the possibility of creating fictive families and friends opens up truly liberating and consoling worlds, as it did for Anne Frank when she created a 'friend' called Kitty, as a reader for her diary letters (Frank, 1954).

Much of the research indicates that children as young as 2 years may start to fictionalize the self and talk like a book if they are immersed in a book-sharing culture (Fox, 1993; Jones, 1996; Whitehead, 2002).

Cultural symbols

Literate and oral cultures enrich the evaluating process of individual storying through the cultural symbols of contemporary literature and traditional myths, legends and folk tales. As individuals we take over the patterns and the values of the stories we find and adapt them to our own needs. Young children probably make their earliest moral judgements in terms of the powerful opposites found in stories: weak/strong, good/bad, happy/sad. This mythic framework of values is reflected in children's story-telling and writing throughout the early years. Clearly this is an influence that will vary in specific details according to the dominant culture of the individual and the shared patterns of community beliefs. The evaluating typical of all narrating cannot emerge from nothing – it develops from the complex mix of different stories, proverbs, assumptions and social reactions that surround us all from birth, in any community. This means, of course, that any description of the development of individual storying must be tentative and related to the unique aspects of every individual's early experiences and to the culture in which the individual lives. Young bilingual children and their families criss-cross cultural boundaries in their encounters with the story traditions of their home community and the stories encountered in mainstream group settings and schools. It appears that grandparents are often crucial in integrating and interpreting children's experiences of multiple worlds of stories and culture (Gregory et al., 2007).

Learning and teaching suggestions

- Introduce the practice of adults in the setting, including visitors and family members, telling the children simple autobiographical anecdotes: 'When I was a little girl/boy not much older than you, … ' Encourage the children in their own personal and fantasy narrating. Find ways of recording these tales and turning them into books and electronic recordings. Invite families to come in and help with making and organizing these collections (provide support with writing and talking for adults who are unsure of their own literacy skills and welcome non-English versions, as well as offers of translations).

- Build up a collection of recorded oral stories, songs, poetry and reminiscences (use some published material but also ask families and members of the local community to record material for the children).

Scholars who focus on the early years of childhood identify narrative as highly significant in the development of a sense of self, as well as forming the foundations of literary understanding and literacy skills. This leads Jones (1996: 141) to claim that 'narrative form is a turning-point in a human being's understanding both of the world, and themselves'. In similar vein, Engel (1995: vii) works from the premise that 'The stories we tell and listen to shape who we are' and proposes a five-phase pattern of narrative development. Crucial to this pattern is the adult–child talk and reminiscing which creates a kind of portrait, or biography, of the infant – what Jones (1996: 163) describes as confronting the infant with herself as an object of contemplation. The stories which follow pick out some milestones along the path of narrative development.

Developmental stories

> But if it's a story, even in my head, I must be telling it to someone. You don't tell a story only to yourself. There's always someone else. Even when there is no one. (Atwood, 1987: 49)

From birth there is always someone who shares little stories with or about the baby or who conducts their own storying over and around the baby. Adult-talk to babies as young as 3 months seems to be establishing conversation-like patterns (see Chapter 3). Behind the adults' strings of questions and comments there are many hidden stories: propositions about lost and found, good and bad feelings, consolation and even the promise of happy endings. We might bear in mind that the conversation-like exchanges between carers and infants do not just establish early language learning patterns – they also establish the traditional narrative roles of teller and told.

The first two years

In the first two years of life it is the people constantly with the baby who tell most of the stories but around the second birthday many infants make a bid for the role of teller. Research identifies examples of first stories at around 2 years of age. One white British child, with support from a parent, developed a pretend account of a shopping expedition to buy some sweets. The stimulus for this fictional narrative was the child's noting and commenting on the absence of a man who had previously been working in the garden (Wells, 1981: 107). In similar fashion, a black 2-year-old in the USA developed a narrative commentary based on recalling a memorable first visit to church:

> It a church bell
>
> Ringin'
>
> Dey singin'
>
> Ringin'
>
> You hear it?
>
> I hear it
>
> Far
>
> Now (Heath, 1983: 170)

Around 2 years of age many children are already speculating out loud – creating little narratives in which they shape their raw experiences into explanations or propositions about life. The storying is usually embedded in conversations, play or commentaries on events and builds on the patterns of interaction established in early infancy: someone telling someone else that something happened!

Around 4 years

Around 4 years of age it is possible to hear and observe a much more conscious story-telling stance. The impact of early encounters with the traditional stories of the culture is increasingly apparent in the form of the stories as well as in the content. Children sometimes use ritual openings and standard plots, endings and characters (Ezra, 3 years, 6 months): 'It's gonna be long/once upon a time there was a big monster' (Fox, 1993: 88). Some children begin to address their chosen audience very firmly and demand the proper attention due to a story-teller (Adam, 3 years, 6 months):

> Hey listen to me ...
>
> I'm going to tell a story ...
>
> Once upon a time ...
>
> there were three little crocodiles ...
>
> named Flopsy, Mopsy and Cottontail ... (Sheridan, 1979: 12)

The sense of threat, of disasters narrowly averted and of powerful desires or wishes permeates many of the collections of children's early storying. It seems as if the content of traditional stories children take over and use in their own storying provides symbols for discussing their own life chances. It is a way of thinking about 'me' in the world.

Around 3 to 4 years

As children progress from around 3–4 years, the influence of the cultural blue-prints (Hughes, 1988) for story forms and content becomes more noticeable. But we should be wary of dismissing this as simple imitation or just retellings of stories heard and seen in early years settings. Children use these story patterns for their own purposes to go over and shape the raw material of their own lives. The complexity of the world, as growing children encounter it, has to be simplified and controlled – perhaps matched, somehow, to the categories of good and bad, love and hate, and so on. This is no easy task, but stories for young children help by concentrating on small segments of experience, on clear categories of behaviour and limited characterization.

Most importantly, stories provide endings in which the possibility of sorting everything out or testing experience to the extreme limits exists. It is not surprising that young children's vocalized storying sometimes reveals a preoccupation with myth-like issues of hatred, abandonment and despair, with everybody dead at the end. But the serious and tragic is not the only mode for making sense of experience, as a crocodile called 'Cottontail' has already indicated. At the age of 2–5, children can be both comical and rude as they sort out the inconsistencies of social life and the complexities of being human.

Up to 5

The early years of childhood are a peak period for indulging in nonsense. Nonsense storying is a traditional and respected way of speculating upon the possibilities of reorganizing the world. There is a great deal to be said for the usefulness of houses that can run around on chicken legs, fully furnished wombs that can be returned to in times of stress (Chukovsky, 1963: 38) or even garden brooms that can be turned into horses. Playing with possibilities is a central activity in early childhood and is not just restricted to straightforward storying – it occurs in storying linked to play materials, found objects, energetic physical activity and social play with other children.

Imaginary worlds in a bag

The West Yorkshire Playhouse pioneered a project in early years settings in Leeds to support and extend young children's story-making and creativity. The children were presented with a large bag and invited to explore the contents: these usually included such items as a length of fabric, a torch, some shells, feathers, nuts, and so on. The children were then encouraged to speculate about where the objects came from, what they looked and felt like, who might have owned them. They were invited to play with them and make up stories and dances about them and later they painted their experiences. The project was documented through photography.

(West Yorkshire Playhouse, 2000)

Learning and teaching suggestions

- Provide simple story bags or boxes containing fabrics, shells, torches, feathers, gloves, and so on and invite the children to invent stories and dances with them.
- Collect items for small world play scenarios that might inspire storying while playing (an acorn, small safety mirror, an egg cup, finger puppets, and so on).

After the early years

The necessity of having another person to share our storying with appears to diminish gradually in the early childhood years. This is not because the need for a listener to tell it to has lessened; on the contrary, we ensure that 'there's always someone else' by taking over the function of listener to our own tales. In psychological terminology, we internalize our language partner. This idea is not strange to any of us: the remarkable two-person dialogue of our earliest language learning experiences is still preserved when infants talk aloud to themselves or adults silently rehearse and debate their thoughts and dilemmas. The original dialogues of early infancy gradually turn inward to shape the inner speech functions of controlling, planning, recalling and predicting, as discussed in Chapter 3. But the voice of storying can also be added to this list. We become the tale, the teller and the told.

Around 8–9 years of age, the cultural models of stories are often used in talk and writing to explore the mysteries and worries that surround beginning to grow up. The expansion of life experiences exposes children to conflicts and threats that must be faced and identified. These conflicts between children 'in the middle years' of childhood often lead to musings on the rights and wrongs of peer group loyalties and disputes.

The important issue of the individual's relationship to society or cultural groups becomes central in adolescent and adult storying. The best evidence for this is our own insights into the personal storying and narratives that preoccupy us as private individuals. The unwritten autobiographies we are all composing as we go along consist of a set of well-shaped stories we can live with:

I was born,

my childhood,

I went to school,

my accident, my illness,

my love affairs,

my career …

Memory is the dominant form but the process of selective recall allows for a great deal of serious evaluating and the framing of significant moral judgements.

Learning and teaching suggestion

- Seek out any possible contacts with elderly people, through residential homes and age reminiscence centres, for example, and ask them to tell the children (or write or record) tales about their childhoods, schooldays, first employment, and so on.

Storying in the early years setting

The possibility of enriching children's own storying is a significant educational responsibility. Storying affects children's understanding of the learning we organize in the early years curriculum as it is a powerful way of linking together organized learning in group settings and informal learning in the community. Young children use narrative as a means of putting the abstract and highly organized knowledge of education into the context of their everyday under- standings.

The knowledge defined by the curriculum is predominantly subject-based (in the UK) but young children still absorb and process experience as it comes to them, as a totality. For example, the early years practitioner may plan a walk in the local park with a group of children and perceive it as 'knowledge and understanding of the world' (DCSF, 2008). However, this experience will mean many things to individual children. It may be memorable and significant because of the sheer excitement of leaving the building, or a bit frightening! Some children will remember the warm sun or the cold wind, or the caterpillar

they found by the tennis courts, or the lavatories that were covered with interesting writing, or the big house with slippery floors called a 'museum'. Many
stories, speculations and daydreams will need to evolve and be told and retold,
played out and re-enacted, drawn or painted, before these differing ways of
knowing can be linked to formal learning and knowledge and understanding of
the world. The children's storying and the adult's role as an essentially supportive partner and experienced story-maker must build the bridges between
everyday experience and more formal learning.

Telling stories

This view of individual storying in the context of early care and education
emphasizes not simply the value of having lots of possible stories to play with,
but the actual ways in which stories are first told, shared and mediated. The
storyteller is the lifeline between the tale and the listener, and oral story-telling
is a special kind of experience for children and practitioners. Placing the skills
of narrating at the centre of the language curriculum highlights this art: early
years care and schooling can be so exclusively organized around books and
literacy that children miss out on the patterns and strengths of oral literary
language. Yet the limitations of human memory and concentration have pared
down the told story to a clear plot, strong actions and the most essential
characterization.

However, the linguistic devices of repetition, alliteration, musical refrains,
rhymes and conventional metaphors can be used to support and enrich the memories of tellers and listeners. These features impart a mesmerizing quality to
language. Good story-telling sessions are magical because no books or pictures
come between the participants and the tale. Imagination has to work on words,
emotional tone, vocal changes, eye contacts, facial expressions and gesture. This
list should be familiar: it is what the infant has to work on in the earliest days of
human contact: it is part of the foundations of language and learning.

The adult storyteller models ways for children to create stories and helps
them to tune in to even more narratives and to reshape their own ongoing
storying. To do this well the adult must

- value and enjoy the chosen story
- have a clear sense of its shape
- have an inner picture or image of its characters and events
- feel a real desire to share it with an audience.

These features of story-telling will also be brought to bear on the children's
early experiences with books and act as bridges between the story told and the
story read. However, the early years practitioner must not become trapped
behind or between the covers of the book – the remembered phrases of a story
or a poem well told are an inner possession and go with the children into a
future we can never predict or guarantee.

A 'story' is a set of events, real or imaginary, and 'narrative' is the spoken or written account that tells about the story's events. Narrative is thus essentially a 'telling', and this emphasizes its selectivity in interpretation. It seems that the mind is disposed to function narratively; disposed to evaluate and tell about particular sequences of experiences. From this it follows that the process of education, if it is a process concerned with the development of mind, must also be concerned with narrative. It also follows that the early years curriculum must preserve a distinct emphasis on oral storytelling (by adults and children), substantial talk about stories and experiences, and much shared reminiscing.

Narrative is a structure that creates and binds together the stories we find in communities; it is also the best way children have of making sense of the formal, self-contained knowledge typical of school subjects. If links between the worlds of early years settings and communities are to develop and be productive they must involve much more in the way of mutual narrative exchanges between settings and the communities they serve. Exchanging stories is just as crucial in the early years of care and education as the organized exchanging of books, toys, outgrown clothes and recipes. It should be given at least as much time, space and respect.

Summary

- Narratives contain at least one, if not more, propositions, for example, shopping for sweets is good or bullying must be resisted.

- Narratives are commentaries in which someone is telling someone else (increasingly that inner person we all talk to continuously) that something happened.

- Narratives are often autobiographical: explorations of our encounters with the world of social and cultural norms and conventions. How are things done? What are the expectations?

- Narratives are also shaped in form and content by the story traditions or patterns of the culture.

- Narratives develop and probe the extremes of human feelings and possible ranges of values.

- Narratives are continually sorting out the complexities of self-knowledge, the relationship between the self and the social world, the possibilities and the probabilities of life's chances.

⚷ Key terms

Narrative: a telling of a sequence of events.
Story: the events or topics to be narrated.
Storying: the activity of creating narratives.

Further reading

Bruner, J.S. (1990) *Acts of Meaning*. Cambridge, MA: Harvard University Press.

Engel, S. (1995) *The Stories Children Tell: Making Sense of the Narratives of Childhood*. New York: Freeman.

Goouch, K. (2008) 'Understanding playful pedagogies, play narratives and play spaces', *Early Years: An International Journal of Research and Development*, 28(1): 93–102.

Hughes, T. (1988) 'Myth and education', in K. Egan and D. Nadaner (eds), *Imagination and Education*. Milton Keynes: Open University Press.

Paley, V.G. (1981) *Wally's Stories*. Cambridge, MA: Harvard University Press.

Notes

1 Sara Coleridge, 'The Months', in Opie and Opie (1973: 169).
2 Attributed traditionally to John Ball, from the text of his sermon at the outbreak of the Peasants' Revolt, 1381.

CHAPTER 7

BOOKS AND THE WORLD OF LITERATURE

This chapter includes:

- early experiences with books
- a discussion of literature and emerging literacy
- guidance on teaching reading and supporting young readers.

The experience of books is personal and unique, and perhaps the beginning of literary experiences can only be described accurately for each individual. But we can at least presume that whenever an infant comes into contact with books, magazines, newspapers and comics the potential for involvement with literature and literacy is there.

Families and researchers have documented individual children's early encounters with books; there is also the anecdotal and personal dimension to refer back to – many of us have some memories of our first books and comics, or of listening to story readings. However, many accounts are mainly based on early experiences at home but, for many children, it is childminders, play groups, children's centres and schools that are the settings for their first encounters with books. This does not necessarily make the home-based accounts irrelevant: it is a central claim of this chapter that the implications of such informal encounters have relevance for learning about literature and literacy in group settings and schools, and that whenever or wherever children first meet books, relaxed and informal approaches should be nurtured and not rushed through or devalued.

Early experiences with books[1]

First encounters

For many infants and small children, books are objects you may stumble over, clutch possessively or move from place to place like building-blocks. Books can also be tasted, sniffed and stroked and this sensual delight in the texture, taste and smell of books may linger into adulthood. The American artist and author, Maurice Sendak, has traced his own passion for creating books back to his childhood and the first book he owned, sniffed, fondled and chewed (Sendak, 1977: 242). This is a reminder of the pleasure to be gained from books as objects, toys and possessions.

Many infants gaze with great interest at the pages of books and scrabble with their fingers at text and illustrations, as if attempting to lift them from the pages. The black outlined images and bold print of Dick Bruna's books are particularly arresting for some infants. There is one outstanding account (Butler, 1979) of an 8-month-old baby focusing her gaze on the bold print and later on the pictures in a Bruna ABC (1967). However, it is not necessary to turn to studies of remarkable babies and exceptional parenting in order to support the claim that books as objects and toys fascinate very small children.

Books designed to encourage young children's sensory investigations are among the most popular (interestingly, these special book techniques are regularly appearing further up the age range). Books as toys for young children may feature holes in their pages, apparently eaten by a very hungry caterpillar (Carle, 1970), or be stained and chewed by rodents (Gravett, 2007). Sometimes they have elaborate pop-up devices and figures, and the paper engineering can become extremely complex and even be used to illustrate almost anything, from the organs and functions of the human body to cross-sections of cities (Biesty, 2002)! Books can feature half-pages, hinged flaps, a graded series of sliced pages (Gravett, 2008) and pages which open out to double their size and extend the pictorial narrative (Deacon, 2002). Some of the most popular books contain extra features such as removable notes and letters that extend the playful possibilities of the story beyond the book. This discussion of books, simply as toys and beautiful objects, should be kept in mind when planning book provision for the early years of care and education.

First encounters with books in early childhood are usually mediated or shared with an older person and become associated with warmth, embraces and total security (Figure 7.1). This strong emotional feeling becomes part of the total attention and concentration associated with books. The experience of temporary withdrawal from the world of practical and external demands, coupled with feelings of safety and comfort, may stay with us in our later reading careers. For many children and adults the favourite places to read are in bed, or in the bath, and small children can be found reading behind curtains, under tables or curled into the bottom of cupboards. They may also find their own quiet places in well-planned early years settings (Figure 7.2).

Figure 7.1 **Sharing a book with a key person (24 months, EAL)**

Figure 7.2 **Reading in a quiet corner of the garden (4 years)**

An emphasis on rooting early reading and involvement with books in secure emotional contexts is more significant than just a means of ensuring that reading is associated with pleasure, important as that is. The sense of safety and well-being may go some way towards explaining the extraordinary fact that children and adults can tolerate considerable threats and terrors in their encounters with literature.

Outside group settings, infants probably become aware of books and reading material as things that take over the time and the attention of otherwise devoted adults and older children. People apparently enjoy this and also take very special notice of babies and toddlers who want to join in. Squeezed between the adult's lap and the pages of the book, infants also find out that books are special: books receive special treatment.

For young children, sharing the 'looking-at-books' game is one way of participating in the importance of books and for many it is a significant way of being like the people they love and depend on. Furthermore, in the early days with books there is less discernible threat or pressure linked with the cultural prestige of reading, so that time with books and a carer is a matter of choice, pleasure and of becoming a person who participates in valued social activities. In terms of later education, this raises such issues as, do young children see teachers and other professionals as admired and respected models of being a reader? Are early years group and school experiences of books, literature and stories unpressured, enjoyable and supportive of children's self-esteem and desire to succeed in activities valued by the culture?

There have always been some families who shared books with very young babies (Campbell, 1999; Jones, 1996; White, 1954; Whitehead, 2002), but there are now well-monitored efforts to help many more parents and carers do this. One of the most successful is the Bookstart project which was originally piloted in Birmingham and involved cooperation between the City Library Services, the local health authority and the Children's Book Foundation. Free Bookstart packs containing a book, a poetry card, a poster, an invitation to join the local library (and other information) were distributed by health visitors to 300 parents/carers of 6–9-month-old babies in three inner-city areas.

The evidence from the families indicated that sharing books with a baby spilled over into enthusiastic sharing of books with all the family – including toddlers, older children and adults. In some cases this led to joining the public library and also buying books. The project is still evaluated regularly (Collins and Svensson, 2008; Wade and Moore, 2000) and has now been extended to all areas of the UK and is supported by funding from children's book publishers and the national government.

Currently the available packs include rhymes and songs, dual languages and two Welsh language packs, one for babies and one for toddlers. The original Bookstart for Babies pack has been joined by a Bookstart Plus pack for toddlers (around 18 months) and My Bookstart Treasure Chest for pre-school children (up to 4 years). There is also a Booktouch pack for blind and partially sighted babies and pre-schoolers that includes 'touch and feel' books and useful advice for carers. The Bookshine pack is designed for deaf babies and toddlers and also supports carers and families. There are advisory booklets available for parents and professionals on 'Finding books to suit different needs' and 'Finding inclusive books'.

Summary

- Infants come across books as objects that appeal to their senses and offer opportunities for certain kinds of exploration and playful investigation.
- Early experiences with books are shared with caring adults or older children and associated with emotional security and pleasure.
- Books and reading are clearly of great importance and valued by many adults and by the wider community.
- Learning to read in the early years must be understood in the context of infant development.

Learning and teaching suggestions

- Key persons should plan to share books with babies and toddlers throughout the day.
- Tell stories and read books with small groups of children at different points in the day, outdoors and indoors – avoid just using the end of the sessions when children are tired and families are arriving to collect children.

Some speculations on responses to books

The whole topic of response to books and stories is complex and can involve several academic disciplines – psychology, philosophy, linguistics and literature.

Emotional intelligence

Literature has always been linked with the idea that reading it can make us, if not 'good', at least more sensitive to the feelings of others and more aware of the challenges and shocks of the human condition. Recent psychological approaches support the experiencing of literature from an early age as one way of nurturing children's development of emotional intelligence. The notion of emotional intelligence developed from Howard Gardner's theory of human 'multiple intelligences' (1983), seven to be precise, rather than just one undifferentiated IQ.

In this theory the 'interpersonal' and the 'intrapersonal' intelligences account for the areas of thinking and feeling that have come to be called emotional intelligence. The interpersonal intelligence is essentially the ability to understand and respond to other people and appreciate what makes them tick. The intrapersonal is concerned with our own inner lives: having access to our feelings and emotions in order to understand and manage ourselves in the world.

The complex links and interactions between our inner self-knowledge and our ability to respond to others have become known as 'emotional intelligence' (Goleman, 1996). These theories are far from simple and cannot be taught as activities in an early years curriculum. However, the opportunities in the early years for children to work with the materials and stories that nourish the various human intelligences are crucial and books and literature are at the heart of nurturing emotional intelligence.

Playful encounters

Encounters with books can be seen as essentially play-like or playful: this aspect of literacy is sometimes ignored by more traditional literary or psychological approaches. The playful exploration of pictures and written narratives in books appears to be a major preoccupation with young children who enjoy literary encounters. Pictures and texts are often subjected to rigorous questioning and tentative reorganization. Characters who appear to be lost or alone prompt such questions as, 'Where's her mummy (or daddy or granny)?' Desperately unhappy characters may also be kissed better, gently caressed on the page and reassured. The conventions of illustrations are also sorted out as small children ponder whether the teardrops on faces are rain (Payton, 1984: 49–50) or what has happened to the rest of Peter Rabbit when only his ears are sticking out of the watering-can.

Such questioning is challenging and literally eye-opening for the adult reading partner, but for the young child it also marks the beginnings of encounters with totally new and surprising sets of possibilities. Suppose a tiger came to tea (Kerr, 1968)? Suppose you saw a shark in the park (Sharratt, 2002)? Experiences found in literature begin to combine with bits of the child's own daily life in rich and liberating ways. A small child can be comforted by a story or a book when away from home and familiar adults, or a threatening situation can be eased by the reassurance that a book or story character coped with this or similar difficulties. Success, joy and humour also migrate from the world of books into the everyday world of the young child who is indulging in a little domestic mayhem 'like Noisy Norah' (Wells, 1978), or singing and discovering the pun in 'Nellie the Elephant packed her trunk'. Bits of books and bits of life combine and interact: 'The experience makes the book richer and the book enriches the personal experience even at this level. I am astonished at the early age this backward and forward flow between books and life takes place' (White, 1954: 13). Playful encounters with books and literature allow children to take over and use, in unstructured ways, anything they choose from the events and the values of narrative fictions.

Safe encounters

Play is safe or 'protected' because it does not have to satisfy demands from the outside world for truth, excellence or completion – it enjoys some distance from real-world pressures. This concept of being safely distanced from demands to get on and make something happen in the real world of practical concerns, may be an appropriate way of categorizing literary responses. Security and protection have already been linked with response to books in the discussion of first encounters. The point was made that in shared book and story sessions very young children can tolerate fears and dangers which would be unbearably distressing in reality. Literary threats are not simply tolerated, they are contemplated and mulled over in positive ways because 'everyone is scared of something' (Gravett, 2007). Small children actually begin to evaluate the moral issues in human behaviour, they consider motives, apportion blame and they also face up to the terribly arbitrary and accidental aspects of life: rabbits caught eating lettuces in gardens do sometimes end up in pies. Small children must themselves be brave and resourceful when they are out on the street, and you cannot even be sure about what lurks in the shadows at home (Brown, 2008).

One reason that young children (and older ones too) thrive on terrible tales is usually expressed as the reader or listener being an onlooker or spectator of literary events.[2] In the case of fiction, we are reading or listening to an account or representation of imagined events in which we are obviously not participants. This non-participation gives us the time and the freedom to evaluate more sharply our feelings and attitudes about the events and characters represented – even very small children pick out the kind and the naughty, the dishonest and the brave in stories, but our ambiguous real-life motives and complex reactions involve heart-searchings, self-delusions and frequent misunderstandings. Because literature and play free us from demands to respond in practical ways, they allow distanced but very full evaluations unblurred by personal confusions and involvement.

Poems and stories tap deep responses. Such processes take time and cannot readily be measured or tested by immediate questioning about the surface features of the poems and stories. However, the cumulative effect of our many experiences as spectators of fictional events, feelings and personalities is an enlargement of our imaginative sensibilities and understandings, our emotional intelligence! It is as if the fictional lives, events and emotions we encounter extend the range of our own responses and increase the resources we have for making sense of our own lives. Perhaps small children are eventually stronger for knowing that happiness and security can be found again after a brief period of threat and abandonment (Blake, 1995).

Learning and teaching suggestions

- Place items of clothing and objects that link with familiar stories and books in the dressing-up provision (for example, a big green umbrella for *The Bear Under the Stairs,* Cooper, 1993).

- Set up literature-enhanced play areas inside and outdoors (for example, a bridge for the Three Billy Goats Gruff; a muddy or grassy patch or a cave for re-enactments of *We're Going on a Bear Hunt*, Rosen and Oxenbury, 1989; a large bundle of sticks under a tree to re-create the story of *Stick Man*, Donaldson, 2008).

Complex encounters

The complexities of responses to books and stories underline the familiar claim that literature operates on many levels. This again links literature with play, for play can also be described as functioning on several levels at once. For example, a small child dragging chairs into a line and calling them a train can be enjoying simultaneously the physical pleasure of clambering on and off the chairs; the sense of achievement when the line of chairs is complete; the satisfaction of operating in a totally imaginary world of journeys; and the social negotiations necessary to persuade an adult to make real sandwiches to eat on the chair-train. Vygotsky (1978) captures this complexity in his definition of play as satisfying unrealizable desires for the young child (how can a toddler control a train or travel alone?), but also requiring considerable self-discipline and obedience to the self-imposed rules of the play.

Initially, very small infants just delight in the sounds of patterned language in songs, poems and stories. They may be observed responding with total bodily excitement to rhythms, rhyming sounds, alliteration and words with onomatopoeic qualities: 'splat', 'croak', 'lippitty-lippitty'. We all retain the potential ability to respond to language as pure sound in aspects of literature and song. Children also delight in the impact of obscure or difficult words and chant them enthusiastically – as if tasting them on the tongue – long before they understand their meanings and begin to use them appropriately.

Very young children follow a narrative closely and make comments: 'What happened next?' 'Is that the end?' 'You left a bit out.' The effects of this sensitivity to story structures and plots are revealed when children become tellers and writers of their own made-up narratives. Clearly there are implications for early years settings here. Children will need opportunities for storying aloud in nearly every situation. It is all this energetic storying and discussion that inspires and supports the dictated or independently written story plots of young children as they become writers and authors.

Responses to literature in terms of roles and of worlds bring in complex cultural assumptions and perspectives. Children try on the roles of the story characters they meet, often in such activities as dramatic play, drawing and miniature world play. Trying on the roles of parents, doctors, teachers and naughty children are familiar enough pastimes, but literature provides far more varied and complicated characters and situations for the child or onlooker of any age to savour. Young children delight in going along with the reckless behaviour of Goldilocks when it involves plenty of porridge-eating, but they often begin to worry about the baby bear who is the loser in all the story episodes!

Moral issues are at the heart of responses to the total worlds created by authors. This is a level of response that can be traced throughout a lifetime of reading and sharing poems and stories, but it has its roots in early encounters with narrative and books. Early experiences with books offer alternative worlds for consideration and reflection, and it is highly likely that the possible levels of response consist of far more than the few discussed here.

Summary

- Early responses are playful in so far as they are open-ended and explanatory, linking books, stories and life in creative and uniquely personal combinations.
- Encounters with literature are safely distanced by the book and the reading situation and foster a detached spectator-like evaluation of the imaginary happenings.
- Literature, like play, operates on many levels and can support flexible and personal meaning-making strategies.

Listening to book language

A familiar voice

Response to stories and book language in terms of pure sound has already been touched on but the significance of this for literacy deserves further consideration. First, the voice of the reader mediates and revitalizes the written text for the child listener. All the subtlety and variety of a familiar voice is brought to the task of re-creating the meanings and intentions of the author behind the text. Story and poetry readings are informal demonstrations of the functions of vocal tone, pitch, rhythm, facial expressions, gestures and body language in human communication.

And the good reader, like the good teller, must employ all these skills to bring the language off the page.

However, young listeners must also work hard to pick up and respond to all the cues that tell as much (if not more) of the story as the actual words. Many traditional tales and rhymes depend on the irony, exaggeration and understatement communicated by the manner of the telling. Very young children are able to respond to all this subtle underlying storyline or subtext because it is relayed through the expressive medium of a familiar voice.

Infants are immersed in bits of stories, anecdotes, snatches of songs, rhymes and jingles, in their homes, streets, shops, places of worship and community gatherings. All this basic human language experience sensitizes children to the more consciously shaped patterns of book language as well as incidentally providing considerable snippets of literary and ritual language.

Listening carefully

Listening to book language read aloud introduces children to the consciously patterned forms of literature. Language as art has been shaped, altered, chosen and carefully placed to produce the effects of just those words in just that particular order. The syntax of written language is more considered and more formal than in most everyday verbal communications. We might claim that experiences of listening to book language help children to move from being talkers and listeners only to becoming readers and writers.

Children listening to stories and poems also hear complex, unusual, foreign and even archaic words. That these extend and enrich children's taste for language is one of the important but unmeasurable claims of literature teachers. What formal test of reading would dare include such items as 'haycock', 'stargazy pie' or 'monumental'? Who would invite the child to read 'ablutophobia' (Gravett, 2007) or 'you're cruising for a bruising' (Wells, 1977)? Young children respond to the poetry of memorable phrases and nonsense by collecting them and making them part of their own linguistic resources.

Poetry and story introduce young children to the literary device of metaphor, but the language of everyday usage is also saturated with metaphors. Small children take nothing for granted and so-called 'dead' metaphors may have a stunning impact on them. Little children puzzle out the meaning links in flower beds (Payton, 1984: 55) and clothes-horses, as well as taking on the delights of 'a diamond in the sky' (Jane Taylor)[3] or a 'snow-cone' (Agard, 1983). Sharing more metaphors with children is not just a literary frill for the curriculum: metaphor is a cognitive tool for increasing the explanatory power of language and thought.

Other voices

The greater complexity and eccentricity of literary book language introduces young listeners to other human voices. Listening to stories and poems is also listening to the unique voices of many authors. Young listeners must make some sort of link or relationship with the idiosyncratic style and feelings of the person behind the words. This issue is crucial in early reading and a failure to lock into the voice and created world of the author is one major hindrance to prediction and the setting up of sets of expectations in reading. Authors help their readers by creating predictable worlds and roles and setting out helpful cues in the text. Of course, authors are not boringly predictable and they can sometimes surprise us and upset all our expectations. But particular authors are instantly recognizable, like family and friends, so that children can confidently let themselves go for an outing with Shirley Hughes, Anthony Browne, Janet and Allan Ahlberg, Pat Hutchins or Mike Rosen. Strangely, however, most attempts to produce simple reading books for young children mistakenly start by getting rid of the eccentric human creator behind the text and pictures. This has always been a serious weakness of school reading primers and simplified phonic texts.

Summary

- The role of the familiar voice is crucial in linking the language of books to the language of daily social life and communications.
- The role of listening is important in introducing children to the highly patterned language of literature and books.
- Listening to literature plays a major part in introducing children to the unique voices and worlds of many authors.

Learning and teaching suggestion

- Build up an audio collection of stories, rhymes and poetry recorded by familiar adults (early years practitioners, key persons, parents and other family members, regular visitors). This should be in addition to published books on CD.

Pictures and texts

Young children's first experiences with books will be predominantly centred on picture books. Picture books rely on images to carry the narrative sequence and evaluation, either entirely or in combination with some text. It is still not uncommon for adults to dismiss picture books as too simple and infantile to merit serious study. Apart from ignoring any educational arguments, this reaction fails to acknowledge the existence of sophisticated picture books designed for adults, and the fact that distinguished artists and writers choose to create picture books.

The apparent simplicity of picture books is, paradoxically, the source of the considerable demands they place on the reader. Reading picture books might be likened to 'authoring' or creating a story. The very lack of text means that a picture book is rich in narrative spaces that must be filled in by the reader. Successful creative reading of this kind demands sensitive interpretations of the story possibilities in the pictures as well as the text, if any. *Rosie's Walk* (Hutchins, 1968) is a now famous example of picture story and text story running parallel and depending on the reader to link the two accounts and create the meaning of the narrative. The same pattern occurs in *Come Away from the Water, Shirley* (Burningham, 1977), where a repetitive and rather staid text of predictable adult comments partners a wildly adventurous picture narrative. It is frequently the case that the pictures in these books are the challenging and eccentric element, rather than the written text. Maurice Sendak's night-time world of *Wild Things* (1967), the domestic threat of *The Bear Under the Stairs* (Cooper, 1993), Mini Grey's *Egg Drop* (2002) and Alexis Deacon's *Slow Loris* (2002) are full of wit, anarchy and humour, and demand detailed picture readings. It takes many rereadings and careful examinations of the images to build up these complex narratives. This powerful method of investigating the layers of possibilities in a book has migrated to the older children's and adults' book market (Gamble and Yates, 2008; Goodwin, 2008). Picture books have been used to discuss such issues as the Holocaust, a nuclear disaster (Briggs, 1983), the arms race (Seuss, 1984) and a wide range of conservation issues (Baker, 2002).

In recent years picture books have been the subject of some exciting publications and research. Teachers and scholars from several disciplines have focused on the picture book as a bridge between an infant's developing sense of self and understanding of all that is 'not self' (Jones, 1996); as a crucial tool in the early development of literacy (Marriott, 1991; Watson and Styles, 1996); as a sophisticated literary genre which displays postmodernist features of openness, multiple meanings and excess (Lewis, 2001); as a complex system of images and visual narratives (Baddeley and Eddershaw, 1994; Doonan, 1993; Gamble and Yates, 2008; Styles and Arizpe, 2002); and as a carrier and subverter of a society's dominant ideologies (Stephens, 1992).

This sophisticated level of picture book study has been an important factor in the development of children's literature as a legitimate field of study (Styles et al., 1992; 1994; 1996). Modern picture books may also be credited with expanding our understanding of the subversive, playful and carnivalesque features to be found in literature. Subversion in play and literature involves unpicking systems and beliefs and standing them on their heads – in order to understand them. Carnival in play and literature is also a subversive element that challenges social control and conventions. The playful and carnivalesque aspects of books enable children and adults to explore the wildest possibilities and defuse the deepest anxieties.

It follows that picture books put young children into the role of active readers from the start. Any lingering belief that reading is a passively receptive language activity disappears when we share a *Spot* book with a child (Hill, 1980), discuss the surprising things going on during Handa's walk (Browne, 1994) or read the names of the ingredients going into Meg's cauldron (Nicholl and Pienkowski, 1972). Many of these books actually invite the reader to hunt for a character, to predict the next event on the basis of prior literary cultural knowledge (*Each Peach Pear Plum*, Ahlberg and Ahlberg, 1977b) or to retell the complete narrative without any textual guidelines apart from that most significant story précis, the title.

Because picture book readers must do so much to make the stories mean something, young readers usually create connections between the books and their own lives and experiences. Authors often help by picturing actual places and events some children will know, as in the cityscapes of *Clown* (Blake, 1995) or the Reception classroom when *Harry and the Dinosaurs Go To School* (Whybrow and Reynolds, 2006). Children delight in pointing and telling with the picture book: 'I saw dinosaurs on the telly.' 'We've got a cat.' 'I've been to that park!' Some authors create characters who straddle the literary and the ordinary world by nibbling the pages of the book and leaving their marks on it (Gravett, 2007). Children themselves fill the everyday world with characters and possibilities from their picture books. I was reminded of this vital connection by a young visitor to my home who looked at the chest freezer and said, 'If I was the snowman I'd get in there for a nice cold rest' (Briggs, 1978). Links with books extend children's creative 'supposings', meaning-making and drawing (Figure 7.3). All these new sets of possibilities enrich the children's individual storying and ensure that even more expectations and successful predictions can be brought to bear on subsequent book encounters.

Figure 7.3   'Winnie the Witch and her cat' (4 years 10 months)

Experiences with picture books establish such basic story conventions as beginnings or ways in, complications, problems and challenges, resolutions and satisfying endings. The pleasures of literary shape and predictability can be judged by the demands children make for repeated tellings of stories and their gradual incorporation of literary conventions into their own created stories.

Example: *Alfie Gets in First* (Hughes,1981)

The raw material of daily life and childhood mishaps is sensitively shaped in a totally satisfying way by the author and illustrator, Shirley Hughes. In *Alfie Gets in First* (1981) we are hurtled into the book and its central action by the desire of toddler Alfie to 'get in first' after a morning's shopping. The complication or problem is immediately clear when the front door is triumphantly slammed on Mum and baby sister by Alfie! He is certainly in first, but he is also locked in, alone and unable to reach the door catch. Triumph soon turns to tears, while a procession of helpful neighbours and tradespeople plan various strategies for rescuing poor Alfie. The resolution is delightful in that it comes about through Alfie's own initiative and re-establishes his confidence and sense of achievement. The total success of this book as an artefact that combines pictures and text in an indivisible whole, is reflected in the way in which the book's spine represents the door that comes between Alfie inside and everybody else outside.

The joy of such books as this is that they work for adults too. As I share Alfie with very young children I am also savouring again memories of the emergencies and excitements in my younger daughter's infancy, for she too was a triumphant door-slammer! Time and many family retellings have safely distanced our actual crises but this picture book immediately puts me back in contact with the child that was and the affective quality of our relationship.

Summary

- Pictures and texts play a complex and significant part in introducing children to literature and preparing them for literacy.
- Picture books are recreated by readers who must behave like authors.
- Picture books are a sophisticated literary genre and establish complex patterns of active reading and meaning prediction.
- Picture books stimulate the creation of links between book worlds and everyday life, and shape individual storying in the direction of literary conventions.

Literature and emerging literacy

Literary texts teach

Literary texts teach those extra lessons about authors, audiences and the conventions of illustration, metaphor and interpretation that go beyond the information given by print (Meek, 1988). Extended encounters with literature in infancy and in the first years of schooling reinforce and expand young children's involvement in the human urge to preserve and share feelings, relationships, ideas and places. To take the last item first, many literary texts communicate a strong sense of place and this is certainly not restricted to children's books. Young children's responses to particular storybook streets, viaducts and skylines, or to tales of certain riverbanks, bridges and parks, may enable them to picture for themselves the more remote, archetypal dark forests and great rivers of myth and folk tale. A pattern of interaction between the totally imagined worlds of some literary texts and the carefully located real-world settings of others typifies literary experiences from childhood onwards. Authors and readers of any age can picture Alfie and Annie Rose's Notting Hill, Harry Potter's King's Cross Station, Bloom's Dublin and Hardy's Wessex, because the fictional worlds of literature grow out of the known and shared reality of everyday places.

Children and adults respond to literature's created worlds of people and ideas by drawing on their own sense of self and their own networks of human relationships. For example, sooner or later children may experience the overwhelming grief of being temporarily parted from a parent. In the context of this not uncommon upset, they share feelingly the desperate howl of *My Brother Sean* (Breinburg, 1973) in his nursery class or the deep fears of abandonment underlying *Hansel and Gretel* (Browne, 1981). In lighter mood, Mike Rosen's poems, 'Chocolate Cake' or 'Eddie and the Gerbils' (Rosen, 1983) encourage us to celebrate and share our own experiences of childhood temptations, joys and mishaps. The process is reminiscent of the mutual pleasure and conversational form of first language learning: the professional author, like the caregiver, may say it better and be more experienced, but the young reader or listener, like the infant conversationalist, is an apprentice who can make meaningful contributions to the stories and the poems.

Book language

Literary texts display for their readers the literary uses of language and are examples of powerful new ways of using words. This aspect of literary encounters is usually referred to as 'book language', particularly in studies of early literacy. Clearly, reading literature and listening to readings of literature provide the best possible introductions to those uses of language typical of written forms: permanence, explicit references and cohesive devices. This means that texts can be returned to again and again, and they contain all the necessary allusions and information for making sense of their propositions.

Perhaps the most important characteristic of literary language is its metaphorical rather than literal function. In contrast, the book language of non-literary discourse aims to make as close a match as it can between the language forms and the real state of affairs being presented. Literal discourse may be concerned with, for example, the life cycle of the ant or the technique for making lino-prints and must aim for unambiguous, precise and foolproof language about ants or lino-printing. But literature purposely exploits the ways in which language may be ambiguous, subtle and evocative.

Literature does not aspire to be foolproof but launches itself into the risky areas of reader responses and individual interpretations. Literary discourse takes risks, using metaphor to link diverse and surprisingly disparate areas of meaning. For example, in the created world of Anthony Browne, huge, shambling gorillas, stirring fearful folk-memories of aggression, monster tales and horror films become endearing representations of fun, affection and gentle timidity (Browne, 2008).

Literature plays with language and exploits all of its potential for innuendo and ambiguity, as well as its rhythm and sounds. Metaphors explain much of the delightful ambiguity of literary language, as when the animals in Mr Gumpy's boat revert to 'typical' behaviour (Burningham, 1970). *Each Peach Pear Plum* (Ahlberg and Ahlberg, 1977b) builds on our sensitivity to rhyming sounds as well as our knowledge of nursery rhyme and fairy-tale characters. Young children's earliest encounters with rhymes and poems teach them that they can join in with the highly predictable rhyming end words. This early language skill, which has great significance for later literacy, will also be employed to substitute alternative and less respectable ranges of words in familiar songs and rhymes. Literary texts create spaces for readers' and listeners' contributions and stimulate play with the rules of language and culture.

Literary forms

The language of literary texts also demonstrates the different forms, or genres, narrative and poetry can take. Narratives can be stories in rhyme and metre, as in the traditional ballads or modern picture books: *The Jolly Pocket Postman* (Ahlberg and Ahlberg, 1995); *We're Going on a Bear Hunt* (Rosen and Oxenbury, 1989). Narratives may preserve the patterns of folk tales and fairy tales with their oral conventions of ritual openings and closures, traditional characters and predictable situations.

They can also tell tales of recognizably contemporary dilemmas and successes in streets, schools and supermarkets. They may hurtle us down rabbit holes, through secret wardrobe doors or bring the forest and the night into our bedrooms. Then, in language still very similar to that with which we buy vegetables and make dental appointments, they tell us of awful dangers and dilemmas that will be resolved at the end of the story.

In contrast, the language of poetry is musical, rich in images and economical in the use of words. Poems literally take up less space on the page and their impact is sharper and intensely concentrated:

Tiger! Tiger! Burning bright

In the forests of the night,

What immortal hand or eye

Could frame thy fearful symmetry? (William Blake, *The Tiger*, 1794)

The distinctive shapes made by poems on the page are a reminder of the physical characteristics of literary texts. Actual texts teach their readers the conventions of books and print – how books work and how readers must behave. Children who are beginning to write often pretend to have the speed and flow of the skilled writer; they also experiment with the shaping and orientation of letters and they liberally sprinkle their writing with full stops and other punctuation. Similarly, they may investigate and imitate the layout of books, the appearance of covers and title pages and the varied ways of arranging blocks of text and illustrations, pagination, lists of contents and dedications. Clearly the literary text also needs the supportive and mediating human 'teacher' who highlights these conventions and models or demonstrates them in writing activities with children and promotes discussion of their functions.

Making sense of text

The literary text teaches us to be readers because it urges us to turn the page and make the meanings the author intended. Young children's questions and comments indicate that they work with great resourcefulness and commitment to make sense of texts and illustrations: 'Why's he crying?' 'Where's the dog?' 'She's not very kind.' 'That's a funny hat.' Good authors support the child's first endeavours to read the text alive, by providing verbal and pictorial clues about the events; rhythmic and enjoyable repetitions of phrases and names; and invitations to make predictions about the possible outcomes. This means creating devices like the large spy-holes in the pages of *Peepo* (Ahlberg and Ahlberg, 1981), which entice the reader into turning the page and finding the whole scene. Or it may be the provision of the picture clues in *Piggybook* (Browne, 1986), which chart the increasingly 'pig-like' changes in people reflected in furniture and artefacts. Constant and joyful repetition of phrases ('But where is the green parrot?', Zacharias and Zacharias, 1965) or names ('Come back my Scelidosaurus, my Stegosaurus, my Triceratops!', Whybrow and Reynolds, 1999) provide not only the means to drive the narrative forward, but also small and memorable chunks of text and distinctively patterned and easily recognized combinations of letters.

Good readers are good predictors of what will be the likely outcome of the initial events and possibilities in the poem or story: once a stranger interrupts a cosy domestic setting, we expect problems; once a wolf or a fox appears, we predict danger and possibly death.

Success in predicting outcomes and amazed delight when the author lulls us into a false hypothesis and 'turns the tables' on our predictions is one of the most potent rewards of reading. Real readers of any age find their rewards in the actual encounter with the text. They read to please themselves. Readers who only read to please others run into difficulties if the external reward and motivation is withdrawn. Reading for pleasure, or for a personally felt need for information, is its own reward. This is not necessarily a solitary pursuit. We may be so moved by the pleasures of the text that we want to share them with others.

Good literary texts allow for endless reruns or repetitions of the experience. Children's delight in hearing a story again and again or poring over favourite books does not just indicate the power of simple pleasurable repetition, although that is important. Literature is only fully understood as a complete entity. We grasp it in retrospect, and in the light of the ending we go back and make sense of the whole pattern. Written texts are ideally suited for going back over, again and again: they are not a succession of fleeting sounds or rapidly changing visual images. Books exist as unchanged objects, playthings that can be returned to at will. Children's requests for 'that book', 'that poem' or 'that story' are testimony to their willingness and need to go over again the experiences they encounter in literature.

Non-fiction books

- Some of the very first books intended for babies and toddlers are texts that teach about colours, shapes, pets, families and vehicles. Many early factual texts introduce such concepts as numbers, alphabets and words for familiar things.

- Young children probably learn even more about the world from the kinds of picture books discussed in this chapter (see the Bookstart references).

- One research example focuses on a boy who enjoyed picture books from 8 weeks old and was, by the age of 3, an expert on sharks, trains, zoo animals, trucks and dinosaurs (Whitehead, 2002).

- Some of the best information books for young children use a narrative style and quality illustrations and photography. Exciting developments in this genre are now the subject of serious study.

- The work of Margaret Mallett places early years non-fiction in the context of young children's language and cognitive development, and good early years practice. 'Early information literacy, like other kinds, fares best when it is situated in lively practical contexts like role play, practical tasks and forays into the wider environment' (Mallett, 2003: 12).

Learning and teaching suggestions

- Create an attractive book corner or area – carpeted, cosy and curtained if possible – with floor cushions, comfortable chairs, plants, pictures and display space and storage for books, CDs and story props.

- Start or extend a book collection and organize it thematically and in genres, using child-friendly boxes and open shelving. Include big picture books (see Chapter 8); books with textures, flaps and holes; wordless and minimal text picture books; picture books and story books; a variety of alphabet books; books based on traditional tales and myths (including modern versions and subversive re-writings); books focused on animal characters, families and challenging issues (loneliness, death, prejudice, fear and jealousy). Include some books that provide a longer text in chapters for early fluent readers and for sharing with adults (*The Owl Who Was Afraid of the Dark*, Tomlinson, 1968; *Clever Polly and the Stupid Wolf*, Storr, 1955).

- Vary what is available in the book area, do not overwhelm the area and the children with clutter. Change the books, recordings and materials according to seasons, festivals, developmental needs and individual and group interests and experiences.

Summary

- Literary texts teach children that literature is an aspect of human communication. Texts build links between imaginary worlds and daily realities.

- Literary texts display the literary uses of language and support children's explorations of the possibilities of the written forms of language.

- Literary texts show and teach the conventions of books and print and the strategies readers must use in order to read for meaning.

- Literary texts teach children about the roles and preoccupations of authors.

- Many books written for young children are rich sources of information about the world. Children do not perceive tight distinctions between 'fact' and 'fiction' and these early experiences with 'information' are among the pleasures of book sharing.

Teaching reading and supporting readers

The reading debate

The debate about reading and literacy is apparently endless and it is not surprising that issues of such psychological complexity and cultural significance do not yield easy answers and quick-fix solutions. A brief review of the 'debate' indicates how sophisticated and tentative are the conclusions of those who actually engage in research and teaching in the fields of early reading instruction and initial literacy. Researchers have warned that 'phonics alone is not enough' (Adams, 1990; Dombey, 2006; Goswami, 2007). Young children must be helped to use both global, or top-down, reading strategies and alphabetic and phonic (bottom-up) strategies.

In the 1980s and 1990s a research-based shift in phonic approaches to the early reading debate occurred when researchers demonstrated a powerful connection between young pre-school children's phonological awareness and their early success in reading (Bryant and Bradley, 1985). The crucial factors were:

- early knowledge of nursery rhymes
- ability to detect rhyme and alliteration
- ability to produce rhyming and alliterative words.

A further refinement (Goswami and Bryant, 1990) suggested that pre-school children are sensitive to regularities in the sound of words. Particularly, the regular phonological patterns in

- the beginning sounds of words or 'onset' (especially of a consonant preceding a vowel)
- the end units or 'rimes' (which produce rhymes).

Factors in learning to read

Experienced professional teachers of early literacy have to interpret the many complex findings of research and clarify the issues in discussions with other professionals and young children's families. Factors which need to be considered include, current knowledge about the brain and children's different developmental stages, learning styles, cultural, social and home literacy experiences. Learning to read is affected by brain development in infancy (Goswami, 2008; Wolf, 2008); it can be adversely affected by poverty and inequalities of many kinds (Freire and Macedo, 1987; Lambirth, 2007; Snow et al., 1991); successful reading depends on a rich background of enjoyable and meaningful encounters with literature and print of all kinds (Smith, F., 1994); reading is complex and children beginning to read require a range of strategies and information about language and print, as well as close individual support in the early days of settling into statutory schooling (Brooker, 2002; Riley, 2006); reading and writing are two sides of the same coin and should be taught together as a whole literacy programme (Browne, 2009; Makin and Whitehead, 2004; Smith, B., 1994; Whitehead, 2007; 2009).

Literacy progress must be monitored closely in the early years; it should be the dominant and joyful focus of the early years curriculum and it should be at the centre of the genuine partnership between early years settings, schools and parents (Goouch, 2007; Gregory, 2008; Kenner, 2000; Nutbrown, 1997; Serpell et al., 2005; Weinberger, 1996).

One reasonable conclusion from all this research would be that there is no one single approach or method that will always teach all children to read. Phonics alone is never enough because of the nature of the irregular phonological and orthographical relationships in written English. Teaching the single sounds of letters as isolated decoding tricks does not work. Children must build a considerable sight vocabulary in the course of enjoyable reading and writing activities and gradually have their attention drawn to letter-sound relationships, the sounds (phonemes) in words and their letter symbols. They also have to be prepared for exceptions and not be defeated by them. Only significant and rewarding encounters with language and literature can sustain young children through the complexities of literacy. However, recent curriculum legislation in England is not in agreement with this eclectic approach and early years practitioners are required to teach synthetic phonics and adopt the 'simple' view of reading.

Learning and teaching suggestion

- Create a poetry collection, including nursery rhymes, nonsense verse, tongue-twisters, jokes and songs. Use this material in daily language play sessions: exploit the rhymes, alliteration and sounds and invent amusing word families (sun, bun, fun, run) to illustrate and incorporate into stories, chants and raps. Create some home-grown alphabets to add to the traditional 'A was an apple' versions.

Synthetic phonics and simple reading

In the English-speaking world the debate about the place of phonics in the initial teaching of reading has gone on for more than a century. It has also become highly politicized as governments insist that they have the 'answers' to problems with literacy and, of course, national literacy rates are an indicator of economic success and political stability.

Legislation in many states of the USA and in England requires the teaching of phonics as the dominant, if not the only, method to be used in schools. English legislation has set out a systematic programme and guidance for teaching synthetic phonics 'first and fast' and prescribed goals to be achieved at the end of the Early Years Foundation Stage (EYFS) when children are 5 years old (DCSF, 2008). These goals require children to:

- hear and say sounds in words in the order in which they occur
- link sounds to letters, naming and sounding the letters of the alphabet
- use their phonic knowledge to write simple regular words and make phonetically plausible attempts at more complex words

- write their own names and other things such as labels and captions, and begin to form simple sentences, sometimes using punctuation.

The last two goals have recently been 'reviewed' (DCSF, 2009) in response to widespread criticism that they are far too abstract, arbitrary and developmentally inappropriate for all 4- and 5-year-olds to achieve. However, the decision has been made to retain them as valid aspirational goals and to produce additional guidance for practitioners on supporting children's early writing and reading.

Facts about phonics

- *Phonics* is a method for teaching reading that focuses on the relationship between sounds (phonemes) and letters (graphemes). A phoneme is the smallest unit of sound in a language but it is not necessarily a single letter: 'ee' in 'bee' is a phoneme. There are approximately 44 phonemes in English.
- *Synthetic phonics* is the required approach in English state schools and it is also the oldest and most traditional phonic method. It is based on the assumption that simple decoding is all that is required in reading and teaches the sounds of individual letters and the 44 phonemes. Children are taught to sound out the letters in order in words and 'blend' them together. Thus beginner readers make 'mer'-'a'-'ter' into 'mat' but struggle with the more complex words in a simple text, such as 'said' or 'the', for example. To get round this, frequent 'tricky' words do have to be remembered and read on sight!
- *Analytic phonics* is based on modern linguistic research and children are taught to look at segments of words and at the frequent patterns in sounds and words. The approach begins by focusing on the beginning, or initial, sounds of words, called 'onset' and at the end phonemes called 'rimes'. This involves lots of enjoyable play with the alphabet (alphabetic awareness) and the sounds of letters (phonological awareness). Children can be helped to enjoy the *alliteration* of same initial sounds in tongue twisters and the same, or similar, end rimes found in words that *rhyme* in songs, poetry and verse.

Early years and primary practitioners have 'guidance' (DfES, 2007) on how to tackle a simple reading programme in six phases. This programme reaches down into the EYFS, although it runs counter to the play-based, active, individualized learning of that stage! In practice, children under 5 could be spending 20 minutes a day, or more, 'sounding out' and 'blending' such words out of context as 'cat' and 'bus' and move on to 'fast' and 'milk'. Sometimes this intense drilling in phonics yields early 'results' but there is little evidence that these gains are retained in the long term. Furthermore, fast drilling of this kind produces anxiety and stress in young children.

Problems, problems, problems

The serious mismatch between current reading legislation in England and the philosophy of the EYFS has been referred to above. But it is important to emphasize the very young age at which children across the UK are in Reception classes (often they are only just 4 years old) and subjected to narrow curriculum requirements. Furthermore, literacy programmes of this kind push all children along at the same pace and do not consider individual developmental differences, gender and special educational needs.

The status of the research on which the English legislation is based is weak in terms of critical peer review and limited to a very small Scottish study (see Goswami's analysis, 2007: 136–40). To date, there is no empirical evidence that justifies the Rose Review's (DfES, 2006) conclusion that teaching synthetic phonics in English classrooms offers 'the vast majority of beginners the best route to becoming skilled readers' (ibid.: 19).

Goswami (2007; 2008) and many other linguists point to the fact that English is a difficult language to learn to read, particularly at the micro-level of phonemes. English has a complex syllable structure so it is better to avoid phonemes and concentrate instead on onset and rime. Similarly, English spelling and the representation of sounds by letters is not regular, so the onset and rime patterns are far more helpful. And, of course, many English words must be learnt and remembered as visual patterns. Where better to start than with picture books and stories that cheerfully present such words as 'elephant' and 'aeroplane' to the young reader?

Because of all these potential problems, a prime focus on 'the big picture' of reading is essential. This means going for meaning first as well as prioritizing pleasure and enjoyment. It is ethically unacceptable to pursue teaching methods that may cause anxiety and stress. It is also illogical to promote children's well-being, self-esteem and emotional intelligence as part of the curriculum, while seriously undermining them in the initial teaching of literacy.

There is a long and contentious history of systematic phonics instruction in the USA which educators in English-speaking countries should consider. Gardner (1991) noted that American educators relied too exclusively on phonics while neglecting the *reasons* for reading (ibid.: 212). More recent research evidence (Altwerger, 2005; Meyer, 2002) again questions the advantage of promoting only one kind of phonics and a 'one size fits all' approach. This unimaginative approach forces all young children, regardless of their individual literacy skills and experiences, to go through the phonics sausage machine. Meyer (2002) records the boredom and the stress shown by many young children and the undesirable lessons they are learning:

- They learn to over-rely on phonics and do not use semantic and syntactic clues.
- They learn a limited definition of reading (that reading is vague, unpredictable and unreliable).
- They learn to comply with doing what they do not understand (do not ask questions, just follow orders).

Finally, most critics of enforced programmes of 'synthetic phonics only' agree that the only people who flourish and do well out of the programmes are the publishers of controlled phonics texts!

Reading books (primers) and phonic texts

It seems inevitable that, with the imposition of national methods for teaching initial reading, primers and controlled phonic texts will also become the official approved reading material to be used in early years and primary classrooms. An example of the kind of text that can be decoded by sounding out and blending is cited by Altwerger (2005: 1).

> Mom has a pot
> Mom has a hot pot
> Mom has a spot
> Dad has a mop
> Dad mops the spot

This is not so different from the early reading primers, with all their drawbacks, that have dominated the initial teaching of reading for decades.

Problems with primers

- *Language.* Primers often make the mistake of simplifying the rich complexity of spoken and written language and by doing so they remove all the most helpful features of book language: not only meaningful narratives and humour, but memorable, frequently repeated phrases. Other helpful features of real book language include rhyme, alliteration and the choice of beautiful, archaic or foreign words. These give stories and verse a unique and unforgettable quality.

- *Illustrations.* Illustrations in primers fail most dismally in terms of their total lack of aesthetic quality or value as art. There is an absence of sensual delight in colour and texture and some very poor drawing skills. If we allow such schemes to be the dominant experience of books for children in the early years of schooling, we deprive them of a world of books that explode with vibrant colours, display delicate line drawings or exploit techniques of engraving and collage. We may also deprive our children of subtly tinted pages, holes, flaps, moving parts and elaborate end-papers.

- *Themes and characters.* In primers no one dies, no one hates and no one loves, but children's books do not flinch from greed and jealousy, rage and loneliness, mourning and death. Primers, however, lack powerful issues and they often ignore contemporary lifestyles, and unthinkingly perpetuate racial and gender stereotypes. Girls and mothers are still limited to the domestic role while boys and fathers are 'doers' and explorers.

Undoubtedly, early years practitioners and primary teachers who feel confident about the reading materials and approaches they use make an enormous
contribution to motivating and sustaining children's successful reading development. However, it is essential that a practitioner's personal preference for
structured reading schemes does not lead to any lessening of the children's
experiences of literature.

Real texts and readers

The advantages of reading books of literary and artistic merit in early years settings and schools are improved motivation, increased literary skills and an
enhancement of the educators' and carers' role. With regard to motivation, the
young child who is invited to read from quality books is being treated as a serious reader from the start. The resulting pride and self-esteem make a positive
and sure foundation for successful literary learning. The use of such books also
entices the child to move on to more and more texts because of the lure of further delights in store. Improved motivation is not restricted to learners:
educators and families who help young readers are also encouraged by the
sheer pleasure of sharing good books. Many parents and educators have in the
past come to dislike intensely certain schemes and their vapid 'characters'.
These negative feelings must have been sensed by generations of struggling
readers. In contrast to this response, educators and families are often the first to
get hooked on *Burglar Bill* (Ahlberg and Ahlberg, 1977a), *Where's Spot* (Hill,
1980), *Avocado Baby* (Burningham, 1982) and *Titch* (Hutchins, 1972)!

The complex skills involved in literacy and its development are at the heart
of the arguments about the best way to approach reading. Controlled and simplified texts are not, paradoxically, the best way to help young readers.
Complex human texts that contain recognizable issues, motives and emotions
described in recognizable language are essential for the emergent reader. If
young children are to get a toehold on a text they need as rich an array of clues
about its meanings as possible. The clues must refer to the contextual aspects
of the text: is it a letter, a cookery book or a story? The pictorial aspects are significant: are the images telling about the text and/or expanding it? The semantic
clues will be those that help to answer such questions as what does it mean and
what is likely to happen next?

Orthographic and phonological clues will enable the young reader to recognize frequently recurring and significant words on sight, to begin to notice initial
consonants and distinctive clusters of letters, and to hear similar and rhyming
phonemes.

Linguistic clues indicate the grammatical category of possible words and their
range of functions. When in doubt over a reading we rely on the linguistic context to indicate whether at this point the text is naming referents, indicating
actions or describing and enlarging upon a state of affairs. In order to use these
clues and possibilities children must be motivated enough and confident
enough to question the text, as we have already seen, and bring all their previous experiences to bear on it. To put it another way, the beginning reader

must take on the whole package from the start, going for meaning or compre-
hension before breaking down the text into its component parts of words,
letters and sounds. Reading is not like painting by numbers and we do not help
children by starting them off as if it were. Real readers need rich and complex
reading materials and good quality texts meet this need.

Learning and teaching suggestions

- Prioritize daily 'shared reading' sessions (see Chapter 9).
- Plan daily activities to promote, (1) *phonological awareness* (use rhymes,
  songs, tongue-twisters, nonsense verse, I-spy games and make collections of
  objects or names that start with the same letters, and so on) (2) *alphabetic
  awareness* (letters, alphabets, print sets, drawing letters in the air, or in sand,
  mud, water, and so on) and (3) *context and meaning* (lots of story telling and
  story reading, talk about what happened, what might happen next, motives
  and problems, and so on).

Practitioners who use literature for teaching reading, as well as for pleasure,
need support and guidance.

1. They must read every book they plan to put into the hands of the children.
   They must be able to speak from first-hand experience of the assumptions
   the book makes, the quality of its presentation, illustrations and language
   and the opportunities it potentially opens up for its readers. Does it raise
   important issues for reflection and discussion? Does it lead to other books
   or activities in early years settings or in the community? Does it extend the
   reader's language experience with new words and new ways of using
   words? Does it offer opportunities for focusing on initial clusters, rhymes
   and groups of letters?
2. The practitioner's choice of books for the classroom must be both varied
   and ample in quantity. There must be a wide range of poetry, story and
   information books and a great diversity of presentational styles or formats.
   Books in the classroom collection should contain pictures only, pictures
   and captions, toy-like techniques that pop-up or have holes or flaps, as well
   as increasing amounts of text. Professional guidance for practitioners and
   carers is now available in regularly compiled and annotated lists of available books and in journals that specialize in children's literature.[4]

As practitioners and carers we must be alert to new publications and new
developments in the book world. We also need to pursue a personal programme of regularly reading children's books for pleasure and information.
Reading quality texts places the power of behaving like readers literally into
the hands of the children. It puts the responsibility for making informed professional judgements and acting as models of what readers do back in the
hands of practitioners, carers and families.

Learning and teaching suggestions

- Regularly set up thematic or genre displays featuring, for example, fairy tales, monsters, poems, reference books, a popular author and/or illustrator.
- Provide some carefully chosen reference and information books. Look for high-quality photographs, art work and diagrams as well as reliable and accurate facts (using some books intended for older children and adults if necessary). Check that reference and information texts have clear and helpful lists of contents, indexes, diagrams and so on, so that you and the children can begin to practise study skills.

Reading with an adult

The use of quality books and literature challenges the traditional approach to 'hearing reading'. Literary texts are multilayered and must be shared, commented on and interrogated in a mutually supportive reading triangle of learner, teacher and text. In the early stages children need time to experience a whole book at a sitting. Initially this may involve the adult in reading the book first and allowing the young beginner reader to follow the performance, before encouraging the child to re-enact the story with the help of the context, the pictures, known letters and words, the adult and a variety of clues.

Young readers will also require the time and the security in which to discuss and evaluate the story and link it to their own lives and experiences. Such important human interactions take time and one-to-one teaching, with all that this implies for large class sizes in early years settings. These readings are also unpredictable and cannot be controlled as tightly as the kind of 'hearing reading' that consists of checking on a child's ability to recognize a few words by sight in a book of regular size and controlled vocabulary and sentence structure. Practitioners who use a range of quality books do not aim to 'hear' individual children read every day. They plan to share one, two or even three complete books with each child every week. However, they have other ways of supporting readers on a daily basis.

All the shared anecdotes, discussions, negotiations, poems, songs, rhymes and stories told or read in the group or class support reading. All the contacts with written materials in the school and the community support reading. Children, practitioners and families read newspapers, posters, letters, notices, street signs, carrier bags, food packages, greetings cards, invitations, recipes and the labels on clothes, cupboards and furniture. Parents, families and other members of the community also support young beginner readers by sharing the books many group settings and schools now send home on a regular basis. The young readers themselves contribute to this network of support by sharing their emerging skills with other infants and their peers who are just getting into literacy. At home young readers may read to their baby siblings or family pets, and in school they can share their developing competence with any other children who will listen.

Children can be helped to create a reading network or community if they are provided with books, time, pleasant spaces and, most importantly, an ethos that values books and reading for real. The issue of ethos and attitudes is crucial in approaches to sharing reading. Real readers take risks and they must feel that it is safe and rewarding to do so. They take chances, not only with the choice of book (there are no numbers or colours to guide you on your way in a life-time of real reading) but also with linguistic decisions.

Reading for meaning needs to be fairly rapid so that the thread of the narra-tive sense is not lost. Clues must be picked up on the run and chances taken – is it 'Mam' or 'Mummy', a 'horse' or a 'house'? This highly skilled predicting can be more finely tuned and corrected in retrospect if the reader is given the opportunity to go back and self-correct. Once the reader knows that the hero-ine must have escaped by climbing onto a big, black, horse and not a 'house', the correction is sensible and rewarding, and not without some humour. Amusement and delight in self-correction rely on confidence and space and time in which to reconsider. The supportive practitioner does not rush in too soon to fill this particular kind of pause. Knowing when to help, and when to hold back and let the text and the child reader do their own work, is a matter of professional judgement, experience and sensitivity: sensitivity to texts and to children is the most significant quality the 'reading teacher' in any setting can develop.

As part of the process of teaching reading and supporting readers, the prac-titioner makes links between books and children's lives. In the first place this is done whenever incidents and characters in stories or poems are talked about and linked with events, people, and places the children know well. Clearly, practitioners can only make a few of these connections because of their limited access to the children's personal lives. However, the children themselves will be willing contributors to the shared and valuable gossip of the classroom, always assuming that such talk is valued and respected.

Yet another way of linking the worlds of children and of books is through the creation of varied 'story props' that bring poems and stories into the play and general activities of the children and also draw the children into the world of the book. These props can be versions of the characters drawn by children, parents and practitioners, and then firmly mounted on card and backed with felt or magnetic tape and used on flannel boards or metal surfaces. Characters and objects from favourite stories can be played with and manipulated on these boards, accompanied by retellings and re-enactments of their adventures. Playful narrative activities of this kind are further enhanced if similarly mounted photographs of the individual children themselves are available. Children in the group are then able to narrate about themselves and place themselves into Mr Gumpy's boat (Burningham, 1970), or in hot pursuit of the elephant and the bad baby (Vipont, 1969).

Children can be further motivated by displayed photographs of other young children enjoying books and storying, or talking and playing with story props. Sometimes the actual objects mentioned in a narrative can be provided and used in playful book re-enactments – for example, a large saucepan and a wooden spoon for *Pumpkin Soup* (Cooper, 1998); some fruit for Handa (Browne, 1994); a bucket for Harry's dinosaurs (Whybrow and Reynolds, 1999). Appropriate puppets, dolls, toys and situations (such as sets of graduated bears, spoons, bowls, chairs and beds; or a patch of mud and long grass in the garden for going on a Bear Hunt) can also be used as powerful invitations to become a reader and enter the storybook world.

Storysacks

'A storysack is a large cloth bag containing a good quality young child's picture book' (Griffiths, 1997: 2).

The sack also contains a soft toy, doll or puppet to represent the book's main character, plus some objects that feature in the story. A non-fiction book that links with the story's theme in some way is included, as well as an audio-taped reading of the book (commercial or home-made). The storysack can also be extended with poems, a language or maths game based on the story and a card of suggestions to help parents use the sack and develop listening, reading and writing skills around the book.

Storysacks can be made by parents and friends of the setting and used as a library resource for the setting and the children's families.

Storysacks enrich and extend children's experiences with books and provide opportunities for flexible play with narratives and stories. Storysacks can also increase active parental involvement in their children's developing literacy.

Storysacks have continued to increase their range of ready-made sack collections and now produce some storysacks for children learning English as an additional language (EAL).

Learning and teaching suggestions

- Start a collection of story props (see Chapter 8). Use a plastic 'zip' bag to hold a book and sometimes a CD of the story, plus the relevant props (cut-out drawings of characters backed with magnetic tape or Velcro; character puppets, soft toys and objects from the story).
- Get together with parents and friends to build up a home-made 'library' of storysacks for the setting and the local community. Plan some simple fund-raising activities so that you can purchase some storysacks from the commercial company.

New literacies

An overemphasis on the roles of phonics and primers in early reading can obscure the fact that very young children are also learning about a vast array of other literacies. Often described as 'new literacies', these powerful symbolic systems of communication include, logos, electronic signs and icons, simplified text messaging systems (texting), moving picture narratives (film, television, video and DVD), ICT and email, computer games, advertising media, digital photography and satellite navigation systems.

The interesting aspect of these literacies that are now embedded in our lives is that they present very young children with communication systems that are very much part of home and community life. They are also visually arresting; often multilayered (visual, aural, mobile); requiring fine muscle control (for clicking a mouse, touching a screen icon, pressing a button); they are often an activity shared with others; they provide immediate feedback and exploit a fairly sophisticated level of understanding of phonology (Crystal, 2008).

This is all a great contrast with the slower, linear build-up emphasized by synthetic phonics training! The drawbacks for young children and their families of some of the new literacies are their commercial power to sell and persuade and their lack of genuine interactive communication. For example, babies do not learn to communicate and talk with a programme on a screen, but toddlers may find ways into literacy as they recognize frequently displayed advertising signs, logos and names, or start to decode and encode text messages. Early years practitioners must always be open to the likelihood that very young children may be sharing a huge range of new literacies with their families and in their communities.

In early years settings the use of digital cameras and simple video recorders is widespread and this kind of technology is often sent home so that families can record their children's interests, dispositions and schemas (Whalley and Pen Green Centre Team, 2007). The sharing of this visual material can feed into official records of child development and assessments of children's learning and progress. Because the technology is so user-friendly, it can also be used by the children themselves as a way of recording their preferences, interests, anxieties and achievements (Clark and Moss, 2001).

Children are not only becoming expert at reading visual narratives and information, they also hear the complex language of directions and distance as they travel in cars fitted with satellite navigation systems! I have already overheard in the nursery garden the phrase, 'You have reached your destination'! This is fun, but it can be very helpful in early literacy when children ask how to write a word or a letter. We can draw in the air, in mud, or dust or sand, and we can enrich the movement experience by also using the language of directionality at the same time: up and down, forward, back, round, turn. Perhaps the new literacies have as much to teach the practitioners as the children in the early years.

Summary

- Reading is something we do for pleasure and for information, and this is learned from satisfying experiences with books.

- Overdependence on the use of reading schemes and controlled phonic texts in schools exposes children to the problems inherent in most primers. These problems include their limited and unrealistic language; the poor quality of illustrations; their inadequate themes and characterization; and their lack of support for the reader.

- Overdependence on a daily literacy and phonics session tends to downgrade the inside and outdoors areas as prime sites for literacy learning and discoveries. The overemphasis on correctness, rote learning and whole-class texts undermines reading for pleasure and limits children's opportunities to explore books and experiment with writing.

- Literary approaches to the teaching of reading involve a careful focus on the nature of written texts, different perspectives on hearing young readers read and a broader view of the place of reading in children's lives.

- The new literacies challenge the narrowness of phonics instruction and the dominance of written texts and open up many opportunities for children and families to excel at reading a huge range of complex communication systems.

Key terms

Genre: a distinctive form of writing or text – a poem, a cookbook.
Literacy: the ability to read and write a language or languages.
Literature: any written text, but more often used about fictional texts.
Metaphor: the language of one subject area used to illuminate and revitalize another – 'spidery writing', 'crowning achievement'.
Phonemes: the smallest unit of sound in a language (not to be confused with single letters) for example, 'ee' in 'bee'; 'ea' in 'beat'; 'e' in 'evil'.
Phonics: a method for teaching reading that trains beginners to recognize the sound values of letters and 'blend' them together in words.
Phonology: the study of the organization and patterning of sounds in languages.

Further reading

Browne, A. (2009) *Developing Language and Literacy 3–8*. 3rd edn. London: Sage.

Campbell, R. (2009) *Reading Stories with Young Children*. Stoke-on-Trent: Trentham Books.

Featherstone, S. (ed.) (2006) *L is for Sheep – Getting Ready for Phonics*. Lutterworth: Featherstone Education.

Gamble, N. and Yates, S. (2008) *Exploring Children's Literature: Teaching the Language and Reading of Fiction*. 2nd edn. London: Sage.

Goouch, K. and Lambirth, A. (eds) (2007) *Understanding Phonics and the Teaching of Reading: Critical Perspectives*. Maidenhead: Open University Press.

Lewis, D. (2001) *Reading Contemporary Picturebooks: Picturing Text*. London: Routledge Falmer.

Mallett, M. (2003) *Early Years Non-Fiction: A Guide to Helping Young Researchers Use Information Texts*. London: Routledge Falmer.

Marsh, J. and Hallett, E. (eds) (2008) *Desirable Literacies: Approaches to Language and Literacy in the Early Years*. 2nd edn. London: Sage.

Meek, M. (1988) *How Texts Teach What Readers Learn*. Stroud: Thimble Press.

Meek, M. (1996) *Information and Book Learning*. Stroud: Thimble Press.

Meyer, R.J. (2002) *Phonics Exposed: Understanding and Resisting Systematic Direct Intense Phonics Instruction*. Mahwah, NJ: Lawrence Erlbaum Associates.

Riley, J.L. (2006) *Language and Literacy 3–7: Creative Approaches to Teaching*. London: Paul Chapman Publishing.

Wolf, M. (2008) *Proust and the Squid: The Story and Science of the Reading Brain*. Cambridge: Icon Books.

www.bookstart.org.uk

www.storysack.com

Notes

1 This chapter contains allusions to the events and characters in many children's books and the full references will be found in the list of 'Literature referred to in the text'.
2 See Britton (1992: 97–125).
3 Taylor (1973: 122).
4 For example, *Books for Keeps*, 1 Effingham Road, Lee, London, SE12 8NZ, www.booksforkeeps.co.uk

CHAPTER 8

EARLY REPRESENTATION AND EMERGING WRITING

This chapter includes:

- literacy in cultures and in schooling
- early representation and symbols
- emergent writing
- appropriate practice in early years settings.

This chapter is about writing in the broad context of children's language and literacy development and raises the following questions about the sources of young children's understanding of writing.

- Where does writing emerge from?
- What behaviours and insights come before the ability to write meaningful messages and understand written communications?
- What is special or distinctive about writing?
- How is writing related to spoken language and even to thinking?

Questions also arise about the nature of writing in a cultural group or society.

- What can be said about the relationships between a writing system and the society in which it has evolved?

And, in the context of this book:

- What can be said about literacy and early education?
- What is the role of the early years practitioner in young children's development as writers?

Some of these questions about literacy will be returned to in Chapter 9, but they emerge from the issues considered in this chapter. Before looking in some detail at the beginnings of mark-making and writing in the individual child's development, we need to review briefly some general ideas about writing and society.

Process and product

It is clear that we use the term 'writing' in two different ways. In everyday communications the context of the situation (as well as of the language) ensures unambiguous understanding. We know that 'writing' may be referring to the psychological and physical processes involved in actively creating a meaningful message. This is reflected in such possible classroom exchanges as 'What are you doing, Delroy?' 'Please Miss, I'm *writing* my Armada story.' 'Writing' is also an end-product of the writing process and so it can be 'Our class *writing* about the Castle visit', or the collected *writings* of Susan Isaacs. Although we are rarely confused by the functioning of the term 'writing' (whether as verb or as noun), we may be less aware of some of the hidden assumptions that colour our responses to 'writing', just because it is both process and product.

The very fact that there is always an end-product to the activity of writing concentrates attention on the 'final' or 'finished' piece of writing. Not only has this tended to detract from interest in and knowledge about the psychological process, but it has also placed excessive emphasis on notions of beautiful, tidy, perfect, grammatical or correct writing. This school tradition of concentrating on the correct end-product inevitably undervalued the first attempts at writing made by very young children. Many parents, teachers and children still think of 'writing' as first and foremost 'handwriting' or 'calligraphy', rather than a form of thinking and communicating (see Chapter 9). When the writing process was considered in the early years of education, it was the physical business of controlling pencils and forming letters that received most attention, and this manual-skills approach is still dominant in many early years group settings and classrooms (where tracing, copying, holding pencils 'correctly' and practising 'letters' continue to obscure the nature of young children's early-writing behaviours and insights).

Historically, the emergence of literacy changes a society so radically that becoming literate is always a personal, political and cultural watershed. Families are acutely aware of this (even if they do not put it into so many words) and their fears and anxieties for their children, as well as their ambitions for them, are reflected in the pressure they sometimes put on staff in early years group settings and schools to get their children reading and writing. If early years practitioners are to respond with sensitive understanding and educative good sense to such inevitable pressures, they need to know something of the relationships between literacy, schooling and societies.[1]

Literacy, culture and schooling

The evolution of a written system in a society leads to the writing down of the significant beliefs and lifestyle of the culture, and a lessening of group dependence on memory and word-of-mouth 'tellings'. The inevitable consequences of this over generations include:

- an enormous accumulation of written traditions
- historical awareness of the past
- huge variations in individual and group literacy skills
- the evolution of new ways of thinking shaped by literacy.

All these important consequences are now 'natural' features of our current lives, permeating society at large, local cultural and community groups and early years settings and schools.

Consequences

Taking these consequences separately, the sheer volume of written material that relentlessly builds up means that none of us can ever hope to see and read all that is produced. This may lead confident literate adults to reject what they do not wish to read (Pennac, 2006), but young beginning readers may still fear that 'everything' has to be read once they acquire the skills. Similarly, some families (unfamiliar with the literacy traditions of schooling) may demand to know exactly what their children must read in order to be educated and successful. This link – presumed to exist between success in school literacy and success or achievement in society – is taken for granted by many parents. It is the 'reading between the lines' message in many educator–parent discussions about literacy.

The sheer proliferation of documents in a literate society leads to the second consequence: a sense of history. Our awareness of the past highlights many inconsistencies, differences, doubts and changes within societies. The facts of a documented past make it possible to question legends, religious beliefs, nationalism, social conditions and political views. But the written word is no more honest and reliable than those who use it – history can certainly be rewritten to reflect a particular viewpoint or a more convenient set of facts and assumptions.

As educators we need to bear in mind the third consequence, that literate societies are nowhere near as uniform in their acquisition and use of literacy as we might be tempted to believe: there are huge variations in the literacy skills of individuals and of groups within any society. Literacy can identify, categorize and value people and groups (socially and economically) in terms of the amounts and kinds of reading and writing they use and produce. These literacy differences are also associated with different value systems in schools, families and peer groups.

The literacy highly valued and rewarded by literate societies and inevitably linked with the more privileged socio-economic classes is the 'school literacy' of formal education. This is the literacy of books and essays, and it requires mastery of book language and formal written style. Many of the characteristics of book-based literacy have been discussed in Chapters 6 and 7, but the main feature is its disembedded or decontextualized nature. Book-based literacy is self-explanatory, free-standing and explicit, rarely depending on events and features beyond it to convey meaning. The best metaphor for school or book-based literacy might be 'library learning' – it can be pursued in solitary fashion by the use of books, documents, computers and other recorded information. The great power of this 'school literacy' is its potential for distanced and reflective evaluation and comparison.

However, the sort of 'literacy events' (Heath, 1983: 200, 386) that all of us participate in for much of the time and that may be the dominant or total literacy experiences of some children and groups are the shared interpretations and production of writing rooted in social and cultural life (for example, the joint letter from a group of residents to a local council asking them to install a light in a dark walkway or the shared attempts by a family to make sense of the instructions for assembling an electric lawnmower). Such group literacy is embedded in the talk, the shared experiences and the cultural assumptions of the participants. However, its closeness to people's common-sense understandings and real-world concerns does not limit it to negotiating public notices, or letters from government and welfare agencies. On the contrary, literacy events can be a sort of shared commenting and thinking and newspapers, magazines, books and internet sites are frequently explored in this way.

Group and community literacy is the basis of 'school literacy', and the only reasonable means of access to it for young children. Where else can our 'library learning' about fictions, official reports or history, for example, have originated but in human lives, communities and language? It is possible for formal education to ignore the shared literacy events children have already known and impose school literacy on them, but this often results in superficial levels of reading and writing, an alienating gulf between schools and communities and serious underestimations of young children's abilities and potential.

Literacy is not just a performance skill with the written system of the language but a cognitive tool that transforms our capacity for self-reflection, mental reorganization and evaluation. In the histories of cultures such cognitive gains are indicated by the development of the reflective and analytical studies of philosophy, logic, linguistics and literary criticism. At the personal and professional levels we use the cognitive tools of literacy daily when we write our 'reflections' or evaluations of our own professional practices, or set down on paper our priorities and policies for specific curriculum areas, or educational issues. Children are performing this same sort of reflective and self-evaluating thinking when they write with genuine interest about their new baby, or the television news film they saw. Writing is not just for conveying information and instructions, nor is it just for sharing pleasure and messages – *writing is for thinking*.

Summary

- The term 'writing' can refer to both physical and psychological processes as well as to an end-product.
- The writing system of a society has, in its gradual evolution, changed the nature of the culture and provided a new tool for individual thinking.
- The consequences of these literacy changes have an impact on our approaches to, and judgements about, school literacy and community literacy.

Early representation and symbolizing

In order to understand the complex process of writing, we need to know something about the cognitive developments and strategies that precede it.

- Initially, thinking develops from the internalizing of actions, movement and images. This is known as *sensorimotor* and *iconic* representation, and is well established in the first two years of life.
- The appearance of gesture, language and make-believe play are signs of a developing ability to represent thought *symbolically*.
- This development is accompanied by mark-making, drawing, the pretend writing of messages and, eventually, recognizable conventional writing.

All these developments, once established, continue to exist, interacting, affecting and supporting each other. For example, early mark-making is highly dynamic and shaped by children's bodily exploration of space and their discoveries of what materials and tools can do.

Example

Eighteen-month-old children in a nursery garden excitedly daub paint, crayon and food over flat and vertical surfaces, as well as their own bodies. This total bodily experience is also linguistic and social as it is accompanied by vocalizing, single words or a brief explanatory narrative.

Early representation originates in the first weeks of life when routines of feeding, sleeping and waking form regular and predictable patterns, but the speed of the ensuing developments varies. Some 3-year-olds begin to form recognizable letters and create emerging writing while other children only achieve this around 8 or 9 years of age. These differences are likely to occur in a complex process that is both personal and cultural, and constructed out of interactions between individuals and their unique life experiences. Young children develop many of the necessary brain structures for thinking and understanding (sometimes called cognitive structures or intelligence) in the process of 'going over' or 'internalizing' their experiences of physical actions and shared interactions with special carers (parents, grandparents, key persons, and so on). However, the development of more complex thinking, including symbolic thinking, depends on the gradual freeing of thought from its links with very specific actions, people and objects.

For something like reflective thinking to develop, there must be a means of holding on in the mind to actions, perceptions and events, after they have occurred. This begins when actions, people, events and objects are remembered – held in the mind – as images of people, activities and things in the world. This capacity for picturing or 'image-ing' in the mind some general features of the environment develops in the second year of life, or even earlier. The very young child has now made the crucial first moves in freeing her thinking from immediate stimuli and its rootedness in the here and now.

Example

Representational thinking is clearly happening when young children recognize pictures of cats, for example, in books, and name them or react by eagerly setting off to search for their own cat, or respond in the same way if they overhear the name of their pet cat in a general conversation, or are directly asked, 'Where's Sammy?' Being able to think about people, animals, objects and experiences *in their absence* means that, in a special way, we can still have a hold on them. The hold is special because it is created mentally and is not subject to immediate reality or facts. Furthermore, we can experiment with these representations: we can play and pretend with them. Young children, from at least the second year of life, will say 'miaow' like a cat, or climb into the cat's basket and curl up to sleep. They even label their own marks and drawings as 'cat' or 'Sammy'. This is not necessarily because the marks are attempts to produce an image of a cat, but may be because the actual making of the marks was a way of imitating with movement, gesture and a marker cat-like actions and the child's own feelings about 'Sammy'.

The repetition and playful trying-out of representations or thoughts about experiences is a process that actively builds knowledge or the mind. Children show us that they know something,

- by doing it
- by creating or responding to a picture-image of it
- by using an abstract symbolic means such as number or language to represent it.

Writing development adds a further level of complexity to this 'three-modes' view of the growth of thought. *Spoken language uses words and syntax to stand for, or symbolize, people, objects, places, and so on, but written words and sentences that represent this spoken language are at a further remove.* If this is complicated and confusing to read about, how do we account for the 3- and 4-year-olds who confidently write a birthday letter to a granny who lives thousands of miles away, or create a name label for the gerbils' cage in the nursery? The answer seems to have at least two major components:

- the power of cultural influences in children's lives
- the power of images and marks.

Symbols and the creation of meanings

At the heart of symbolic systems and behaviours as varied as pretending to be a cat or 'eat' plasticine cakes, is the human gift for making meanings out of arbitrary movements, sounds, marks and gestures. There is nothing cat-like about the words 'cat', 'chat' or 'Katze' and cats do not actually say 'miaow'. Moulded lumps of plasticine are not really cake-like and holding them near the mouth while making chewing movements with the jaws is not 'eating'. And as for language, 'What's in a name? That which we call a rose/By any other word would smell as sweet' (Shakespeare, *Romeo and Juliet*, II. ii. 43). The possibility of meaning and communication in all these symbolizing activities is created by the human makers, children and adults alike.

Teddies and blankets

The activity starts in the earliest months of life, most noticeably when the infant endows a soft toy or blanket, and so on, with a great wealth of feeling and significance – so much so that comfort in stressful situations or in the minutes before falling asleep appears to depend on it utterly. This drive continues as children cuddle and talk to objects and toys, pretend to be things and try to interpret the marks they notice in their world. These behaviours are clearly reflections of children's ability to make meaning out of arbitrary signs.

Drawings

Young infants are readily generalizing their experiences when they recognize significant people in all sorts of changing circumstances, movements, clothes and moods. Young children do the same when they draw their first people as stylized signs with big heads and tail-like legs; this is the 'tadpole' stage in drawing. Similarly, Western children live in a great variety of dwellings, and few have open coal fires, but the usual 'my house' drawing is a standardized square with windows in the corner angles, a central door and a chimney belching smoke. These drawings of people and houses do not appear to be attempts at artistic realism but are cultural signs, abstract representations of the meaning and significance of 'my dad' and 'my house'. This tendency to use a *generalized sign* is probably the bridging activity between thinking with actions, images and symbols and communicating through a conventional writing system.

Drawings, signs and writing

In the early years of childhood, drawings and writing are produced together and, like so much play and pretending, they may be doing many things: communicating messages or standing for experiences, ideas and sensations. Many researchers (for example, Bissex, 1980; Ferreiro and Teberosky, 1982; Hall and Robinson, 2003; Kress, 1997; 2000) emphasize the significance of the drawings that precede and then accompany writing. The importance of drawings lies partly in their contributions to the total meaning of children's written communications and also in their links with general thinking strategies. *Children use drawing as a dynamic, exploratory, problem-solving activity.* Their marks on the surfaces of paper, board, tables, pavements or walls are creative: they are totally new in the world, they were brought into existence by individual children. But, once made they are fixed, unlike actions or talk, and they can be worked on, repeated and altered in many ways.

Representations of a surprisingly regular kind emerge as children exploit the possibilities of drawing (see Matthews, 2003). Space is enclosed by a drawn line and then adapted by the addition of certain minimal 'signs' into representations of people, animals or buildings. For example:

- Circles with dots and dashes added become faces or human figures that can be minimally altered to represent fishes, cats and cows.
- The face 'sign' is just as easily changed into suns, flowers, balls and spiders.
- A squared enclosure can be a car, a parcel, the park or a house.

Other conventions for indicating space, location and boundaries become very familiar to observers of children's drawings:

- the marking out of earth and sky with parallel horizontal lines
- the careful drawing of a border that follows the edges of paper, board or table top.

Complex and intangible emotions are also indicated in children's drawing systems by minimal marks:

- jagged, saw-like teeth suggesting greed and ferocity
- the upward curving ends of a line producing the 'smiley' mouth of happiness.

These comments are a reminder of the sign-like and even 'writerly' aspects of an area of children's early representational thinking that is sometimes undervalued. We need to be aware that under-5s are accustomed to creating and working with their own graphical systems of flexible signs; this is what drawing and mark-making is, and its potential for supporting and extending writing competence has not yet been fully explored in educational practice. Taking drawing seriously could transform children's communication and literacy achievements in the early and primary years of education (Figure 8.1).

Figure 8.1 **Taking drawing seriously – a self-portrait (4 years)**

Ironically, the interest in early, or developmental, writing may have had the effect of diminishing attention, support and resources for drawing in the early years curriculum. Young children's pictures and experiments with markers are sometimes scanned by practitioners for letters, numerals and letter-like forms but their intrinsic value as drawings is in danger of being ignored. This is not just an early-childhood education issue – pressure for writing in the later primary years drives drawing out of the literacy curriculum. Older pupils in primary schools still need opportunities to draw their messages and extend the total impact of their writing by using imaginative illustrations, diagrams, some appropriate observational drawing and the range of graphical signs, logos and symbols found in a literate society, including electronic symbols, logos and texting abbreviations and conventions.

Learning and teaching suggestions

- In the outside areas provide water and big brushes for bold marking.
- Make pavement chalks available for hard surfaces and fix chalkboards on walls and fences.
- Big markers and rolls of cheap paper can be used outside and remember that damp sand and mud are irresistible media for mark-making (Figure 8.2).

Figure 8.2   **Mark-making with sticks in mud (Reception)**

Summary

- The emergence of writing is dependent on the earlier development of cognitive modes for representing and symbolizing actions and experiences.
- These modes of representation are developing rapidly during the first three or four years of life and build on the internalization of actions and images, making them general symbols for what were originally specific perceptions and events.
- Early representation gradually frees thought from specific stimuli and circumstances and enables the symbolic systems of gesture, language, pretend play and drawing to develop.

- The ability to hold on to experiences and feelings by means of internalized actions and images is revealed in the tendency to transfer strong feelings and associations to arbitrary or 'found' objects in the environment. Things (toys, ribbons, blankets), and even people, come to stand for whole sequences of emotions and experiences: they are symbols.
- Drawing and mark-making are part of these complex developmental processes and form powerful links between early representation and the symbolic nature of written sign systems.
- Drawings and marks use arbitrary signs to communicate meanings and stand for experiences, ideas and sensations.
- Playing, pretending and spoken language are crucial symbolizing activities that support and share many characteristics with early writing development.

Emerging writing

WARNING! Infants under 3

Infants who are under 3 years old can be found in most children's centres and other early years care and education settings. For these babies and toddlers, other activities are far more important than writing! The priorities for them must be communicating, signing and talking; forming stable relationships with key workers and a small number of other adults; the sensory exploration of materials and investigating outdoor and indoor environments; mark-making and painting; playing alongside other children and singing, dancing, running and climbing!

Emerging writing is a phrase that places a clear emphasis on the process by which children investigate and exploit the possibilities of writing. The phrase is also used here to suggest links with the emergence of spoken language in infancy and the development of playful activities involving pretending and problem-solving. There are problems to be tackled in literacy learning, problems that arise mainly from the differences between spoken and written communication. However, the ways in which young children set about investigating the challenge of print (Figure 8.3) should not be thought of as different in kind from their general strategies for thinking about and resolving other problems.

Figure 8.3 **The challenge of marking on paper on the floor (24 months)**

Making sense

The view that young children's learning and thinking is based on the construction of meanings, or making sense of things, is very prominent in developmental psychology and linguistic theory. This approach describes early learning in terms of strategies and processes that enable infants to sort out and to organize things that are new, important, appealing, strange and disturbing. The significant strategies in this learning include the *careful observations* of features of the environment (including print), and of human behaviour, including talking, writing and reading. Lengthy periods of observation by young children culminate in *selective imitations* of bits of the noticed world: for example, a gesture may be tried out or part of a word or phrase repeated. Similarly, there may be an attempt to draw a few letters or numerals.

Very young children also *pretend* to perform a skill or activity in its entirety. This is obviously happening when an infant babbles a 'conversation' into a pretend or toy mobile phone, with all the meaningful non-verbal features of pauses, rising and falling pitch and the accompanying nods, smiles and gestures. We also see this totality of *pretence and imitation* in operation when a young child does pages of scribble writing, re-creating both the speed and the flow of the physical actions as well as the spiky, linear appearance of a written text. This pretending or approximating behaviour is part of the *hypothesis-forming* that characterizes human thinking. Hypothesis-forming includes:

- *Abstracting*. Abstracting the essence, the distinctive core, of an event or feature of the world goes on during the lengthy periods of observation and non-production that precede the emergence of many skills, including talking and writing. Abstracting probably plays an important part in the creation of mental representations of actions, persons and events.
- *Hypothesizing*. Hypothesizing and constructing are reflected in the highly selective imitating and pretending that follow from abstracting. Hypothesizing about 'what it is' and constructing 'ways of doing it' occur in early talking, drawing and writing, as well as in a whole range of playful activities.
- *Revising*. Revising can be thought of as the reshaping and improving of pretending, in the light of helpful feedback and closer observations of discrepancies and conflicts. This revising can go on indefinitely, until the pretence approximates more closely to the observed behaviour, or satisfies the child's purposes and sense of 'rightness'. One example of revising in early language learning is the process by which the flow of an infant's babbled 'talk' is gradually modified and shaped. Actual sound combinations occurring in the home language (or languages) are focused on and repeated by child and caregivers until real words are thought to be 'recognizable'. Similarly, in the young child's marks and drawings, approximate numeral and letter shapes identifiable in the culture are recognized, praised and gradually come to be repeated intentionally by the child.

Child + people + culture

The active, thinking, hypothesizing child is one element in this complex learning equation but the other crucial elements are the human social and cultural environments. Young children become thinking, communicating people because they are involved in social life from birth – regardless of race, socio-economic class or status. Children's moves into spoken and then written communication can only be properly accounted for in terms of the support and the stimulation they find in their personal and cultural situations. Research identifies three recurring features of this social discourse (Bruner and Haste, 1987: 21; Gerhardt, 2004; Gopnik et al., 1999; Trevarthen, 2002):

- Older and 'wiser' people appear to support or 'scaffold' all aspects of a baby's learning in the culture, presenting just enough manageable stimulation and information, as well as demonstrating examples of how to react and what to do. Even older children can be as useful in this way as adults.
- Meaning is mutually constructed or negotiated between babies and their caregivers. This implies that the infant is learning to share references and meanings as an equal partner and, in doing so, is exposed to the agreed

meanings of the particular culture.
- The culturally specific nature of the values and the assumptions shared with very young children are significant.

Language, both spoken and written, will be a major carrier as well as a dynamic creator of these cultural values: we do not just tell babies how to say 'hello' and 'goodbye' – we demonstrate when, where and how the expressions are spoken and gestured in our particular social world, by being particularly attentive in our own greetings and farewells to babies.

This theory of learning emphasizes that learning is what the mind does and children develop powerful strategies for thinking and problem-solving long before schooling starts. Furthermore, studying language is one way of studying the mind, and children's earliest attempts at writing and reading give us extra insights into their language and thinking.

Research evidence

Research evidence about young children's early literacy learning has accumulated steadily over the last three or four decades. Although literacy is rooted in spoken language and communication, it does present novice learners with special challenges. Two questions sum up the problems facing the literacy beginner:

- How do I share my meanings in this special system?
- Who can help me?

The crucial helpers for the child will always be older and wiser members of the family and community, but the question of meaning is closely tied to the differences between speech and writing.

Speech

Speech is experienced immediately and its physical production can be both heard and seen. It is also varied and coloured by accent, dialect, situation, and so on, and spoken communications are further clarified by vocal emphasis, pauses and rhythm, and so on. The immediate face-to-face nature of speech makes it highly flexible, changeable and responsive to feedback from others and to the total social context in which it occurs. Spoken language communicates meanings immediately, negotiating any difficulties and repairing any misunderstandings and confusions as it goes along.

However, we should set against these positive advantages the fact that speech does not communicate over distances, nor over long periods of time and, as we all learn to our cost, spoken words cannot be unspoken, or destroyed (although they may, in time, be forgotten or forgiven).

Writing

Writing does not rely on a face-to-face situation – it must be self-sufficient and self-explanatory, carrying all its intended meanings in linguistic signs and conventions only. In written communication everything must be fairly explicitly stated; arguments and sequences of thinking must be logically set out and developed. These features and limitations make writing more formal and impersonal than speaking but they are also the source of its power. Writing communicates across space and time, and it can be preserved, returned to and even changed. For the beginner, however, writing does mean that you are on your own, a difficult move away from sharing and building a verbal interaction. Emerging writers are always in the process of learning to be alone and independent. At any time they are operating along a continuum, always being somewhere on the line from oral to graphic expression – from receiving the feedback of a conversational partner to developing the ability to be both sides of the communication, the teller and the told. It all seems overwhelmingly difficult, yet the observational evidence is clear: many very young children demonstrate a great deal of initiative, pleasure and creative experimentation in their encounters with print. This is the same sort of creativity and pleasure that older children, adolescents and many adults demonstrate in their daily texting on mobile (cell) phones (see Crystal, 2008).

Young children's hypothesizing about print would appear to be powered by the desire to answer two questions (or question clusters):

- What is it for and what's in it for me?
- How do you do it and which marks really matter?

These are oversimplifications, but they do get us into the crucial areas of *composition* and *transcription*. The question of what is composed in writing is a question about meaning and function – what is it for and what's it about? Many young children discover that writing carries messages and, although these kinds of messages have often been shared in verbal interactions, written messages really make people sit up and take notice, so, print is powerful as well as communicative. Some 2-year-olds start on written greetings, such as 'kisses' on notes to friends and family or 'welcome' banners. Some 3- and 4-year-olds progress to unconventional yet readable instructions and complaints: 'I HIVANT HAD A TR IN PAD (I haven't had a turn in playdough)' (Newkirk, 1984: 341).

In their homes and communities, young children may attempt to add the name of their favourite sweet or cereal to a shopping list, and they often recognize the names and logos of supermarkets and fast-food restaurants. Sometimes they discover that they can leave an important message for Mum (Figure 8.4 – I'm in the playground, by Nicolas Lee).[2] This really is a remarkable discovery about writing: you can go away and leave it to speak for you. The ability to write messages defeats time and distance but it also brings personal independence.

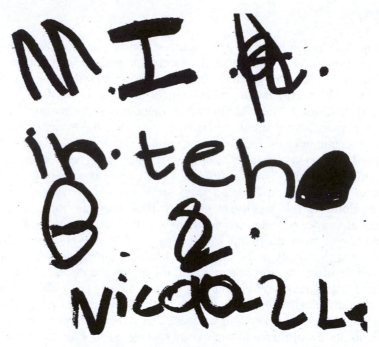

Figure 8.4   I'm in the playground. Nicolas Lee

Ownership, power and control over their own writing and, eventually, their own lives, rests with readers and writers: they are full members of the literacy club (Smith, 1988). Writing has been equated with 'finding a voice' (Graves, 1983; 1984), and young children seem to be on their way to achieving this when they ask us, 'What does that say?' Until these crucial links between print and the power of voicing meaningful messages are made, the learner-writer of any age will be merely copying without real purpose.

Central as these questions of 'what is it for?' and 'what's in it for me?' are, many young children do not wait passively for complete answers. They often settle for hunches about meaning while simultaneously investigating 'how do you do it?' In fact, young children's spontaneous learning strategies are rarely tidy or organized into neat hierarchical stages. It is important that adults develop some awareness of the complex patterns of interaction between finding out that real writing means something important, and finding out how it is done and what counts as writing. Children demonstrate for us daily these networks of interrelated discoveries as they attempt to write their own names. Personal names are charged with meaning: they embody our sense of self-worth and our place in the world. Furthermore, the adult community usually places great value on very young children's ability to write their own names and welcomes the achievement enthusiastically. For the child, the ability to recognize and write that name conventionally also gives some control over a set of known and meaningful letters that can be easily identified. This known set may stimulate a great deal of experimenting and theorizing about complex written conventions.

One 4-year-old boy in a nursery class I was visiting wrote part of his name, Dennis, as a fairly random scatter of 'D' 'e' 'n' 'n' . He then stopped, turned to me and said, 'I can write my name, it's got two of those' (pointing to the second 'n'). He completed the writing with 'i' 's', including a second attempt at the 's' (Figure 8.5). Dennis was spontaneously demonstrating his knowledge of conventional orthography, as well as his interest in practising and improving his control and skill with the marker (a biro pen), and the formation of the challenging letter 's'.

Figure 8.5 **Dennis: I can write my name. It's got two of those**

Children exploring writing systems

Research into children's understanding of the nature of writing systems has produced evidence of child hypotheses that are not conventional but are attempts at answering the crucial question, what is writing? Pre-school children in a very poor, urban, Spanish-speaking environment in South America (Ferreiro and Teberosky, 1982) apparently evolved a 'minimum quantity hypothesis'. When deciding what was 'readable' these children theorized that a minimum of three graphic characters must be together if a piece of writing could be read, anything less was called a 'number'. However, this hypothesis was eventually abandoned because it did not account for all the one- and two-syllable words the children used regularly in Spanish, including their own names.

Literacy, however, is more than collections of words and word recognition. The gradual discovery of writing as a system different from speaking hinges on the ability to create and manipulate sentences. Sentences belong to writing (Kress, 1994; 2000) not speaking; they are the really significant chunks of text around which writing is organized and built up. We do not talk in sentences unless we are reading or reciting prepared statements, lectures, letters and stories. The significant unit for spoken utterances is not a sentence but the meaning-bearing clause that constructs shared understandings 'on the run', while we are thinking on our feet.

The constructed sentence of the written language features one main topic, and young children come to understand these differences if they are encouraged to play with the possibilities of creating their own statements about pictures, photographs and activities. Simple topic sentences in children's early writing may seem repetitive to adults, but many children are delighted to find they have discovered a sentence formula that can be exploited almost endlessly. In the early stages of writing it is appropriate and powerful to be able to generate lots of sentences of the 'I like my … ' or 'we saw a … ' type.

Children exploring conventional graphics

This discussion has already indicated that children's unconventional hypotheses and constructive errors about writing present them with some stimulating conflicts. The processes of trial and error, feedback and reformulation also characterize children's experiments with all the conventions of mark-making, letter formation and the spatial arrangements of print. Young children's written messages emerge gradually from scribbles and drawings that may contain attempts at letters and numerals.

In an influential analysis of this emergent writing, Clay (1975) identified stages in which children seem to be sorting out particular aspects or 'principles' of writing:

- The first stage for the young child is making a distinction between drawing or pattern-making and writing. This indicates the emergence of the *sign concept* because it suggests some insight about writing as a system of signs. At this stage distinctly letter-like forms appear in children's drawings and strings of pretend writing are produced.
- Understanding that writing is a sign system for conveying messages and some skill in producing letter forms is a beginning, but the production of writing involves other important principles. These principles are concerned with the conventions for combining individual letters to form words, sentences and continuous text. The *recurring principle* focuses on the way in which writing uses the same shapes over and over again. This repetition of loops, circles, sticks, squiggles and crosses produces most of the

conventional forms and, in children's early attempts, a few near misses or invented forms.

- The *generative principle* highlights the fact that words and sentences may be produced ad infinitum by combining and recombining a limited set of letter forms.
- The *principle of flexibility* imposes some limitations on the number of letter-like forms that are acceptable as signs. The invented letters children come up with will eventually have to be dropped from their written repertoires.

Children encounter many different printed forms, typefaces and graphics but this exposure ensures a useful focus on the essential and distinctive features of letters.

A further group of principles (Clay, 1975) is concerned with the conventions of page arrangements and the spatial orientation of print. Young children will experiment with the directional flow of writing and reading, its distinctive linear organization and the conventional uses of spacing. Some children appear to stumble upon solutions and conventions that have been, or still are, used by human groups in various parts of the world. For example, British and American children's writing can temporarily flow from right to left, as in Arabic and modern Hebrew, or it may be written in vertical columns. Some young writers organize their script to move from left to right, right to left in the ancient Greek pattern known as boustrophedon ('as the oxen ploughs'). What more sensible solution to page limits and directional flow can there be, than moving to and fro across the page, as if ploughing a field?

The gradual discovery that conventions matter because they significantly affect the communication of meanings in a particular culture, occurs as a result of pretending, sharing and practising reading and writing in families and communities.

The work of professional researchers in the USA, South America and Britain has drawn attention to the 'scientific' ways in which young children formulate hypotheses about writing and demonstrate curiosity about the variety of written forms they meet. This is exemplified by a monolingual British 6-year-old, of Scottish descent, in an East-End London school who was teaching herself to write the Bengali characters she encountered in the school and the community (Figure 8.6).

Children behave like teachers of writing, for themselves and for their peers. These teacher-like behaviours include self-imposed practice and self-correction and the redrafting of drawings, writing and spellings. Some children even set out practice lists or inventories of what they know and can write confidently. Recent research has confirmed that young children's spontaneous marks and representations about their mathematical thinking emerge in similar ways (Worthington and Carruthers, 2003). Lists of known letters, mathematical graphics, numerals and favourite words appear frequently in some children's drawings and writings, and seem to function as personal checklists. But it is in the context of learning about standardized spelling that children can behave like fairly independent teachers and researchers.

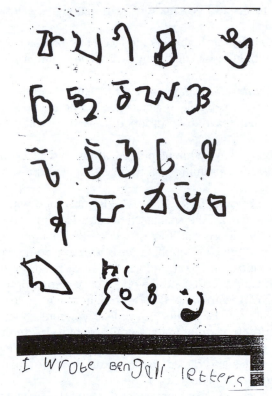

Figure 8.6 **I wrote Bengali letters**

Learning and teaching suggestions

- Create attractive and well-maintained writing areas, corners or groups of tables – outdoors as well as inside – and provide a range of markers, papers, erasers, straight-edged rulers and pencil sharpeners. Include fine pencils and biros as well as thick pencils, stubby crayons, coloured felt and water-based pens. Occasionally introduce inks, pens and small brushes.

- Extend the range of drawing, marking and messages in your setting: encourage spontaneous drawing (this is not just a matter of supplying materials, but valuing, talking about and displaying children's drawings). Provide a group/room/class message board for the use of children, adults amd families; set up chalkboards and flip charts indoors and outside so that the children can draw, mark and write on large surfaces. Focus on the use of lists and help the children record such items as: names of children in the group, names of practitioners, key persons, other carers, family members and friends; lists of favourite foods, pets, colours, clothes; names of local streets and landmarks; shopping and ingredients lists; favourite storybook characters. Use these lists as counting and sorting data, as discussion points and as the focus of alphabetical and phonological investigations and learning.

- Create literacy-enhanced play areas for older children and plan with the children lists of possible extensions for the play (Hall and Robinson, 2003). Take the children on visits to places like shops, clinics, bus and train stations if you plan to set up play versions of them. Use unexpected 'events', mishaps, or complications to inspire more play and problem solving and meaningful literacy (ibid.).

Children exploring spelling systems

I used the phrase 'fairly independent' above in order to highlight the innovative approach young children often have towards the spelling system. This approach gives rise to non-conventional spellings, but a closer analysis of these errors in English orthography indicates that they are real attempts to represent the sounds children utter and hear themselves, using the alphabetic names and sound symbols they know. Children's invented spellings reveal the extent, as well as the limitations, of their current knowledge of the sounds of their language, or languages, and the relationships of these sounds to an alphabetic system.

Read (1986) described children's invented spelling as creative, systematic and highly phonetic. The strategy is creative in the sense that rather than copying or imitating a model, early spelling reflects children's own attempts to work out some systematic regularities and patterns that might underlie spelling. Children's initial hypotheses about spelling are phonetic judgements about sounds, the physical basis of speech, and how to represent them systematically. One detailed case study that illustrates just how very systematic children's invented spellings can be is Bissex's (1980) analysis of her own son's development as a writer. A clear pattern of developmental stages in spelling has been outlined by a researcher who reanalysed the material of the Bissex study (Gentry, 1982).

The analysis suggests that learning to use the standardized spelling system is rooted in the young child's desire to communicate messages and share in the general writing activities of the home and community. This drive to join in and share leads to:

- the *pre-communicative stage* of spelling in which scribbles, numerals, letters or odd words are the pretend writing often found on shopping lists, labels, letters and story books.
- The *semi-phonetic* and *phonetic* stages indicate growing understanding that there are letter and sound relationships. The names of the alphabet letters do themselves suggest speech sounds and syllables and the names of letters can be used to represent the sounds of spoken language. At first this is a fairly rough or semi-phonetic approximation, producing such delightful examples as 'RUDF' ('are you deaf') (Bissex, 1980: 3) and 'PAULSTLEFNMBR' ('Paul's telephone number') (ibid.: 7), written at 5 years, 1 month. These semi-phonetic strategies now look very familiar to adults and children who regularly do 'text-messaging' on mobile phones.
- In the *phonetic stage* a more complete attempt at representing all the sounds

of words appears in the spellings, and the messages become more complicated and more confident: 'DO NAT DSTRB GNYS AT WRK' ('do not disturb
genius at work') (ibid.: 23), written at 5 years, 8 months. The highly phonetic
nature of this strategy is tellingly revealed in the reflection of a particular pronunciation feature, the 'NAT' [not] of standard American English.

• The move from phonetic spelling to the stage of 'correct' or standardized
  spelling passes through a transitional phase. During this period some of the
  conventional and historical but not phonetic features of standard English
  spelling begin to appear in children's work. Increased experiences of reading add greatly to children's visual memories of many distinctive words, as
  well as commonly occurring digraphs, letter strings and word patterns.

The work of Goswami and Bryant (1990) suggests that school instruction in
reading and writing alphabetic script helps children detect and recognize
phonemes and this supports their early spelling strategies. It is only at a fairly
late stage in spelling development that instruction will benefit children. This
conclusion – that any formal teaching of spelling should be delayed until children have started reading and are able to evolve their own strategies for
understanding the nature of writing and spelling – brings the implications of
research evidence for school and classroom practice into sharp focus. Children's
early experiments with spelling are part of a complex process of making meaning (Kress, 2000) and demands for conventional accuracy must not be allowed
to overwhelm children's creative play with letter and sound relationships.

Appropriate practices

WARNING! Supporting boys

Recent perspectives on child development and studies of the brain in
infancy confirm what experienced practitioners have long suspected:
that literacy learning in boys follows a very distinctive path. Furthermore,
traditional approaches to the teaching of early literacy may actually disadvantage boys and fail to pick up on their strengths. Practitioners must
focus on the highly energetic and active learning styles of boys and tar-
get the outside learning areas and the desire that many boys have to
pursue meaningful literacy while 'on the move'. Many boys are often
strong on practical problem solving and investigations and their interest
in literacy should be inspired by these kinds of interests. Practical guidance for practitioners is now available in England and makes an informed
contribution to the debate about ways of supporting the development
of boys' early literacy: *Confident, Capable and Creative: Supporting Boys'
Achievements* (DCSF, 2007).

It is clear that very young children may learn far more about print and the functions of writing in their communities than has been acknowledged by traditional teaching approaches. However, opportunities to use and extend such out-of-school learning within school or other early years settings are dependent on the attitudes of professional educators and carers. Self-directed, independent pupils who have the potential to function like researchers themselves (Featherstone and Featherstone, 2008) need tolerant and flexible professional tutors – tutors who know that there is now a strong case for asserting that children may learn more about reading and writing from the captions, cartoons, signs, advertisements, labels and slogans of their environment than from the carefully controlled words in school primers and textbooks. Words in the environment are not graded and controlled but they are always purposeful: they carry real messages and are supported by a rich array of contextual clues.

We have to respect and extend not only the spoken language children bring to school but also the judgements and hypotheses they have constructed about written language. Failure to do this carries the risk of massively underestimating the experiences and abilities of young children. A complete break with the spontaneous processes of play, invention and experimentation, which characterize out-of-school learning, may leave young children helplessly confused in classrooms for weeks as they attempt to puzzle out the rules of the strange new regime. Practices that avoid a damaging gulf between out-of-school and classroom- or group-based learning and that build on children's existing knowledge of language and literacy are the most appropriate.

An appropriate set of guidelines for the teacher of early literacy must consider:

- inspiration
- real needs
- supportive environments
- informative feedback
- new thinking skills.

This may seem to be a surprising list because it does not include the usual checklist topics, such as spelling, punctuation, sentence structure and handwriting. But these important areas are more usefully addressed and understood as they occur in purposeful early literacy developed from the spoken language and social experiences of young children.

Inspiration

Arousing children's desire to write is an essential part of the literacy teacher's role. The inspiration for writing arises partly from children's perceptions of it as a high-status activity – something that is done by significant people in their social world. This is one good reason for providing children with daily experiences of being at the elbows of important and admired persons who are writing for real. The potential of these experiences is enormous if we try to ensure that much of our genuine writing as practitioners is an open, public and educational activity. Young children might sometimes observe and make oral contributions to the writing up of their records by practitioners, as well as being invited to choose examples of their work to be dated, annotated and added to these records. We can arrange to plan and write letters, notes and invitations to 'outsiders', while children are around to comment and offer helpful suggestions. Occasionally the children can be taken on a writing expedition around the setting to discover other writers at work, in the kitchen, the medical room and the office, for example. For one Reception class, a walk in the local woods inspired thoughts, ideas and associations with woods, all of which were recorded as a wall display (Figure 8.7).

Figure 8.7 **A display about woods (Reception)**

Inspiration for young writers is furthered by providing a wide range of writing materials, some especially pleasant places to write in, including the outdoor areas, and examples of 'writing' to investigate and try out. These could include the many kinds of print encountered every day, as well as varied scripts and any different writing systems used in the community, several styles of graphics, a selection of manuscripts, typescripts, printouts and some different conventions of print and layouts in prose and verse.

A wide range of writing materials means much more than some regulation-size school paper and thick pencils for young children. These basics have their place, but inspiration for real writers demands range and variety, according to need, function and even whim! The really stimulating writing area extends the possibilities of writing and of drawing with a range of markers and a variety of papers and surfaces.

A selection of printing devices in the early years setting can enlarge the potential for producing print repetitively and speedily; they also enable young children to produce what is beginning to look like 'real' published writing. Computers, printers and digital cameras increase the sophistication of children's published work and can, if shared with adults and other children, nurture rich experiences of alphabets, orthography and the conventions of print. Even experiences of printing with oddments of scrap materials and cut vegetables, for long a traditional part of the early years curriculum, can support children's understanding of the nature of print and printing technologies.

Inspiration for writing is fostered by an educational environment which acknowledges and extends the huge variety of scripts and writing technologies which exist in society, and introduces children to a new community of writers.

Learning and teaching suggestions

- Writing areas should stimulate children's interest in the range and functions of writing: help the children to collect samples of print from the environment (recipes, haiku, knitting patterns, crosswords, word searches, invitations, greetings cards, postcards, receipts, bills, addressed envelopes, fast-food take-away menus, carrier bags and photographs of street signs, shop logos and other public signs). Arrange displays of scripts from several cultures and examples of messages, information and food packaging in many languages (involve families, the community and all the members of the setting in contributing to this).

- Several technologies for writing should be available: rubber pads and ink stamps, computers and printers with word-processing software, concept keyboards for the younger children as well as qwerty (ICT can extend children's alphabetic knowledge and their awareness of punctuation signs, spacing and typefaces).

Real needs

Real needs for writing in early childhood must be considered carefully and related to such broader literacy issues as the place of writing in a culture; the potential for social and political independence and choice that literacy can give individuals; and literacy as an extended way of thinking. These perspectives were outlined in the earlier sections of this chapter and should provide a rationale for daily decisions about writing and writing tasks in the early years setting. However, approaches to writing at this stage of education should also be informed by a keen sense of the appropriate place for writing in the individual child's existing range of communicative skills.

Most children in early years settings are already skilled communicators in the modes of gesture and body language, talking and listening, drawing, modelling and constructing and playing. It is misleading to think that teaching children to write is teaching them to communicate efficiently: writing should be seen as another means of enriching and extending children's existing communicative skills and satisfying their own needs for the tools of literacy.

In this respect it is important to be aware of the range of writing needs we as adults model for the children. Do we only write lists, memos, institutional notices, names on pictures and models, correct spellings and isolated demonstrations of good handwriting? Do the writing tasks we impose on the children amount to nothing more than redundant writing about already expressive and communicative pictures and models? Or very limited sentences about every single event, experience or outing shared by practitioners, families and children? There are, of course, occasions when all these kinds of writing might be just the appropriate response for adults and individual children, but a simple blanket response of putting labels on everything and writing reports about everything trivializes writing and does not advance the development of young writers and thinkers.

Purposeful writing must include, memory aids, records, communications, expressive and art-like functions. The use of lists, notes, Post-it pads, mobile phones and personal jottings, as memory aids, is part of many children's out-of-school culture and becomes a significant feature of later school-based literacy. The concept of a list often occurs naturally in play and pretend writing, particularly if home corners and dramatic play areas are thoughtfully equipped with pads and pens for shopping lists and till receipts, telephone messages and prescriptions. Lists occur spontaneously when some young children produce inventories or checklists of the words, letters and numerals they know and can write without help.

Encouraging children to jot down invented marks, names, items, figures or words they like or need to remember can become a natural part of experiences inside and outside early years settings. For example, many different kinds of lists can be compiled and favourite words recorded.

Lists which spring from the children's lives and concerns in and out of early years settings are examples of writing used to pin down and to remember; they also lay the foundations of ease and pleasure in collecting words, using the tools of writing and creating useful records of experiences and knowledge (Figures 8.8 and 8.9).

Simple lists function as records. The beginnings of study skills, such as note-taking from books, can be found in lists of favourite story-book characters and incidents; the collection and discussion of strange, interesting and exciting words and phrases; and the noting of remarkable ideas. We cannot expect older primary children to be able to make useful notes from information books, as opposed to pointless copying of page after page, unless they have had this earlier background. Children should be helped to approach information texts with their own queries in mind (Mallett, 1999). In the early years these enquiries can start from lists of 'things to talk about' or 'things to find out'. The following questions come from a Reception class[3] where projects, investigations (and even the keeping of chickens) are at the heart of the curriculum:

Figure 8.8   Writing a shopping list (4 years)

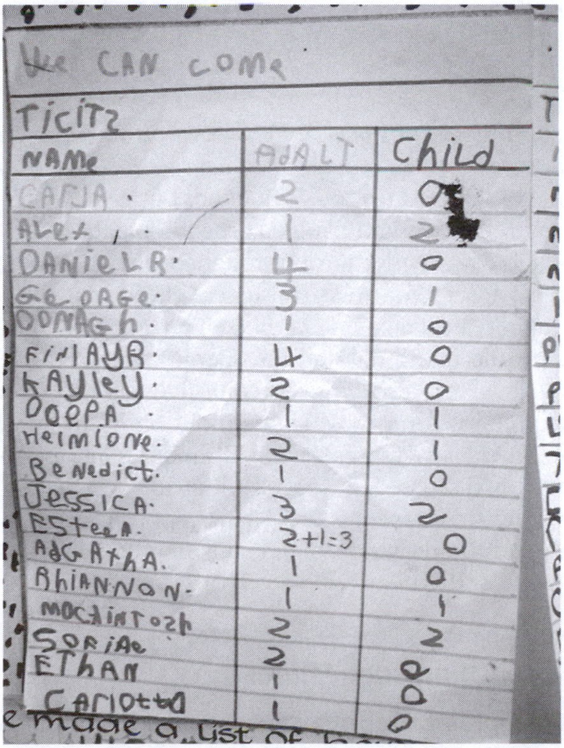

Figure 8.9   A list of people who bought tickets for the dog show (Reception)

- Do chickens have nostrils?
- Do chickens have teeth?
- What makes a fish happy?
- How do you know you are not a bat?

Children reveal their understanding of the communicative function of a written record when they ask if they can take home a copy of a successful recipe or decide to copy out the words of a favourite song or poem to take home. These are good examples of writing as communication that satisfies real needs and crosses the home and education boundaries. Such 'copies for home' are particularly suited to writing up on the computer and then printing off, as many copies as necessary. These instances are far more significant, in communicative terms, for the individual writers than a compulsory sentence under every drawing or the copying of a class letter in order to learn letter-writing conventions.

Real letters that go by post (or sometimes by hand) to real recipients are potent and sensible motives for learning a society's highly conventional forms of personal address, as well as the crucial importance of accurately written envelopes. Real letters also reflect a whole range of possible styles, from affectionate and chatty notes through to formal and precise communications, and they introduce children to the notions of:

- intended audience
- purpose
- appropriate form.

We should ask of all the kinds of writing that go on in early years settings and schools, at any age or stage of education, what *is it for and* who *is it for?*

Writing is always directed towards someone, but it must still be shaped and tried out by being rehearsed and planned. This preparation for writing happens inside our heads, is vocalized out loud, roughed out on paper, typed up on a screen or even tried out on a trusted listener. These trial runs are part of the process every writer must attempt of imagining an audience, but the effort brings a bonus. In the trying out and the shaping we find that we cannot just talk to ourselves, we can also write for ourselves as the intended audience. Writing as an expressive form in which we hold on to and understand experiences, joins the other early representational modes such as gesture, play, talk and drawing, already discussed. Respect for individual experiences and privacy; sensitivity to writing that demands a human response, prior to any correction and assessment; and the provision of a stimulating literacy environment are all part of a supportive and writerly classroom or group setting.

Learning and teaching suggestions

- Raise the literacy profile of all other curriculum areas: place writing materials (paper, pads, pens, crayons and pencils) in the outdoor area and with the science, maths, blockplay, home and role-play provision. Think of using magazines, newspapers and comics in theses areas and providing written notices, guidelines, instructions, information and lists.

- Vary the paper: children need small pieces for little notes and lists; large sheets that can be used flat on the floor/ground, or fixed to walls and easels (giving children the experience of bold marking and writing); good-sized strips of paper that facilitate experiments with the linear organization of comic-strip style drawing and writing; and some lightly tinted paper is a great attraction.

- Create a small workshop area (it can even be a well-organized box or trolley of materials) for the making of simple books. Provide paper, card, staples, glue, needles and thread and some basic instruction cards on 'How to make a stitched book', 'How to make a zig-zag book' and so on. Think of the possibilities for making books across the curriculum: books about music, science, games, the garden, computers, mathematics, and so on.

Supportive environments and feedback

Creating supportive environments involves such issues as time and opportunities to write and rewrite, and the provision of informative feedback about writing. Time to write means ensuring that there are reasonably long and uninterrupted blocks of time in which writing and many other activities can go on. One of the most important reasons for resisting the increasing fragmentation of the early-childhood group and school day into rigid timetable slots and 'hours' for literacy and mathematics is so that children may develop and sustain serious involvement with a wide range of curricular experiences. For the same reason, we need to look critically at the number of interruptions we allow for radio and television programmes, choir and assembly practices, or other worthy distractions.

If well chosen and well set-out writing materials are available, as well as the time to become involved, children are able to exercise the independence and choice that characterize real writers, and they are more likely to be satisfying their own needs and finding their own writerly voices in the process. They are also more likely to explore and experiment with the actual nature and organization of print and texts, the pattern of narrative and the conventions of spelling. Children need opportunities for practising writing, but their own meaningful self-imposed tasks can be far more rigorous than any arbitrary exercises, as the example indicates (Figure 8.10). In this instance,[4] a child who enjoyed unpressured blocks of time, the security of a real writers' classroom and the appropriate materials (including scrap paper for rough work, as well as final draft sheets of paper), has been able to work through to the standard spellings of 'chips' and 'fish'. Clearly, lots of trying, looking at the visual patterns and rejecting some versions was involved. This is a particularly good example of a spontaneous approximation to one of the most reliable approaches (see Mudd, 1994; Peters, 1985) to learning standardized spellings: look, cover, write, check with the standard form, try again if necessary.

Figure 8.10 **Spelling 'chips' and 'fish'**

Beginning writers need feedback that is informative about writing and supportive of their own approximations and hypotheses. Practitioners need to know what children can do already, how they are thinking about language and literacy, and what they are aiming to do next. The organization of groups and classrooms must be directed towards maximizing the time available for practitioners to talk to children, individually and in small groups. Such talk can focus on the messages intended and relate the attempted forms to known letters, words and texts. In a room full of meaningful writing about many things this should not be difficult. Sometimes the practitioner might write a word or two of comment and encouragement on a child's work. Gradually the discussions will involve the nature of some standardized spellings, as relevant, or conventional forms of sentence structure or syntax, and issues of presentation. This kind of feedback means spending time discussing children's work with them rather than accepting it in order to look at it later or even taking it away to mark.

Demonstrating writing and discussing it with children is a top priority and might well replace some of the time spent on unproductive correct copying, routine 'writing-about everything' exercises and the traditional way of 'hearing' readers. The group setting and the classroom are potentially supportive writing communities and children usually take a great interest in each other's activities and investigations, so they too can be encouraged to help each other (see Chapter 9).

Research into early writing from several countries puts considerable emphasis on classroom writing conferences and the production of rough drafts rather than 'one-try-only' finished pieces. Writing conferences in which groups of children sit down, with or without a teacher, to discuss and edit their written drafts may be some years away from the earliest developmental stages of writing in early years settings. However, something very like a writing conference happens for the younger children when the practitioner organizes a shared writing session, acting as scribe for a small group, verbalizing a whole range of linguistic decisions and issues, pen in hand (see Chapter 9). Young children also enjoy just being with each other in attractive writing and drawing areas, indoors and outside.

In the early years of education there must be warm acceptance of tentative private writing and spontaneous, unpolished pieces which have clearly stretched the young child's resources. But to ensure literacy development, time must also be found for the regular discussion, drafting and editing of writing for publication in and around the setting or the school. When practitioners act as scribes and linguistic informants for young children they are tackling the young writers' greatest problems about getting started on independent writing:

- the physical business of *transcription*
- the language and thinking process of *composition*.

In the early stages the two processes need to be clearly separated. Initially, the young writer must be released from the demands of conventional transcription and spelling and freed to concentrate on the cognitive and creative processes of composition. When this temporary separation is well handled and the adult–child writing partnership flourishes there is far more going on than the satisfying production of individual and group books, news-sheets and letters – important as these are. It is likely that children's thinking, their cognitive potential, is being changed and extended by the writing process.

Learning and teaching suggestions

- Look at the setting/classroom/school/outdoor learning areas and environment as rich sources of words and information about writing and spelling. Let the children help by creating, lists of words and phrases they use regularly; labels for displays and materials; name cards and notices, including laminated signs and notices for the outdoor learning area. Prioritize daily 'shared writing' sessions in the later stages of the early years (5–7) and maximize the roles of adults as scribes, secretaries, proofreaders, publishers and correspondents for the children.

New thinking

New thinking has already been associated with the acquisition of literacy in the earlier discussion of the changes literacy brings about in a society. For the individual, particularly the young child, becoming a writer reflects a remarkable fusion of personal, individual experiences and needs with the symbolic communication system of the culture. But it is far from being a simple process of learning to use the written forms of the culture: writing, like talking, develops an inward-turning aspect, becoming a new means of organizing and restructuring thought – a new cognitive tool. The role of our earliest writing partners (parents, other people and professional educators) is as significant as that of our first conversational partners. In this respect, we should note the claims of Vygotsky, that the child's thinking potential is extended greatly in partnership with an adult (1978: 84–91). It is as if the child is a head taller when working with an involved, supportive and more experienced adult. Children reading and writing in partnership with adults are thinking at full stretch.

Writing, by its nature, provides a way of holding on to experience, of going over it, shaping and evaluating. This is a special way of rerunning experiences in order to understand them fully. Writing in process is also productive of totally new ideas and points of view, as experienced writers confirm. It is often in the act of writing about something that we are surprised by apparently new insights and conceptions that emerge on paper, or on the screen. Writing as an act of externally forming and clarifying ideas is a virtual distancing of experience from ourselves. This may well allow for more efficient and perceptive contemplation and understanding.

Objectives for writing (England) (http://nationalstrategies.standards.dcsf.gov.uk)

- There is some emphasis on the marks made by young children from 22 to 36 months and an expectation that they should begin to give meaning to their marks as they draw and paint, as well as ascribing meaning to marks they see around them (30–50 months).

- From 40 to 60 months there is an emphasis on breaking the flow of speech into words and using writing as a means of recording and communicating. Attempts at writing for different purposes, such as lists, stories and instructions, are expected at this stage. The two very challenging and contentious requirements that these young children should (a) use their phonic knowledge to write simple regular words and make phonetically plausible attempts at more complex words and (b) write their own names and labels and captions and begin to form simple sentences, sometimes using punctuation, remain as an 'aspiration' for practitioners (DCSF, 2009)!

- By the end of Key Stage 1 (age 7) the objectives for writing have multiplied in number and complexity, ranging from planning and consistency in narrative and non-narrative writing, to using simple and compound sentences and using present and past tense consistently. At this stage many of the requirements will challenge the understanding and competence of practitioners as they are framed in very abstract terms. Perhaps the best message to hang on to, from the recent review of the primary curriculum in England, is the great emphasis placed on talk and oral communication in the early and primary years and the lovely truism that, 'If they can't say it they can't write it' (ibid.:60).

Handwriting

Handwriting is a craft skill and should be stimulated and nurtured throughout the years of schooling, as a separate issue from becoming a writer. Of course, there is a link in that the thinking writer needs to evolve a personal handwriting style that communicates efficiently and pleasantly, but this is hardly a priority in the process of thinking and writing. After all, we know that handwriting suffers as our ideas flow and outpace the hand. In fact substantial writing of a professional, academic or commercial kind depends on the services of secretaries and computers. Perhaps we should try to free the issue of 'good' handwriting from all the moralistic and social etiquette associations it has acquired. The aesthetic quality of the handwriting is not a direct reflection of the quality of the ideas and thinking it encodes, even less is it a reflection of the worth of the person writing. However, handwriting can provoke strong feelings that are closely associated with cultural attitudes and the assumptions we make about individuals (Sassoon, 1995).

A serious issue is involved here. If we make powerful subconscious judgements about writing, based on what it looks like, we are confusing the cognitive achievements of literacy with mere display and performance: literacy is the development of human mind and that is why we want children to be readers and writers. This is particularly important now that word-processing and rapidly developing new technologies remove the chores of transcription and place powerful new writing tools at our fingertips. What children and educators do with the new technology is dependent on their understanding of the interactive nature of language and literacy, of writing for real audiences and real purposes, and of using writing as an extension of thinking skills.

All the materials and activities that support artistic, creative and physical education in the early years setting and primary classroom also support the development of competent handwriting. General muscle tone, balance, eye and hand coordination and the fine muscle control of delicate finger and wrist movements are developed and sustained by brick construction, sand play, printing with junk materials, painting and drawing, and so on. Visual sensitivity to colour, spacing, harmony and aesthetic form is fostered by exposure to the displays, fabrics, pictures, artefacts and writing children see in their early years settings. If we cannot point to high standards of provision in all these areas of the curriculum and the educational environment, we cannot claim to be seriously concerned about handwriting.

Specific provision aimed at stimulating interest in the craft of handwriting and providing opportunities to practise it may be focused on a calligraphy area or small display. Even an attractive container of calligraphy materials and examples stored in the writing or language area of the classroom, a well-lit corridor display, or the outside area writing trolley, can be a simple but adequate resource. The basic materials must satisfy two different purposes: first, to provide good examples and demonstrations of the craft and, second, to provide the tools and materials for practising the skill. Examples of the craft should include well mounted samples as well as illustrated books of different styles, including some traditional school classics such as Marion Richardson and italic, and examples of modern computer-generated calligraphy on book-covers, documents and commercial material. There is also value in having cards of basic unadorned roman script and examples of the other scripts used in the local community.

The meaning or content of any written material used as handwriting examples for children should have some intrinsic value, so that calligraphy is also a way of sharing a poem, a riddle, a proverb or counting rhyme. Some examples of complete alphabets and numerals, zero to nine, are also useful as stylistic guides.

Tools and materials for practising handwriting skills should include the usual variety of pencils, pens, felt markers and paper, including both rough draft and final draft qualities and firm clipboards and pads. In the early years, it is generally better to provide unlined paper for most writing as this is far more flexible for the children's own drawing and writing strategies. Delaying the introduction of lined paper fosters the development of the children's visual sensitivity to spacing, linearity and the impact of blocks of print and colour.

I am unconvinced of the usefulness of whole-class writing lessons in the early and primary years, or of interference with the ways in which very young children habitually hold their pencils and markers. The greatest spur to efficient handwriting is the desire to share and value an important message, and the most influential models of effective and pleasing personal handwriting are the early years practitioners children meet. Practitioners working with the younger children (3–5 years) might consider using such old-established practices as 'writing' favourite and familiar letters 'in the air' in big bold movements. This linking of letter formation with movement and strong muscular sensations is a very helpful experience for young writers. Children also enjoy describing the shapes and directionality of the letters as they form them, using such vocabulary as 'up and down', 'up, round and down', 'straight up' or 'down, up, down, up'. Educators of the older children (6–7) should set aside time to talk about handwriting and demonstrate to individuals and small groups the most efficient ways of forming individual letters. This is not done by plodding illogically through the alphabet, but by taking groups of letters which are formed by similar strokes (Sassoon, 2003).

The excitement of this particular approach is the continued emphasis on handwriting as the visible trace of a hand movement; the links with other motor and artistic activities, the belief in finding comfortable and rapid personal styles; and the early introduction of 'exit strokes' to help the move to joined up writing (cursive). Handwriting teaching in the early years must be based on observing young children's writing experiments and practices, and offering appropriate guidance and useful techniques at the right time.

Objectives for handwriting (England) (http://nationalstrategies.standards.dcsf.gov.uk)

- At the end of the Foundation Stage it is expected that children can hold a pencil effectively so as to form recognizable letters, most of which are correctly formed. But this will build on lots of experiences in using a range of tools and equipment, learning to manipulate objects with increasing skill, drawing lines and circles and beginning to form recognizable letters.

- In the first year of Key Stage 1 (5–6) there is an emphasis on comfortable and efficient pencil grip and the achievement of clear spaces between words. Children should also be able to use the space bar and keyboard to type their names and simple texts.

- At the end of Key Stage 1 (age 7) children should be writing legibly, spacing correctly between words, using upper and lower case letters appropriately, as well as using 'the four basic handwriting joins'. They should be able to word process short narrative and non-narrative texts.

Summary

- Young children's attempts to make sense of print are demonstrations of their powerful strategies for making sense of their lives and experiences. This problem-solving in early learning is characterized by active and creative abstracting, hypothesizing, constructing and revising.

- Research evidence on young children's early literacy learning indicates the ways in which they tackle questions about the nature of print, how it works in their communities and how they themselves can use it. The research suggests that young children create reasonable hypotheses about print, spelling systems and texts, and modify and develop these hunches and experiments in the light of helpful feedback from models, demonstrations and talk with other writers.

- Practices and policies in early years settings must build on and extend children's existing knowledge of literacy and develop their strategies for experimenting, hypothesizing and making sense of new experiences and new materials.

(Continued)

(Continued)

- Practitioners need to give close attention, in their planning and provision, to inspiring children to write; to creating real needs for writing in their groups, schools and classrooms; and to providing supportive environments and informative feedback about writing. Most important of all, however, is their own understanding of the part played by the writing process in reorganizing and extending the thinking of children and adults.

- Handwriting or calligraphy is a craft skill and, although it can be stimulated and nurtured in the early years curriculum, it must be treated as a separate skill from the process of becoming a thoughtful and communicative writer.

Learning and teaching suggestions

- Firm and portable writing pads can be improvised for the children by covering strong cardboard, or thin hardboard, with decorative gift-wrap paper or tinted brushwork paper. More experienced writers in the 6–7 age range may enjoy using straight line guides for special writing assignments: these can be made from strong white card with bold black lines drawn at the desired widths (the guides are placed beneath a child's writing paper and the dark lines show through faintly).

- Maintain a focus on the craft of calligraphy: display examples of scripts (italic, Sassoon, Marion Richardson, roman, Arabic and illuminated letters). This can provide an ideal opportunity to write out some poems, rhymes and folk sayings in some of these scripts. Encourage the children to start decorating their own special writing and experiment with calligraphy. Provide some examples of modern styles that are often computer generated (documents, book jackets and commercial advertising materials). Provide cards of the script preferred in the setting or school and examples of numerals zero to nine – these can be taken home by families. There are times when practitioners should make specific opportunities available for practising handwriting with small groups of children who are old enough, able enough and interested enough to benefit. However, the years from birth to 7 cover a vast developmental phase and generalizations about handwriting 'lessons' would be unhelpful!

⊶ Key terms

Graphics: the smallest units in writing or text (for example, 'b', 'B', 'f', 'F').
Orthography: the use of letters and the rules of spelling in a written language.
Representation: a major form of thinking that uses actions, gestures, pictures, words, and so on, to stand for ideas and experiences.

📖 Further reading

Anning, A. and Ring, K. (2004) *Making Sense of Children's Drawings*. Maidenhead: Open University Press.

Bissex, G.L. (1980) *GNYS AT WRK: A Child Learns to Write and Read*. Cambridge, MA: Harvard University Press.

Clay, M.M. (1975) *What Did I Write?* London: Heinemann.

Crystal, D. (2008) *txtng. the gr8 db8*. Oxford: Oxford University Press.

Hall, N. and Robinson, A. (2003) *Exploring Writing and Play in the Early Years*. 2nd edn. London: David Fulton.

Hall, N., Larson, J. and Marsh, J. (eds) (2003) *Handbook of Early Childhood Literacy*. London: Sage.

Kress, G. (2000) *Early Spelling: Between Convention and Creativity*. London: Routledge.

Marsh, J. and Hallett, E. (eds) (2008) *Desirable Literacies: Approaches to Language and Literacy in the Early Years*. 2nd edn. London: Sage.

Pennac, D. (2006) *The Rights of the Reader*. Trans. S. Adams. London: Walker Books.

Sassoon, R. (2003) *Handwriting: The Way to Teach It*. 2nd edn. London: Paul Chapman Publishing.

Curriculum Frameworks (England): www.standards.dcsf.gov.uk/nationalstrategies

Notes

1 These issues are fully explored in Hall et al. (2003), Heath (1983), Kress (1997; 2000), Marsh and Hallett (2008), Olson et al. (1985) and Ong (1982).

2 I am grateful to my former colleague Jan Lee for providing this example. It was written by Nicolas (5 years, 10 months) and reflects his phonetic knowledge: the substitution of the sound symbol 'B' for 'p' is a feature of his own pronunciation (as well as creative ingenuity) using the known 'B' and 'g' sounds in 'playground' but indicating missing letters with dots. The capital 'A' (written over a lower case 'a') apparently represents the sound of the stressed 'm' in 'I'm'.

3 I am grateful to the children of the Reception year at St John's Roman Catholic Infant School, Norwich, for their questions and to their teachers Mary Fisher and Shelagh Swallow for sharing them with me.

4 I am grateful to Miranda Higham for this example from her teaching-practice classroom and to my former colleague Gill Hilton for bringing it to my attention.

CHAPTER 9

THE EARLY YEARS PRACTITIONER AND LITERACY

This chapter includes:

- literacy beginnings for babies and toddlers
- moving on with literacy
- emergent literacy
- children with complex needs
- parents, families, communities and cultures
- records and assessment.

This book highlights three major aspects of literacy:

- the complex interrelatedness of communicating, listening, talking, reading and writing
- the roots of literacy located in a general symbolizing development in infancy
- the role of this symbolizing power in the creation of meanings.

These aspects of literacy are rarely acknowledged when literacy programmes or curricula for the early years are being devised. It is all too easy for early years practitioners to be rushed into complying with requirements for early learning goals, targets, tests, unrealistic aspirations and phonics lessons, while ignoring questions as fundamental as, what is reading and writing really doing for readers and writers? Or, why do we teach children to read and write? If these basic questions are rarely asked, it is hardly surprising that such complex matters as the interdependence of language modes and the roots of symbolizing activities are not considered at all. However, if we hope to foster early literacy we need to be sensitive to all these fundamental aspects of human development and learning.

Our studies of language and the role it plays in individual development and in education should convince us of at least one thing: language is all pervasive and bound up with much of what we think, feel and do as individuals and as members of particular social groups and communities. If it is difficult to untangle language from everything we experience as people, it is almost impossible to separate out the tight mesh of the four language modes of listening, talking, writing and reading. I would also argue that if we attempt to separate these forms of 'languaging' we do irreparable harm. At best, a trivialization of language activities occurs when we begin to cast around for lists of things to do in daily literacy sessions. At worst, we facilitate the imposition of inappropriate checklists of achievements at certain ages in listening, reading, speaking and writing 'skills'.

If the interrelated nature of talking and listening, reading and writing is sometimes lost in current practices, the connection between communication, literacy and early symbolizing activities is rarely made and understood. Yet literacy is rooted in a general symbolizing ability that develops in the first year of life and this symbolizing is so distinctive of human thinking and behaviour that it can be thought of as the distinguishing feature of human development. This bold claim highlights the fact that the teacher of literacy is in the business of nurturing not just 'a language for life' (DES, 1975) but the very quality of life of the learner. We need to develop and value the many symbolizing activities which support and enrich early literacy, such as facial expressions, gestures, movement and dance; role play and dramatic representations; scribbling, drawing, painting and modelling; mapping, building and the construction of miniature worlds.

Our own understanding of the nature of symbolic representation is crucial. The point is not that we should always be able to interpret or share these complex symbolic representations but that we should respect them as powerful intellectual strategies. Symbolic activities are particularly interesting for the early years practitioner because they are a fusion of the unique personal experiences and concepts of an individual with the systems of shared meanings specific to the culture.

Literacy beginnings for babies and toddlers

'Read them,' said the King.
The White Rabbit put on his spectacles. 'Where shall I begin, please your Majesty?' he asked.
'Begin at the beginning,' the King said, very gravely, 'and go on till you come to the end: then stop.' (Lewis Carroll, *Alice's Adventures in Wonderland*, 1872, ch. XII)

To begin at the beginning with literacy means going back to the earliest patterns of communication that can be observed in the 'conversation-like' behaviours of babies and their caregivers (see Chapter 3). The earliest interactions of babies with their caregivers establish not just language structures but the prototypes of narrative form and story-telling behaviours. But perhaps we can extend these ideas and see the very early prototypes of reading and writing as present in the beginnings of language. This is not such an extreme idea if we bear in mind the fact that it is now generally accepted that language begins with non-verbal communicative behaviours, and literacy is developed by the desire to communicate.

Reading people

From the start, babies are 'reading' the eye contacts, faces, gestures and postures of those significant persons who care for them (Figure 9.1). This must involve scanning, focusing, anticipating and predicting responses and making contacts. The infant starts by 'reading' for emotional responsiveness and this is beautifully demonstrated by every baby who fixes an adult with a wide stare and accompanies this with appealing smiles and mouthing, and arm, leg and whole-body movements. Babies also 'read' the faces of their carers (Figure 9.1) in order to check on the appropriate emotional response to new or surprising situations.

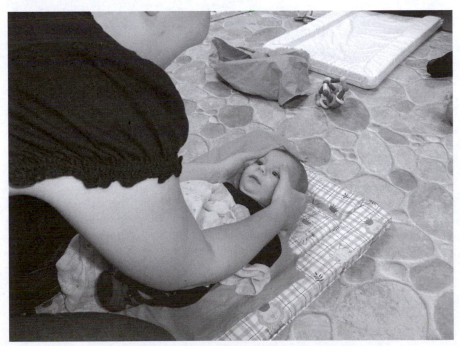

Figure 9.1 A baby reads his mother's face carefully (4 months)

Listening

Very young infants are sensitive listeners and this supports their reading of persons and situations. The listening skills of newborn infants are highly developed, they are able to discriminate voices from other noise and rapidly come to recognize the particular voices of their constant caregivers. Again, it is emotional tone and mood that are picked up by the sensitive reading and listening infant. It is probable that patterns of intonation and emphasis are particularly important to young infants and help them focus on the meaning-bearing segments of speech, such as beginnings and endings, nouns and verbs. It is essential to think of young babies as 'reading' people and situations and listening for response and meaning in their earliest interactions because it establishes them as communicators and meaning-makers long before schooling starts.

Sounds and rhythms

It is equally important to note that infants are sensitive to words as pleasurable sounds and they delight in words linked with rhythmic movement, bouncing and rocking. So from the start it is not just words as messages that are attended to but words as poetic forms. Rhyme, rhythm and repetition are the earliest language play we can share with infants and, interestingly, are features of the earliest literature we share with children: the literature of nursery rhymes and songs. We begin, it seems, with play and learning thoroughly mixed up together.

Babies and the language curriculum

As the impact of official curriculum requirements is felt in early years settings, as is the case in England and other parts of the UK, practitioners will need to consider the indirect effect these requirements may have on babies and toddlers (the under-3s). The very existence of written 'aspirations', descriptors' and 'goals' for the early years puts subtle pressure on practitioners and parents to compare and assess very young infants and, perhaps, find them lacking! The resulting temptation to 'bring them on', or coach them, will impede the drive infants already have to communicate, form secure attachments, explore sounds and language and their immediate environment, and express their own thinking in vocalizations, movements, gestures, marks and play with people and objects. The early development of very young children is a holistic process and any distortion of their experiences in order to promote learning in language and literacy, or any other curriculum subject, may result in a few early gains and many later problems.

Moving on with literacy

Moving on with literacy depends on the success children achieve in sharing meanings and becoming communicators. Research makes it clear that very young children are actively engaged in 'meaning': in investigating and questioning the significance of all human activities and responses. Such intellectual curiosity ranges from questions about where significant adults go to all day, to exhaustive interrogations about the economic basis of window-cleaning services (Tizard and Hughes, 2002: 96–7). These lively explorations of the meaning of human behaviour and motivation need not be left at home; they should come into early years settings and be applied to the people, the talk, the literature and the other planned experiences of the early years curriculum. If young children are to continue their development as communicators within group settings, they need an environment rich in opportunities for symbolic play and representation. Moving on with literacy comes down to sharing and negotiating meanings through the use of sounds, words, images, gestures, objects and signs. Learning to read and write, in and out of early years group settings and schools, depends on involving young children in reading meanings and making messages.

Early care and education needs to create bridges between the common-sense, everyday shared meanings children are already exploring and the specialized meanings framed in literary and other forms of knowledge. Young children know a great deal about their families, homes and communities but they need time and opportunities for relating this knowing and these meanings to the 'facts' of science, mathematics and book literature. Book language (the prestigious written form of the culture) is best introduced by pleasurable participation in rhythmic language games, rhymes and poems.

Telling tales and sharing books

Early literacy thrives when it is nourished on a rich diet of gossip, anecdotes, reminiscences and story-telling. Oral story-telling is the oldest and most powerful way of sharing and passing on the knowledge, experiences and beliefs of a community. We all feel confident about launching into a good story about a professional 'hiccup', or a modern myth about the profligacy of government, or the madness of 8-mile traffic jams. Yet we hesitate about risking telling (not reading) a story in the early years setting. This reluctance can be overcome if we understand that it is legitimate to be as free with our own version of 'The Three Bears' as we are with our versions of 'The Night I Locked Myself out of my Own Car!' Furthermore, the use of story props (as described in Chapters 6 and 7) supports the concentration and the confidence of tellers and listeners, and the gains are incalculable. The total focus on establishing and maintaining a rapport between the teller, the tale and the listeners enriches classroom relationships, nurtures listening skills and sensitizes young children to the rhythmic, formulaic qualities of poetic language.

For young children, story-telling is also the best kind of introduction to the features of extended, explicit prose: the 'book language' central to all further literacy experiences. Oral story-telling leads children from the informal, face-to-face qualities of everyday verbal interactions to the formally organized patterns of the written language.

Many approaches to early literacy start with sharing picture books with young children, and the books certainly provide important experiences of listening to a tale told, hearing book language and looking at a story carried forward by pictures as well as text. But the connections between the book and the child's world need to be built by sensitive talk at the appropriate times. Children need opportunities for conversations about books and stories and time to examine books closely and sort out their feelings and responses to them. Meanings are created in these ways and the layers of story or subtext are gradually unpacked. Sometimes the picture tells one story and the text is less explicit, as with *Rosie's Walk* (Hutchins, 1968).

If favourite books are available and in the hands of children, expectations about them are not restricted to narrative form, plot and character. Close textual investigations lead children to look at the black marks of text and to discover familiar letters, repeated letters and even whole words they know. The puzzling conventions of illustrations are also analysed as children learn what is inside or outside the picture frame. Learning to read pictures is a sophisticated skill and continues to develop as part of a general ability to 'read' photographs, film, video and television images. But perhaps the most interesting and exciting literacy development in these early stages comes when children begin to put themselves and their worlds into the books, the excitement of knowing that 'My Nan's got one of those', or 'There's my baby's buggy!' or 'I ran away once in the supermarket' is the motivation for going on looking at books. Books are meaningful in human terms.

Sharing meanings is a richly complex feature of human behaviour and literacy will not be promoted by simply sticking to books and talk about books. The experiences children bring to group settings and schools and the new experiences they find there must be re-enacted or tried out in many different symbolic ways – singing, dancing and music-making, drawing and painting (Figure 9.2), dressing-up, play artefacts, natural objects, moulding and sculpting media and construction. These are the foundations of early literacy and not just 'optional extras' that bridge the gap between home and playgroup, nursery or school, and help children settle in early. It is not the actual things that bridge the home–school gap and make for emotional security, it is what children are doing with and through them, plus opportunities to share their thinking and learning with significant key persons, that enable the children to feel 'at home' in the world and culture of early years group settings and schools and make their own significant contributions.

Writing and reading messages

The children's contributions in the forms of stories, anecdotes and narratives must not just be accepted, they must become important components of the early years literacy programme. They are usually preserved as group-made books of imaginative stories or accounts of shared experiences in and out of the setting. From the start of early years education, children's stories can be copied down by adults, taped for later transcription, or the children's activities and outings can be recorded on video film or in sequences of photographs. These visual narratives can later have text added or, sometimes, be left as open-ended invitations to 'remember when, remember how?'

Figure 9.2   Exploring marks and paint (George, 22 months)

High-tech book-making in an early years centre

Children at Earlham Early Years Centre (2-, 3- and 4-year-olds) use simple sturdy digital cameras ('jam-cams') to record their favourite places
and activities around the setting. Their choice of subjects is entirely personal and has included the grassy slope, potato printing, mates, the ball
pool and the snack table. They are supported by the enthusiasm and
expertise of their nursery educator, Margaret, who helps them print their
pictures from the computer and put them into simple folded paper
books. Margaret will scribe titles and captions if the children request
them, and most of the books contain emergent writing. These books are
shared with the families and kept in the children's own diary folder of
their progress and achievements. These photo books are a way of giving
young children a voice in their own education. They are quite literally the
child's view of early education. They give professionals and families
insights into the children's perspectives on the setting and the experiences it provides. And for some anxious and unsettled children, the
camera is an irresistible lure into the outside learning environment and
cooperative activities with other children.

This sort of material may often be group inspired, but highly personal stories fascinate both authors and classmates. It is often the case that families and neighbours are willing to make up simple books about their children and their daily lives, and many schools have developed a policy for inviting families in to make such books with their children. This approach has proved to be a powerful incentive for families from diverse cultures to bring their languages and their worlds into the centre of literacy learning and multilingual book-making in the nursery (Kenner, 2000). Most practitioners who embark on a course of listening to very young children and inviting them to tell stories find that they have released a torrent of powerful material. Furthermore, the children become involved and proud collectors of stories; however, the proper respect due to their work must be reflected by careful transcribing and mounting, attractive display and suitable storage of all class narratives.

The most significant piece of meaningful writing in every child's life is probably her or his first name (see Chapter 8). 'Games with names' can be a powerful way into early writing and communication if we follow the children's developing interests and observations and provide ample examples of names in use. The obvious starting point is the labelling of children's property and of the pictures and models they create. This can lead to the easy recognition of initial letters and children's names can be grouped according to these salient letters. Many children will point to letters in the environment and announce that 'I've got one of those', meaning that the letter occurs in their name. Other interesting features such as double letters in names seem to provoke considerable interest, as the previous chapter indicated.

This orthographic awareness can be extended by labelling children's own books, the seeds they plant in the garden, their seating places for meals, and so on. Names on cards can be sorted on a daily basis to 'record' who is here and who is away, a practice known as self-registration in many early years settings. Considerable enthusiasm and excitement are always generated by a display of mounted and named photographs of the children as babies, or photographed working in and around the building. The power of names is not to be under-estimated, whether written down or slipped into a familiar story-telling situation for fun. All the power of love and anger that focuses on the names of caregivers, siblings, friends and pets ensures their almost immediate recognition in spoken or written forms.

Children's interest in important words, words suffused with meaning and feeling, is usually accompanied by a desire to write or make them. Even if not positively helped or encouraged to do so, children make their marks in wet sand, mud, clay and dough, or with paints, pencils and crayons. These 'signatures' are often highly idiosyncratic, recognized immediately by families and professional staff, even if they are not in the full conventional form but just a promising initial or a scatter of the component letters. This attachment to the letters of a name is often expressed in terms of real affection and some young children will stroke certain letters and hug special pieces of text (Lierop, 1985).

This serves as a reminder that learning anything, but especially literacy, is bound up with feelings and emotions. In the later stages of education we go so far as to ask pupils to evaluate literature in terms of how they 'feel' about or 'like' or 'prefer' certain texts. However, it is unreasonable to expect such sensitive and feeling responses to literature at the later stages if the early processes of learning to read and write have undervalued feeling and caring about words and texts.

The excitement of children's own names as symbols of ownership and presence in the world should soon spill over into a delight in finding writing almost everywhere. Suddenly it seems that the whole world is neatly named: the inspection covers and drain grids in the outside areas, the fencing round the garden, the school or playgroup sign-board, the lavatory bowls, plastic bottles and so on. Such varied but very informative writing from the environment should not be ignored. Many young children have always learnt to write and read before schooling by investigating such materials and asking questions about them.

We can extend these discoveries by bringing into the early years setting collections of packages and cartons that we can 'read' in order to cook the food, make the model or grow the plants. We can share the children's delight in familiar advertisements, shop carrier-bags, rhyming or repetitive slogans and well-known logos and signs. These materials have real-world relevance and importance, and they make bridges between home and educational settings. They encourage talk and play about the world of out-of-school learning and experiences. In terms of linguistics, such materials provide information about the features of letters, spaces, words and text and allow important insights into the symbol and sound correspondences of the alphabet. Furthermore, these materials are easily collected, easily replaced and perfect for endless play and manipulation.

With a little more effort, and the involvement of families and the wider community, the early years practitioner can also make collections of texts and packages from other cultures that feature more than one language, and even different sign systems or alphabets. 'What does this writing say?' is a particularly interesting question when the teacher does not know the answer! Literacy learning can make us all vulnerable, and young children need to know that it is acceptable not to know about everything. Incidental demonstrations of powerful adults 'not knowing' may be very reassuring for many children. Responses such as 'How can we find out?' 'Could we guess?' 'Who can we ask?' 'Perhaps x will come to our centre, playgroup or school and tell us about the writing', are models of good education in action.

It is important to allow for a great variety and range of experiences and experiments in early literacy. While some children write their names and play with printing sets or plastic alphabet letters, others will create pages of pretend writing, fold sheets of paper into booklets and dash off linear-looking scribbles (Figure 9.3). Young children do need considerable supplies of paper and markers so that they can experiment with scribbled notes, doctor's prescriptions, books of stories, labels, warnings, welcome letters and even music. They certainly need access to the computer as many are already familiar with emailing, blogging, surfing the net and using the keyboard.

Figure 9.3   **Ella writes an invitation to the children's centre (4 years 5 months)**

Some children delight in cutting out and collecting scraps of printed text from magazines and newspapers; others play such games as looking for writing that 'me and my friends' are wearing. Many children are also aware that they see writing on the television and they recognize the names of programmes and products. Some children choose to write, over and over again, all the letters and even numerals that they can 'do'. This is a kind of inventory or checklist of all that they know and can write (see Chapter 8). Some children may have considerable experience of using a mobile phone, a computer keyboard and controlling the mouse, and will be ready to explore the potential of a simple word-processing program.

In the earliest stages of literacy many children will be aware of alphabets because families often buy them as posters and wall charts to decorate children's rooms, as well as buying alphabet picture books. Alphabets are also displayed in clinics and many of the children's treatment areas in hospitals. The collection of alphabets in a care and education setting should be as varied, appealing and relevant as possible. Children can be actively involved in creating their own exciting alphabets of such sets as 'our names'. Any gaps in a group alphabet provide a valuable, open-ended, problem-solving situation for children and educators: 'Do we know anyone with a 'Z' in their name?' Favourite food makes a good subject for an 'ABC' and 'most disliked' food is even greater fun. A more ambitious alphabet can illustrate the children's exploits in the local community, for example:

D is for Deptford Park where we can run round the track.
K is for Keston Ponds. We went pond-dipping and made our own nets.
T is for Totters. They have horses and carts and collect old junk.

All these suggestions for getting started reflect the varied interests and stages that children may go through. I stress that tentative 'may' because becoming a reader and writer is a very personal business and the ways to do it are unique as are the many cultural, ethnic and religious settings in which children get started. But the aim is clear:

- to get the young learners to a stage where they are saying or thinking, 'what does that say?' and
- 'how do you write X?'

Early literacy is dependent on asking the right questions about language and print and on using adults and other children as linguistic informants by directing questions to them. Literacy is also about feeling safe and confident enough to indicate one's ignorance or confusion but, above all, it is based on an unshakeable belief that writing and reading are always meaningful activities.

Literacy in the outside area

Literacy can happen anywhere – it certainly does not need to take place under a roof! So, set up rich literacy learning experiences in any outdoor areas that the children can access.

- Improvise a mark-making and writing trolley to store and move markers and papers outside.
- Find a small trolley or wheeled basket to store and transport books, maps, guides, brochures, and so on outside.
- Provide clipboards and attach pencils so that children can write anywhere outside – or indoors.
- Designate walls and hard ground surfaces for chalking and water painting.
- Make and laminate children's name cards for the outside. Make laminated notices, including 'where to park buggies, trucks and bikes'; 'what we are growing'; 'birthday greetings to children and staff'.

(Continued)

(Continued)

- Put up laminated sets of instructions on how to play popular group games with the children (very helpful for parents and workers).
- Create cosy reading areas and dens with blankets, cushions, wind-breaks and big umbrellas/parasols.
- Scatter some postboxes or pigeon-holes around so that children and adults can leave little gifts and messages.
- Remember the literacy potential of play garages, hospitals and shops. Provide road markings and road signs for purposeful wheeled-vehicle play.

Emergent literacy

Once we have helped to nurture in children a positive passion for stories, poems and books and an expectation that written language carries meaningful messages, we will need to support the development of specific aspects of literacy. In order to avoid any suggestion that literacy is first reading and then writing, with neat groups of hierarchical skills and orderly phases of progress, I have chosen four aspects of literacy that can be focused on throughout the early years:

- the roles of authors and readers
- the significance of collaborative approaches to emerging literacy
- the nature of written forms as both permanent and disposable
- the issues of independence and written conventions.

Authors and readers

The reason for discussing authors and readers is that from the earliest days of education children can and should experience being in both roles. The author–reader relationship is not a one-sided affair in which the reader accepts passively the message given out by the author whose ownership of the text is emphasized by the high status of print. In the act of reading we are all authors as well as readers. Readers must use their knowledge of the world and their linguistic expectations to re-create actively the meanings implied in text and pictures.

These theoretical claims about the blurring of the author-reader role have implications for educational practices. If young children are to see themselves as potential writers and as active author-like readers they need to regard books as communications from real, knowable people. The idea that people write books is fostered initially by a plentiful source of stories made up and told by carers, practitioners, other adults and children as well as heard from books, and by sharing close examinations of the texts and the pictures. The possibility of gradually building up a collection of favourite and 'known authors' is dependent on good book resources and pleasant settings for quiet browsing. Such approaches are enhanced if practitioners, parents and helpers refer to the authors by name when sharing books and refer back to other books by the same writer and/or illustrator. Early years educators can also set up small displays of books by one author so that young children can 'tune in' to the quirky, idiosyncratic and recognizable style of the writer/illustrator.

Particular authors and illustrators become known and loved by children. I visited a class of 6-year-olds who were so enchanted by the gorilla and chimpanzee characters created by the artist and writer Anthony Browne that the teacher and parents had organized a visit to a children's book fair so that the class could buy their own copies of the books. In another class of 8- and 9-year-olds the strangely punning and surrealistic illustrations of some of Anthony Browne's books had inspired working models and writing about fantasy playgrounds and parks. It was not uncommon for my students to find that their story-sharing sessions were interrupted as the name of the author was greeted by 'Where's her photo then?' This is surely a mark of appreciation for a particularly human and interesting publishers' convention.

Establishing authors as persons is now widely reflected in the valuable practice of inviting authors to visit schools and public book events on an ad hoc basis or as part of a 'writers and illustrators in schools' scheme. This can now be linked to the role of the Children's Laureate (www.childrenslaureate.org.uk). Many contemporary authors and illustrators have their own websites; they also regard school visits as crucial to their research and planning for new publications. Early years practitioners and their young pupils are sometimes not considered to be interested in such schemes, but this is a sad underestimation of young children's fascination with people and their work. Young children in an infant school have, to my knowledge, baked and decorated a cake to celebrate the birthday of a favourite storybook character and invited the author to tea!

Supporting this sound appreciation of the person behind the text, will be all the other ways in which young children take on the roles of authors. The planning, writing, illustrating and making of individual, small-group and class books provide essential insights into the nature of the writing process. This personal kind of reading material is highly motivating and allows for a sense of pride in ownership and early success in reading back what is known, expected and expressed in familiar language forms. Books made at home and at school develop from the spoken language forms children know and use confidently, but these books also highlight the nature of written text.

Children can learn an enormous amount about writing from reading. Initially, if teachers and adults write messages and stories for them, children learn that writing is different from talk. Subtle changes occur as the vocal pitch and intonation, the hesitations, repetitions, vocal 'noises' and throat clearings, self-corrections and body language of face-to-face talk are removed from the performance and only the words are retained. Even the difficulties of the adult-scribe, who cannot keep up with the pace of everything the child says, provide useful introductions to the differences between spoken and written language forms.

Young children beginning reading are not just decoding words in order, they are reading groups of meanings blocked together in sentences and paragraphs. They are 'reading' that written words are separate and surrounded by space, in contrast to the continuous stream of sounds in speech. If children read and write with sensitive adults in unhurried situations where words are tasted on the tongue and discussed, they also begin to experience the varied and complex relationships between sounds and their representation by means of letters. Good reading and writing experiences sensitize young children to initial letter sounds and to some interesting sound pairs or digraphs, such as '*ch*', '*sh*' and '*th*' and even to endings such as '-ing' and '-ed' (see Browne, 2009 and Riley, 2006, for detailed advice on introducing phonemes and digraphs).

Making books involves a literacy partnership between children and supportive adults, and the resulting texts can be 'published' for group, home and school use. Publication can be enhanced by children's illustrations, photography, word-processing and traditional book-making techniques (Johnson, 1991). A major study of making books in educational settings (Smith, B., 1994) describes a triangular relationship between the composer/reader, the scribe/good listener and the text which is written, read and edited. This study also has detailed advice on training other adults, parents and older children as scribes and listeners.

As children work with their own books they are increasingly keen to model them on the published books they read. This is another aspect of 'conventions' and of becoming an author, as the children move on from their initial pride and delight in simple ownership of their writing to a wish to see it look 'like a real book'. This leads to an interest in the clear separation of pictures from blocks of text and the idea of meaningful paragraphs is developed from decisions about 'what shall we say on this page or under this picture?' In this phase, title pages and authorial ownership take pride of place, as does an emphasis on 'The End'. Some children become fascinated by publishers' names and addresses, and replicate these features with their own school or class identity. Pages become numbered as writing becomes more extended and the claim that this book is 'mine' or 'ours' is also reflected in a desire to use the conventional copyright logo. All this play and pretending is a powerful indicator of children's rapidly developing sense of the place of literacy in their culture and in their lives.

Collaborative approaches

Literacy is learnt and used in collaborative ways in many cultures, and its initial learning and use need not be restricted to childhood or to educational institutions. Adults as well as children engage in mutually supportive talk and explanations as they negotiate the meanings of written material. Just observe two or more people reading the instructions on a food package or on do-it-yourself equipment and materials! These shared readings are paralleled by collaborative writings, such as the joint writing of a report or mutual agonizing over a difficult letter of condolence or rejection. 'Two heads are better than one' (according to folk psychology), and this certainly applies to the sophisticated demands of literacy.

Life in educational settings can provide many opportunities for shared literacy activities (Rich et al., 2005; 2008), and children and adults should not stop at sharing storybooks and cooperative book-making – there are also posters to design, information to be researched on the World Wide Web, invitations and acceptances to receive and send, as well as the sharing of greetings, enquiries and so on. Initially practitioners play a major supportive role as readers and linguistic informants for younger children, but as the children's own literacy skills develop they can be practised and extended in collaborative ways.

It is possible to boost greatly the amounts of writing and reading children do in early years settings and schools by encouraging them to share both their knowledge about writing and their reading abilities with their peers. Children can read to each other in attractive and informal book corners, library areas, sheltered gardens and playgrounds. This reading can be within their own class or age range but it can also spread to reading to younger and older children, as appropriate. Children playing together in socio-dramatic, or role play, areas can extend each other's literacy if there is good provision for literacy-enriched play (Hall and Robinson, 2003; Makin and Whitehead, 2004).

Example

The Reception year children (4–5 years old) in St John's Infant School, Norwich, enjoy a play-based curriculum and learn through topics that are always rich in language and literacy opportunities. The children and their teachers set up a 'Baby-Minding Company', complete with an office full of notices, signs, message pads and telephones. Every baby doll they had collected for the project was named, registered and wore an identity tag. Records were kept carefully (using words, signs, marks, pictures and numbers) of who was 'minding' a baby, how long for and where they could be contacted! The responsibility was taken very seriously and 'minders' had to keep their baby with them at all times and treat it properly. The appropriate office records also had to be completed when a baby was handed back. All the children participated, whatever their level of 'literacy', and their marks and signs were respected and often tutored by their classmates.

Shared reading

One way of boosting daily reading is by the practice of 'shared reading' using 'big books'. Many children's books of high literary and artistic quality are produced in a 'big book' format which enables a large group of children to see easily the fine details of print and illustrations. In frequent shared reading sessions an adult can demonstrate all the skills and insights which an experienced reader brings to a text. This involves reading the text aloud to the group, first in one uninterrupted reading which establishes the plot of the story, the narrative style and the enjoyment of the illustrations. Second and subsequent readings will begin to engage the children more closely with the text as the adult points out the left to right flow of the printed words as they are spoken and highlights interesting book conventions (title pages, authors' and illustrators' names, publishing details, ISBN codes). Discussions of the plot, the characters and the tales being told by the illustrations develop the children's skills as discriminating and critical readers. As the children are drawn into the practice of shared reading they will also take the lead (Figure 9.4).

Figure 9.4   **Jenson (4 years) leads a big book reading session**

An ever closer focus on the print is ensured as the adult draws the children's attention to recurring names, repeated phrases, rhymes and words, some of which the children may know already from previous book readings, group and classroom word collections and labels, and the environmental print outside the setting. Shared talk about all these meaningful words will be an appropriate way of teaching phonological, alphabetic and orthographic awareness. Furthermore, initial letter combinations (digraphs); end (terminal) groups and rhymes; common patterns in English ('qu', 'ou'); and the double vowel sounds (as in 'sleep', 'food', 'baa'), enable children to identify and group words in 'families'. This close focus on print also helps children and adults to talk about the nature and functions of punctuation as they encounter capital letters, full stops, commas, speech marks and the really exciting dashes, question marks and exclamation marks that occur in literature.

Writing

The biggest problem for the beginning writer is lack of information about words, their component sounds and how these are represented by conventional symbols or letters. Overcoming this difficulty is also the biggest problem for the teacher of beginning writers! The way out of the dilemma hinges on collaborative approaches and a special kind of division of labour. The complex tasks of transcription and composition must be clearly separated (Smith, 1982). Practitioners and other adults have the transcription skills that enable them to write down the message in the conventional form, by hand or machine. Young emerging writers have the ideas, feelings and experiences they are composing or shaping into narrative forms, but they need scribes or secretaries to dictate to, and this is the significance of early book-making as a collaborative venture between child–author and adult–secretary.

Gradually, children will take advantage of any other linguistic aids and props such as small collections of words linked to particular experiences or materials and presented in attractive containers. Personal word collections can develop from these word hoards. Other sources of information include other children who may know and 'own' words. Favourite books and areas of the school and classroom can be checked for 'that word' required. An inspiring account (Geekie and Raban, 1993) of this kind of approach in an Australian reception class charts the empowerment of young children who are taught to interrogate each other and their classroom setting in the dynamic pursuit of literacy. Verbal accounts may be recorded and later transcribed by practitioners and the use of the word-processor can eventually lessen the children's dependence on an adult scribe, although care is needed as laboriously printing up words letter by letter on the screen can become a tedious trap rather than a writing prop. This is a poor use of the new technologies, as is the uncritical reliance on 'reading books' on CD-ROM that simply replicate dreary primers and mask meaningless text with visual tricks and loud music.

Shared writing

Writing is not a simple matter of finding individual words: the child's lively and creative use of grammatical patterns and literary phrases is 'the writing' and it depends on the practitioner for its survival. Approaches that utilize the pleasure of savouring words, discussing problems and creating books together have come to be called 'shared writing'. Practitioners and small groups of children jointly create large books that may be based on personal experiences, the adventures of a favourite storybook character, or some favourite poems and songs, or shared outings and classroom investigations. This approach maximizes the children's creative ideas and composing skills, and also enables the practitioner to share the processes and conventions of writing with several children at once.

The only tools required are a bold marker pen and a flip chart, or some large sheets of paper fixed to a small easel or chalkboard (older children may respond well to an interactive whiteboard). The practitioner/scribe writes at the dictation of the children, but talks herself and the children through every aspect of the process and draws the children's attention to the smallest details. This includes shaping the group discussion and fragments of talk into suitable passages for writing. At this level the children are helped to make the important and complex move from speaking to writing, learning in a meaningful context that writing is different from speech. The conventions of writing are taught as the adult talks about all the detailed decisions writers must make and invites the children to instruct her how to do it. For example:

'Where do we start on the paper?'
'Do we use a capital letter?'
'How do we spell that?'
'What letter does it start with – do we know a word like it; have we used this word before?'
'Is that the end of this part?'
'Do we use a full stop here?'
'How can we show that this is a question?'

These questions lead to constant rereading of the text and re-writing it, lots of linguistic talk and the energetic solving of genuine literacy problems (Geekie and Raban, 1993: 23).

Shared writing is also a way of preparing children to continue tackling their writing in collaborative ways at the later stages of education. In the later primary years a willingness to engage in shared writing conferences will be important. However, in the early stages of literacy writing is often a hard-won achievement for the child, as well as a spontaneous creative experience, and too much redrafting is best avoided. The young child's pieces of writing are often treasured objects to be tucked away in secret places or, sometimes, a gift for a loved person, and we need to exercise great sensitivity about reworking such material.

At the later stages of literacy development it is still advisable to provide time, space and materials for private writing that is not subject to 'handing in' and marking. Of course, such writing might be shared voluntarily with a trusted adult who happens to be an early years practitioner but this is a personal communication and should be responded to in an appropriate way.

Permanent and disposable

Disposable

There is a tendency in language study to make much of the importance of writing in terms of its permanence and, correspondingly, to neglect its equally important 'disposable' nature. We should remember that in one significant sense spoken language is permanent: it can never be 'unsaid' and has a terrible permanence in other people's minds. The neglect of writing as a disposable product has often led to some foolish and 'unwriterly' practices in the early years of schooling. For a start, there has been a reluctance to allow children to have second thoughts about a piece of writing, to erase sections of it, delete it, throw it away and start again. But an interest in redrafting and editing at the later stage of writing implies the tolerance of such messy but very writerly practices as cutting up sections, rejigging them and pasting them down, on paper or on a computer. Real writing involves using lots of scrap paper for headings and useful ideas and, of course, positively cultivating overflowing waste-paper bins. When young children are able to work on a computer they discover the liberating power of the delete key and the possibility of printing out satisfyingly clean text.

Writers, particularly young ones, also like to 'say it out loud', or whistle, wriggle and get up and walk about. Young boys are likely to benefit if they are encouraged to write 'on the hoof' as they build, explore and talk. But this is heady and revolutionary stuff, so let us simply admit that as adults we do not often get writing 'right' first time and we should not expect children to do so!

Permanence

The sort of permanence in writing which is highly significant for education is that which enables us to use writing as an extended way of thinking. Once the idea, experience or phrase is roughly written down it is captured. Ideas, implications and new connections begin to flow from the matter on the page or the screen. In this sense the permanence of writing is bound up with its alterability or total disposability, but it is also an interesting issue of power and control for writers. Who decides for beginning writers what they can keep, alter or destroy? It seems clear that if from the start the young writer has to give over this control to an adult, then writing will never become a powerful mode of personal thinking, communication and a source of pleasure. Response to children's early writing must be sensitive and respectful. We should incorporate into our 'marking' of it such procedures as discussing and altering material with the child's agreement and active involvement. The mistakes made by children should be seen as a powerful teaching aid that enables the practitioner to have some insight into the child's thinking, progress and current strategies for understanding and using written forms.

Children's appreciation of the permanence of writing will be fostered by their awareness of it as a source of pleasure that is always there to go back to. It is a measure of our success when a child flicks excitedly through a book and says 'Where's that poem about ... ?' or demands to know where we have put the story about, 'that dog who got all dirty so they didn't know he was really Harry and they put him in the bath' (Zion, 1960). Children also go home and recommend favourite books to friends and family, or demand that they buy them. And, over the years, no matter how many times we go away, we can always come back and the story is still there. *The Very Hungry Caterpillar* (Carle, 1970) still munches through an amazing menu and *Farmer Duck* (Waddell and Oxenbury, 1991) and his farmyard friends always manage to drive away the lazy old farmer.

Writing is also a permanent record of facts, information and historical change. Books begin to work for children in the early stages of literacy as extra 'informants' or 'teachers' and the use of library collections and reference skills may start from the children's own group-made books. Practitioners, parents and children together can produce highly personal and relevant books about 'our gerbils', 'planting pansy seeds' or 'the avocado book', complete with a recipe for making guacamole![1] Such books form the nucleus of an early years classroom reference collection and are meaningful initiations into using the power of written language to get things done in the world.

Independence and conventions

Getting things done in the world is one aspect of being independent, and early literacy raises important issues of personal autonomy and the nature of conventions. It may seem a little odd to be linking issues of autonomy and conventions together, but many worrying and controversial aspects of early literacy teaching are rooted in misunderstandings about these related issues. Without in any way minimizing the significance for individuals and cultures of a sound mastery of conventional written language, we need to question the high priority still accorded to teaching and learning conventions in the early stages of literacy. History, research and classroom experience suggest that too much concern for the early teaching of conventions and rules, at the expense of independent and exploratory approaches to reading and writing, slows down children's progress and seriously undermines their desire to be readers and writers.

Autonomy

A first priority for early literacy and, indeed, an aim of care and education at any stage, must be personal autonomy: the clear establishment of a sense of control over one's life and learning experiences. If this sounds too grand and vague for the early years we should stop and consider the growing evidence of avoidable confusion and misunderstanding that assails young children in their first weeks and months in schools and has a detrimental effect on early literacy (see, for example, Brooker, 2002; 2008; Drury, 2007; Gregory, 2008). Sadly, it is often the areas of reading and writing in the early years that confront young children with meaningless tasks, pointless questions and unexplained activities. These practices can be found in children's centres, nursery schools and playgroups as mandatory curriculum targets that must be attained come to dominate the activities. We need to question the usefulness of such activities as asking low-level questions about perfectly obvious pictures, colouring in outline drawings of characters from primers, copying out trivial sentences from work books, learning to write letters and numerals by linking up dots, underlining capital letters and full stops, and so on.

The writing that goes on in early years settings between the children themselves and between practitioners, family members and the children should raise the questions that drive children to seek clearer and more effective writing strategies, that is, conventions. We need to raise the issue of writing functions: what is this piece of writing for? The answers will be as numerous and varied as human purposes, ranging from 'fun' to 'dire warnings'. My favourite example of the latter came from a Year 1 (5–6 years) classroom where the cleaner had pinned a hastily written note on the window for the children arriving that morning: 'The window ain't safe. Watch out for bits of glass.'

Audience

Our writing activities must also raise the question of audience. Practitioners must use effort and ingenuity to ensure that children have a wide range of people and even institutions to write for. Children can, with adult help in editing and typing on the computer (those significant conventions again), complain about the dogs fouling their local park or ask a local veterinarian to let them observe a routine surgery. Let us think less about 'marking' the children's writing and more about writing back to them with notes of encouragement or important information. Children's writing in the early years will be highly expressive, full of their personal stance in the world, their feeling responses and shared assumptions. If we try to eradicate from their writing how children feel about their experiences, we are likely to eradicate any desire to write at all. The appropriate tone and style of a piece of writing is gained slowly and is a result of asking and answering for oneself, *'What is this for and who is it for?'*

Progress in writing is bound up with autonomy and although the availability of materials and spaces for writing are essential, children also need to be involved from the start in forming opinions and having views about their own writing successes and difficulties. This can be started by actually writing back to the children about their work, and discussing with them the effectiveness of their writing for its purpose and audience.

'Hearing' readers

Early reading also involves aspects of independence and early years educators need to encourage approaches that will ensure rapid and meaningful reading.

Young children need to tackle reading globally, getting the gist of the message quickly, rather than attempting to decode every word and risking losing meaning. Any tendency to read alone or begin to read 'silently' should be positively supported. Considerable thought and flexibility should govern the practitioner's approaches to the 'hearing' of young readers. Reading aloud to other adults, older children and visitors will help when children are suddenly racing away and anxious to practise their emerging competence. But the old tradition of hearing every child, every day, labouring through short and often meaningless snippets must be critically reassessed.

Less frequent but far more intensive contacts with a practitioner will probably set children off on fruitful meaning-making encounters with books and other written matter. The 'hearing reading', every day, approach effectively devalues all the other important reading for meaning that goes on in early years classrooms.

As part of the process of encouraging independent reading, early years practitioners must find ways of developing children's self-correcting strategies and their self-assessment. If children are allowed to make minor miscues and even lose meaning, they will learn, given a little time and a sense of self-confidence, to go back and self-correct or, at least, question the text and raise the issue of 'that doesn't make sense'. It all depends on the adult's professional sensitivity and judgement about not rushing in too soon with a word-perfect correction but, equally importantly, not leaving a child floundering so long that meaning and confidence evaporate.

Editing and study skills

We can begin to extend young children's understanding of the usefulness of written language conventions by introducing them to the process of editing writing and acquiring study skills as they reach the later early years stage (6, 7 and 8 years). The success of editing depends on using the children's own writing, building on their developing insights into the differences between spoken and written forms, and supporting their desire to communicate more effectively. Early work on editing will tend to focus on the conventions of standardized spelling and punctuation. Success in taking on the conventions of spelling seems to depend on a cumulative build-up of language experiences – a general background of listening carefully to language and playing with its sounds, rhythms and patterns.

Spelling

Specific attention to spelling is most successful once children are confident readers and have a considerable experience of seeing written forms and writing themselves. Children also need plenty of opportunities for attempting spellings without being unduly constrained by the fear of getting it wrong.

Attempts to spell 'as it sounds to you' encourage the investigation of the sound properties of language and the varied relationships between spoken forms and their written representations.

Careful examination of children's writing will reveal groups or patterns of non-standard forms. These can be discussed with individuals and small groups, related to words the children know by sight or to words in favourite books, poems and songs. Once the children are enthusiastic readers and writers they will enjoy linguistic games that involve collecting groups of words similar in appearance, sound or meanings. Class and personal dictionaries can begin to be useful as children's writing and reading skills develop. They may be arranged thematically for some purposes, as well as alphabetically. Frequently encountered digraphs and strings of letters may be explored by making collections of them or building families of words that have these features.

These activities should be undertaken in exploratory ways and in meaningful contexts because they can easily become sterile exercises. Children's investigations of spelling should be pursued in a spirit of linguistic curiosity rather than with moralizing overtones about 'good' and 'bad' spellings. Spellings are neither good nor bad, they are standard or non-standard, but they are an important aspect of clear communication. Eventually the social and occupational well-being of those who are unable to spell in conventional and standardized ways is undermined.

Punctuation

Punctuation is bound up with two issues, the disembedded nature of written language and the concept of the sentence. It is often difficult for practitioners, parents and other adults who have been writing successfully for years to realize that the sentence is not a natural feature of spoken language. It is true that the explicit sentence with its clear subject and predicate and its proper agreements of number, gender and so on, as well as the cohesive devices which link the clauses, has migrated into some spoken forms. When we speak in our most formal registers, as in prepared speeches, we tend to use sentences because we are speaking aloud from the written form, but the language of social interaction and personal expressive talk is based on the unit of *the meaning-bearing phrase*. Daily language use is concerned with conveying and sharing meanings and it is embedded in obvious social contexts which make explicit verbal references and agreements less crucial. The implication is that children need many experiences of listening to book language and creating books and other pieces of text in shared-writing situations if they are to understand what is going on between the initial capital letter and the full stop.

It is much easier to approach the use of punctuation by way of the problems associated with the disembedded, or perhaps we might say 'unembodied', nature of written language. Punctuation partly compensates for the loss of much that is crucial in meaningful face-to-face communications. This includes indicators of units of meaning and their relationships and developments, as in sentences, paragraphs, phrases and clauses. Punctuation markers also replace the vocal into-nation patterns and the pauses and changes of pitch we use to convey questions, statements and hesitations. The best way to develop children's sensitivity to these features of writing is to encourage the reading aloud and sharing of their written communications. Difficulties with phrasing, ambiguities and breathless unpunctu-ated continuity soon become obvious in interesting and unthreatening ways. Asking questions (such as 'what can we do?' and 'how can we make this better?') is always wiser and more educationally useful than the silent condemnation of fairly meaningless red-ink corrections.

Study skills

In the early years of education we can make a positive start on the teaching of other study skills. Good points of departure here are the children's interest in sorting and classifying the group or classroom collection of books, as well as experiences of looking things up in reference books and on website search engines. Interest in different kinds of information books depends, of course, on there being a range of such books available. Interest is further stimulated by placing appropriate reference books and downloaded information next to the-matic displays or collections of materials and artefacts. Thus, a collection of the musical instruments improvised and made by the children can be gathered together attractively and further enhanced by 'close at hand' books and website information about singing games, musical instruments from other cultures or an anthology of the children's own favourite songs. Similarly, a display of stones, pebbles and fossils does need one or two well-illustrated and accurately informative books and photographs to accompany it.

The skills of 'looking things up' and 'finding out about it' in reference books are extended by an introduction to the functions of a contents page, an index and the use of alphabetical order. The use of such books for searching, identi-fying and informing introduces the particular techniques of reading for information. This kind of reading is different from readerly approaches to nar-rative and poetic writing: the forms of imaginative literature need to be read in their entirety. However, reference material can be scanned and only the rele-vant sections attended to. Relevance here is judged in terms of the reader-researcher's question or problem. It is unnecessary to read the whole book, let alone copy it out word for word – a pointless practice often associ-ated with the use of information books for projects in the later primary years. Similarly, knowing what is relevant and being selective are the biggest chal-lenges encountered when using websites and young children will need adult support and guidance. Approaches to early literacy that encourage autonomy, reflection and investigation are one way of ensuring that children use reference books and computers as resources for answering their own independently for-mulated questions (see Mallett, 1999; Meek, 1996).

As they progress through the early years of schooling, children become increasingly interested in the variety and range of books provided for them. This interest can lead to a spontaneous sorting and classifying of the class book collection. If spontaneity appears to be weak, it can be strengthened by displaying the children's own class-made books on special shelves, placing information books next to relevant resources, setting up collections of books by one author and organizing trips to the local public library. These kinds of initiatives often lead children to demand 'let's have a library'. Such a literacy role-play project teaches the children a great deal about the conventions and organization involved in the management of a wide range of books for borrowing. As well as deciding how to classify the available books the children have to organize ways of issuing borrowers' tickets and keeping a check on the books borrowed. Such problems challenge and extend children's understanding of alphabetical order, reading and writing for practical purposes, the classification and retrieval of information, and the nature of 'subjects' or knowledge categories. To these complex study skills we might also add the very important interpersonal skills of courtesy, fairness and respect for shared resources.

Children with complex needs

Every child develops a unique combination of qualities, strengths and needs and follows a personal learning journey towards literacy. For some children, additional physical, cognitive, emotional and social factors make their educational needs 'special' or complex. The broad categories of special and complex needs include:

- a range of developmental delays; problems with communication, eye-contact, turn-taking, responsiveness and appropriate social behaviour (often indicative of autism spectrum disorders); movement difficulties, delayed crawling and walking and clumsiness; impulsivity and extreme activity
- disabling conditions and prolonged illnesses that restrict breathing and movement and confine a child to a wheelchair
- degrees of sight impairment and blindness; degrees of hearing loss and deafness; conditions that limit physical growth
- speech delay, incomprehensibility and muteness; later problems with print recognition and processing
- extremes of 'giftedness' and precocious intellectual power.

Early years practitioners will encounter many of these conditions and they must clarify their thinking and advance their understanding of each child's complex needs. Adequate coverage of the highly specialized fields of special educational needs (SEN) and complex needs are beyond the scope of this book. However, the processes of language development and the early years practices outlined in this text can create a base for sound understanding of all children's individual needs. We can add to this understanding a set of pedagogical principles for ensuring minimal rights and aspirations for young children, whatever their complex needs.

Some pedagogical principles

- All children have a range of needs but children with complex physical and cognitive disabilities will also experience some emotional and social impacts on their lives.

- Children with complex needs must be nurtured and educated with a focus on their holistic development. They cannot simply be defined by their 'special' or 'complex' needs alone.

- Practitioners and families must be wary of developing low expectations when they are raising, caring for and creating learning environments for children with complex needs (Figure 9.5).

- Children with complex needs have their own views, preferences and aspirations and practitioners must learn to take these seriously, find creative ways of listening to and accessing them, and cooperate with families and expert advisers to make them happen.

- Children with complex needs have a right to an imaginative life, to dreams and ambitions and to pleasure and enjoyment. Relationships, communication, language and literacy can make major contributions to children's imaginative lives, hopes and wishes.

Figure 9.5 **High expectations – using the computer (5 years)**

These principles also underpin good practice in the early years with all children, particularly in the early months and years of life when unambiguous identification of many complex needs is not easy. Before rushing to embrace ever bigger and brighter solutions, labels and diagnoses, we must check that the basic requirements for quality care, safe environments and close adult professional relationships are in place for children in the early years. We must then ensure that all the enabling language and literacy factors discussed in this book are found in our settings. We can also remind ourselves that the big breakthroughs in children's reading seem to come, according to the research, when children have closely monitored one-to-one tuition; have approaches that are literacy orientated and involve writing; have meaningful material to read; and, most importantly, receive the powerful message from their families, carers and tutors that they are loved, valued and respected.

Specialist further reading

Hall, K. (2003) *Listening to Stephen Read. Multiple Perspectives on Literacy*. Buckingham: Open University Press.

Logue, J. (2009) *Working with Parents of Children with Additional Needs*. London: Featherstone/A and C Black.

Macintyre, C. (2009) *Dyspraxia in the Early Years. Identifying and Supporting Children with Movement Difficulties*. 2nd edn. Abingdon: Routledge.

Newman, S. (2008) *Small Steps Forward. Using Games and Activities to Help your Pre-school Child with Special Needs*. 2nd edn. London: Jessica Kingsley.

Orr, R. (2003) *My Right to Play: A Child with Complex Needs*. Maidenhead: Open University Press.

Sutherland, M. (2008) *Developing the Gifted and Talented Young Learner*. London: Sage.

Wall, K. (2006) *Special Needs and Early Years. A Practitioner's Guide*. 2nd edn. London: Sage.

Wall, K. (2010) *Autism and Early Years Practice. A Guide for Early Years Professionals, Teachers and Parents*. 2nd edn. London: Sage Publishing.

Parents, families, communities and cultures

All the issues and choices raised in this book lack a crucial dimension if they are not shared with the families and communities who send their young children to us to be cared for and educated. Early years settings should always be open to the families they serve, and as well known and well used as any other community facilities. Ideas about open group settings and schools and partnership with parents have significant implications for many professional choices. Partnership involves the genuine sharing of ideas and mutual support and this increasingly depends on the quality of the conversations and activities parents and professional educators share. Professionals could do more to explain the principles on which they base their practices in sensible human terms. Do we still talk mysteriously, of 'reading for meaning', using 'real books' and 'developmental writing' and leave it at that? Outside care and education settings, these terms are either ludicrously obvious or meaningless! What is a parent to make of 'learning from concrete experiences' or 'writing across the curriculum'? As well as saying exactly what we mean, rather than staying safely in the cocoon of professional jargon, we must help parents and the community to say what they mean.

Many parents still feel that they do not have enough information about what their children are learning in the later early years stages in school, despite plentiful contacts. This suggests that practitioners must continue to work at building true partnerships, real conversations and cooperation. For example, practitioners may talk to parents about 'writing' and mean the processes of composing meaningful messages while, in the same conversation, 'writing' to the parents means neat handwriting and the conventions of spelling and punctuation. Parents' understandable anxieties about the formal achievements of 'correct' and well-presented English can only be lessened if practitioners' priorities and their reasons are presented in unambiguous terms.

The success of many 'reading-with-parents' schemes has been instrumental in helping families to worry less about word-perfect barking at print. In fact, many families have been able to reclaim their pride in their under-5 children's skills of recognizing books, slogans, instructions, labels and names in all sorts of places and at all sorts of extraordinary angles. A rapidly increasing number of projects in the USA and Britain – for example Reading is Fundamental (RIF), and Families and Schools Together (FAST) – continue to extend the notion of partnership by sharing the excitement of books and literacy, and acknowledging that literacy begins at home and then 'goes to school' (Weinberger, 1996).

A 10-year study of children growing up in the city of Baltimore, USA, (Serpell et al., 2005) also charts the significance of literacy activities in the 'intimate culture' of the home. This research makes it clear that the literacy-related activities shared with parents (books, word games, board games, story-telling, meal-time conversations, educational television) promote

- orientation to print
- narrative competence
- phonological awareness.

True partnerships are rarely bland or comfortable all the time and sometimes parents and communities may appear to make demands that worry practitioners. Indeed, a school or early years setting may sometimes feel that a simple acquiescence in certain requests would damage its educational provision and curriculum policies. Parents may ask 'When are the children going to be taught the rules of spelling?' 'Why aren't they copying their letters?' 'Why have the children not got reading books?' This is not necessarily a criticism of the early years setting. It is certainly a request for information and probably reflects an understandable fear of the disadvantages and inequalities suffered by those who are not functionally literate in society. These unnerving questions about literacy teaching are indications of a need for regular practitioner-parent workshops and discussions about language, literature, literacy and child development. Perhaps these questions also indicate that not enough is being done to make families and communities feel that they are co-workers in every aspect of the education of their children.

Families who use the Pen Green Centre in Corby (Whalley and the Pen Green Centre Team, 2007) are involved in ongoing professional training opportunities and become co-researchers and contributors to their children's records and assessments. This commitment to taking families seriously as co-educators is demonstrated by the centre's booklets produced with and for parents. The education theories and pedagogical practices followed by the centre are carefully explained and explored and the observations of the children made by the parents in their homes illustrate the books and are also integrated into the records and planning of the practitioners.

The examples of parental involvement described throughout this book, from Earlham, Pen Green and Baltimore, do not come from privileged communities, but they demonstrate the liberating effect of parents and practitioners working together for children.

Records and assessment

Assessment of young children's learning, language and literacy is not an exact science but an art, a matter of making sound professional judgements. The following features of effective educational assessment provide useful guidelines:

- Assessment must be rooted in everyday reality and should be going on all the time. It should include children's own views about what they are learning and how they feel about it. This can be done by giving children cameras to record achievements and difficulties, or using informal interviews, collected drawings, favourite books and pieces of work significant for the child. Children can also share these personal records of their progress with their families on a regular and informal basis (Figure 9.6).
- Assessment must be based on careful observations of children. These can be in the form of field notes, narrative accounts, sketches, diagrams, photographs and video recordings. The skilled child-observer looks for 'critical moments', or breakthroughs in understanding, and identifies individual children's regular and personal styles of thinking and learning. These learning styles are sometimes tracked and analysed as schemas (Athey, 2007; Nutbrown, 2006) and sometimes as dispositions and learning stories (Carr, 2001).
- All our observations of children are useless if we do not use them to inform our thinking and planning and ensure 'feedforward' for the children. Observations must be reflected on in the light of such questions as, 'What's going on here?' and 'What comes next?' In early years settings where observations of the children are at the heart of the curriculum the children are eager to get involved too and make their own contributions (Figure 9.7).

Figure 9.6 **A 4-year-old girl shares her profile records with her dad**

- Assessment of children's communication, language and literacy requires us to *recognize it*, *record it*, *review it* and *share it*. With regard to the latter, the main purpose of assessment is not to compare children with each other, but to develop relationships with children and their families that give us insights into children's learning at home and in early years settings.

Practitioners can find good advice and models in many publications (Browne, 2009; Bruce, 2010; Drummond, 1993; Hutchin, 1999; 2007). Many of these researchers base their work broadly on the practices for monitoring and assessing language and learning pioneered by *The Primary Language Record* (CLPE/ILEA, 1988). This is still a valuable guide because it goes well beyond simple summative assessments: it provides diagnostic insights for the practitioner; it reflects the richness and breadth of children's language experiences and potential; and it involves parents and carers directly in contributing to their children's cumulative language records. Many early years settings now involve parents in assessment by asking them to contribute their own observations, anecdotes, films and photographs to the early years records of their children's progress.

All these good things are in danger of being ignored in the pre-5 years of education as practitioners are now required to check up on early learning goals for communication, language and literacy and complete a summative assessment at the end of the Early Years Foundation Stage (age 5 in England). The English Early Years Foundation Stage Profile requires teachers to make a judgement about each child's achievements (in all curriculum areas), as expressed by summary statements (for example, 'Recognises a few familiar words'). These statements must be ticked, or left blank, and then scored for ticks! Yet research tells us that young children's 'errors' in reading and writing are a source of valuable insights into their thinking. Research also tells us that learning is a matter of processes and potential, best assessed when children are working with an older and wiser tutor, but not necessarily tapped by one-off solitary performances.

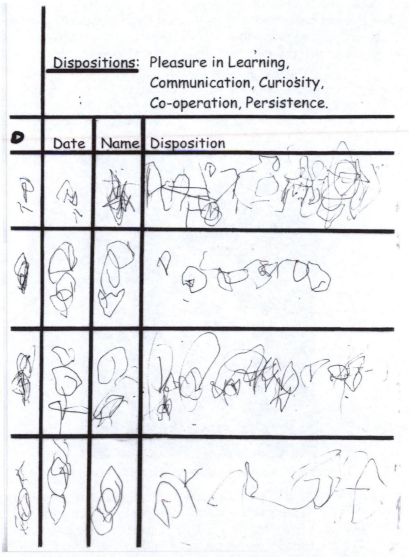

Figure 9.7   Children's contributions on a teacher's observation sheet (3 years 6 months)

Good practice in a reception class (4–5 years) – *Mary Fisher and Shelagh Swallow*

At St John's Roman Catholic Infant School we work as a team consisting of two full-time teachers (ourselves), one full-time Teaching Assistant, two Teaching Assistants that job share and two 1:1 helpers for statemented children with Special Educational Needs – this need varies from year to year.

We share our observations informally on a daily basis and we have regular meetings to discuss these observations and plan the next steps. When the children first join our setting we provide a variety of welcoming experiences and support their transition to school as sensitively as possible. Our classroom is play-based and they have free access to activities which may be familiar to them from nursery or playgroup (Figure 9.8). During this time we assess their *well-being* using the Ferre Laevers method and we also assess their *involvement* using the Ferre Laevers scale. It is then our aim to raise the well-being of each child so that they are able to become more involved in their learning. A high level of involvement leads to deep level learning.

Figure 9.8   **Literacy enriched play – at the vet's surgery (Reception)**

As a team we regularly look at examples of child-initiated work and discuss them so that we become better skilled at recognizing their value and see how they can lead future learning in a new direction. We have compiled a portfolio with a section for every scale point of the Foundation Stage Profile. When we find an example of child-initiated work we look at it and annotate it, noting which scale points it would be evidence for. *Usually a single exam-*

ple of child-initiated work, or an observation, or an anecdote, will be cross-curricular and evidence for at least three areas of learning. We do not plan from the FSP but this exercise helps our whole team to recognize the learning in these child-initiated activities and how rich they are, it also familiarizes us with the scale points and it helps us to plan future activities.

In our setting we have tried to establish a culture where child-initiated ideas are valued and recognized, so that this encourages all the children to share their ideas knowing that they are valued and this in turn raises their level of well-being and involvement and leads to deep level learning.

In our setting we do not use workbooks or work sheets. We display all the children's work and annotate these displays (Figure 9.9), documenting the learning process from the initial idea through the various stages to a variety of outcomes. This process does inform our planning and enables us to evaluate too. It also helps the children to re-visit their learning journeys and it informs parents and visitors. Children often add to these displays with their independent work. For example, in our Mary Poppins topic, inspired by a child's Mary Poppins doll which led to another child bringing in his DVD, we each made a grid map showing Mary finding her way to the children, or the house, etc. When these were displayed the children started making their own grids showing their way home, or started spotting grid patterns in the environment and even in their breakfast! One idea led to another and we had a grid and arrow party. What could have been simply a maths activity ended up as an all-encompassing cross-curricular mini topic.

Figure 9.9   'The Dog Show' – a wall display draws together a whole project (Reception)

Laevers' well-being and involvement theory

Professor Ferre Laevers is a Belgian academic and researcher in early childhood development and cognition. His work charts the effect that experiences, including early learning and education, have on children's self-esteem and behaviour. He describes the body language and behaviour signals of *well-being* (or not) that practitioners and parents can observe, including:

- flexibility
- assertiveness
- enjoyment
- openness/receptivity
- relaxation
- self-confidence.

His work also focuses on signs that children are learning at a deep level and assesses this in terms of *involvement* on a 5-point scale, from completely uninvolved to deep and sustained absorption. The signals of *involvement* include:

- concentration
- persistence
- satisfaction
- creativity
- facial expression/composure
- excited talk.

(See Laevers, F. (1997) *A Process-Oriented Child Monitoring System*. Leuven: Centre for Experiential Education, University of Leuven.)

Good literacy practitioners need not be too distracted or challenged by tick-lists, as these examples show. We do need to range widely in our own assessments and build up rich records of children's responses and developments in talking, listening, stories, books, poetry, rhyme, play with language, music, dance, print, signs, drawing and pictures. Children can be drawn into the assessment process at a very early stage. One valuable practice is building up folders of selections from the children's drawing and writing, along with photographs of the children's activities, and asking the children to choose items for inclusion. These items should be dated and include the child's reasons for choosing them attached, along with notes on the learning by the adults who work with the child. I always included a few examples, which gave a time sequence to the collection: the first drawing or writing the child did with me and some half-termly examples. The sense of progress, or a learning journey undertaken, in such a folder is exciting for parents and child to contemplate. The practitioner gains a new insight about the child's thinking as it is revealed in changing strategies and hypotheses for representing meanings and experiences.

Reading profiles kept by practitioners must include notes on children's attitudes and approaches to books and print and their knowledge of illustrations, print conventions and the clues offered by context, syntax, phonics and semantics. When children read aloud, the teacher will need to note attempts at self-correction, questions about the text and other evidence of making sense of the task. However, complex as the teaching of reading is, there is still a place for children's own views about learning to read – self-assessment can start in the early years. With the help of the teacher's secretarial skills, young readers can keep personal records of what they read in and out of school, what they like and why, and what they have not enjoyed. They can be helped to talk about their reading aloud performance, what gives them trouble and what occasions have been successful. Independence in literacy is about encouraging children to express from the start their own needs, formulate their own questions and hypotheses, and evaluate their own progress. If this approach is established as a priority it will lead to a more meaningful focus on the conventions of written language.

Further reading

Abbott, L. and Langston, A. (eds) (2006) *Parents Matter*. Maidenhead: Open University Press.

Browne, A. (2009) *Developing Language and Literacy 3–8*. 3rd edn. London: Sage.

Campbell, R. (2009) *Reading Stories with Young Children*. Stoke-on-Trent: Trentham Books.

Carr, M. (2001) *Assessment in Early Childhood Settings: Learning Stories*. London: Paul Chapman Publishing.

Drummond, M.J. (1993) *Assessing Children's Learning*. London: David Fulton.

Makin, L. and Whitehead, M. (2004) *How to Develop Children's Early Literacy: A Guide for Professional Carers and Educators*. London: Paul Chapman Publishing.

Riley, J. (2006) *Language and Literacy 3–7: Creative Approaches to Teaching*. London: Paul Chapman Publishing.

Weinberger, J. (1996) *Literacy Goes to School: The Parents' Role in Young Children's Literacy Learning*. London: Paul Chapman Publishing.

Whalley, M. and Pen Green Centre Team (2007) *Involving Parents in their Children's Learning*. 2nd edn. London: Paul Chapman Publishing.

Whitehead, M. (2007) *Developing Language and Literacy with Young Children*. 3rd edn. London: Paul Chapman Publishing.

Note

1 My thanks to Martha Boyd and her teaching-practice class for this delightful experience.

LANGUAGE AND EDUCATION: SOME KEY TEXTS

Austin, J.L. (1962) *How to Do Things with Words*. Oxford: Clarendon Press.

Brown, R. (1973) *A First Language*. Harmondsworth: Penguin.

Bruner, J.S. (1983) *Child's Talk: Learning to Use Language*. Oxford: Oxford University Press.

Crystal, D. (1995) *The Cambridge Encyclopedia of the English Language*. Cambridge: Cambridge University Press.

Donaldson, M. (1978) *Children's Minds*. Glasgow: Fontana/Collins.

Edwards, A.D. (1976) *Language in Culture and Class*. London: Heinemann.

Edwards, C., Gandini, L. and Foreman, G. (eds) (1996) *The Hundred Languages of Children*. London: Ablex.

Hymes, D.H. (1972) 'On communicative competence', in J.B. Pride and J. Holmes (eds), *Sociolinguistics*. Harmondsworth: Penguin.

Luria, A.R. and Yudovich, F.I. (1971) *Speech and the Development of Mental Processes in the Child*. Harmondsworth: Penguin.

Mallett, M. (2005) *The Primary English Encyclopaedia: The Heart of the Curriculum*. 2nd edn. London: David Fulton.

Meek, M., Warlow, A. and Barton, G. (eds) (1977) *The Cool Web: The Pattern of Children's Reading*. London: Bodley Head.

Milroy, J. and Milroy, L. (1998) *Authority in Language: Investigating Standard English*. 3rd edn. London: Routledge.

Piaget, J. (1926) *The Language and Thought of the Child*. London: Routledge and Kegan Paul.

Saussure, F. de (1974) *Course in General Linguistics*. Glasgow: Collins. (First published 1915, Paris: Payot.)

Slobin, D. (1979) *Psycholinguistics*. 2nd edn. Glenview, IL: Scott Foresman.

Snow, C.E. and Ferguson, C.A. (eds) (1977) *Talking to Children: Language Input and Acquisition*. Cambridge: Cambridge University Press.

Wells, G. (1987) *The Meaning Makers: Children Learning Language and Using Language to Learn*. London: Hodder and Stoughton.

Whorf, B.L. (1956) *Language, Thought and Reality: Selected Writings of B.L. Whorf*. New York: Wiley.

Yule, G. (1996) *The Study of Language*. Cambridge: Cambridge University Press.

LITERATURE REFERRED TO IN THE TEXT

Agard, J. (1983) *I Din Do Nuttin*. London: Bodley Head.

Ahlberg, J. and Ahlberg, A. (1977a) *Burglar Bill*. London: Heinemann.

Ahlberg, J. and Ahlberg, A. (1977b) *Each Peach Pear Plum*. Harmondsworth: Kestrel/Penguin.

Ahlberg, J. and Ahlberg, A. (1981) *Peepo*. Harmondsworth: Kestrel/Penguin.

Ahlberg, J. and Ahlberg, A. (1986) *The Jolly Postman or Other People's Letters*. London: Heinemann.

Ahlberg, J. and Ahlberg, A. (1995) *The Jolly Pocket Postman*. London: Heinemann.

Atwood, M. (1987) *The Handmaid's Tale*. London: Virago.

Awdry, W. (1997) *Meet Thomas and His Friends*. London: Reed International.

Baker, J. (2002) *Window*. London: Walker.

Barber, A. and Bayley, N. (1990) *The Mousehole Cat*. London: Walker.

Biesty, S. (2002) *Rome in Spectacular Cross-Section*. Oxford: Oxford University Press.

Blake, Q. (1995) *Clown*. London: Jonathan Cape.

Breinburg, P. (1973) *My Brother Sean*. London: Bodley Head.

Briggs, R. (1978) *The Snowman*. London: Hamish Hamilton.

Briggs, R. (1983) *When the Wind Blows*. Harmondsworth: Penguin.

Brown, R. (2008) *The Tale of Two Mice*. London: Walker.

Browne, A. (1981) *Hansel and Gretel* (The Brothers Grimm). London: Julia MacRae.

Browne, A. (1986) *Piggybook*. London: Julia MacRae.

Browne, A. (2008) *Little Beauty*. London: Walker.

Browne, E. (1994) *Handa's Surprise*. London: Walker.

Bruna, D. (1967) *b is for bear, an abc*. London: Methuen.

Burgess, A. (1987) *The Piano Players*. London: Arrow.

Burningham, J. (1970) *Mr Gumpy's Outing*. London: Cape.
Burningham, J. (1977) *Come Away from the Water, Shirley*. London: Cape.
Burningham, J. (1982) *Avocado Baby*. London: Cape.
Carle, E. (1970) *The Very Hungry Caterpillar*. London: Hamish Hamilton.
Carroll, L. (1872) *Alice's Adventures in Wonderland*. London: Macmillan.
Cooper, H. (1993) *The Bear Under the Stairs*. London: Doubleday/Picture Corgi.
Cooper, H. (1998) *Pumpkin Soup*. London: Doubleday/Picture Corgi.
Dahl, R. (1982) *The BFG*. London: Cape.
Deacon, A. (2002) *Slow Loris*. London: Hutchinson.
Donaldson, J. (2008) *Stick Man*. London: Alison Green.
Dunn, J. and Bate, H. (2008) *ABC UK*. London: Frances Lincoln.
Frank, A. (1954) *The Diary of Anne Frank*. London: Pan.
Gravett, E. (2005) *Wolves*. London: Macmillan.
Gravett, E. (2007) *Little Mouse's Big Book of Fears*. London: Macmillan.
Gravett, E. (2008) *Spells*. London: Macmillan.
Grey, M. (2002) *Egg Drop*. London: Jonathan Cape.
Hill, E. (1980) *Where's Spot?* London: Heinemann.
Hughes, S. (1981) *Alfie Gets in First*. London: Bodley Head.
Hutchins, P. (1968) *Rosie's Walk*. London: Bodley Head.
Hutchins, P. (1972) *Titch*. London: Bodley Head.
Kerr, J. (1968) *The Tiger who Came to Tea*. Glasgow: Collins.
McKee, D. (1988) *Who's a Clever Baby Then?* London: Andersen.
McKissack, P.C. and Isadora, R. (1986) *Flossie and the Fox*. London: Viking Kestrel.
Nicholl, H. and Pienkowski, J. (1972) *Meg and Mog*. London: Heinemann.
Opie, I. and Opie, P. (eds) (1973) *The Oxford Book of Children's Verse*. Oxford: Oxford University Press.
Rosen, M. (1983) *Quick, Let's Get Out of Here*. London: Deutsch.
Rosen, M. and Oxenbury, H. (1989) *We're Going on a Bear Hunt*. London: Walker.
Sendak, M. (1967) *Where the Wild Things Are*. London: Bodley Head.
Seuss, Dr (1984) *The Butter Battle Book*. Glasgow: Collins.
Sharratt, N. (2002) *Shark in the Park*. Oxford: David Fickling.
Storr, C. (1955) *Clever Polly and the Stupid Wolf*. London: Faber.
Taylor, J. (1973) 'The star', in I. Opie and P. Opie (eds), *The Oxford Book of Children's Verse*. Oxford: Oxford University Press. p. 122.
Tomlinson, J. (1968) *The Owl Who Was Afraid of the Dark*. London: Methuen.
Vipont, E. (1969) *The Elephant and the Bad Baby*. London: Hamish Hamilton.
Waddell, M. and Oxenbury, H. (1991) *Farmer Duck*. London: Walker.
Wells, R. (1977) *Benjamin and Tulip*. Harmondsworth: Penguin.
Wells, R. (1978) *Noisy Norah*. Glasgow: Collins.
Whybrow, I. and Reynolds, A. (1999) *Harry and the Bucketful of Dinosaurs*. London: David and Charles.
Whybrow, I. and Reynolds, A. (2006) *Harry and the Dinosaurs Go to School*. London: David and Charles.
Zacharias, T. and Zacharias, W. (1965) *But Where is the Green Parrot?* London: Chatto and Windus.
Zion, G. (1960) *Harry the Dirty Dog*. London: Bodley Head.
Zolotow, C. and Sendak, M. (1968) *Mr Rabbit and the Lovely Present*. London: Bodley Head.

REFERENCES

Abbott, L. and Langston, A. (eds) (2006) *Parents Matter*. Maidenhead: Open University Press.

Adams, M.J. (1990) 'Why not phonics and whole language?' Paper prepared for the Symposium on Whole Language and Phonics, Orton Dyslexia Society, Minneapolis, MN, March.

Aitchison, J. (2000) *The Seeds of Speech: Language Origin and Evolution*. 2nd edn. Cambridge: Cambridge University Press.

Aitchison, J. (2001) *Language Change: Progress or Decay?* 3rd edn. Cambridge: Cambridge University Press.

Aitchison, J. (2003) *Words in the Mind: An Introduction to the Mental Lexicon*. 3rd edn. Oxford: Blackwell.

Aitchison, J. (2008) *The Articulate Mammal: An Introduction to Psycholinguistics*. 5th edn. London: Routledge.

Altwerger, B. (ed.) (2005) *Reading for Profit: How the Bottom Line Leaves Kids Behind*. Portsmouth, NH: Heinemann.

Anning, A. and Ring, K. (2004) *Making Sense of Children's Drawings*. Maidenhead: Open University Press.

Athey, C. (2007) *Extending Thought in Young Children – a Parent-Teacher Partnership*, 2nd edn. London: Paul Chapman Publishing.

Austin, J.L. (1962) *How to Do Things with Words*. Oxford: Clarendon Press.

Baddeley, P. and Eddershaw, C. (1994) *Not So Simple Picture Books: Developing Responses to Literature with 4–12 Year Olds*. Stoke-on-Trent: Trentham Books.

Baker, C. (1996) *Foundations of Bilingual Education and Bilingualism*. Clevedon: Multilingual Matters.

Barratt-Pugh, C. and Rohl, M. (eds) (2000) *Literacy Learning in the Early Years*. Buckingham: Open University Press.

Bissex, G.L. (1980) *GNYS AT WRK: A Child Learns to Write and Read*. Cambridge, MA: Harvard University Press.

Blakemore, S-J. and Frith, U. (2005) *The Learning Brain. Lessons for Education*. Oxford: Blackwell.

Britton, J.N. (1992) *Language and Learning*. Harmondsworth: Penguin. (First published 1970.)

Brock, A. and Rankin, C. (2008) *Communication, Language and Literacy from Birth to Five*. London: Sage.

Brooker, E. (2002) *Starting School: Young Children Learning Cultures*. Buckingham: Open University Press.

Brooker, E. (2008) *Supporting Transitions in the Early Years*. Maidenhead: Open University Press.

Browne, A. (2009) *Developing Language and Literacy 3–8*. 3rd edn. London: Sage.

Bruce, T. (ed.) (2009) *Early Childhood. A Guide for Students*. 2nd edn. London: Sage.

Bruce, T. and Spratt, J. (2008) *Essentials of Literacy from 0–7*. London: Sage.

Bruner, J.S. (1975) 'The ontogenesis of speech acts', *Journal of Child Language*. 2: 1–19.

Bruner, J.S. (1983) *Child's Talk: Learning to Use Language*. Oxford: Oxford University Press.

Bruner, J.S. (1986) *Actual Minds, Possible Worlds*. Cambridge, MA: Harvard University Press.

Bruner, J.S. (1990) *Acts of Meaning*. Cambridge, MA: Harvard University Press.

Bruner, J.S. and Haste, H. (eds) (1987) *Making Sense: The Child's Construction of the World*. London: Methuen.

Bryant, P.E. and Bradley, L. (1985) *Children's Reading Problems*. Oxford: Blackwell.

Butler, D. (1979) *Cushla and Her Books*. Sevenoaks: Hodder and Stoughton.

Campbell, R. (1999) *Literacy from Home to School: Reading with Alice*. Stoke-on-Trent: Trentham Books.

Campbell, R. (2009) *Reading Stories with Young Children*. Stoke-on-Trent: Trentham Books.

Carr, M. (2001) *Assessment in Early Childhood Settings: Learning Stories*. London: Paul Chapman Publishing.

Centre for Language in Primary Education/Inner London Education Authority (CLPE/ILEA) (1988) *The Primary Language Record: Handbook for Teachers*. London: CLPE.

Chomsky, N. (1957) *Syntactic Structures*. The Hague: Mouton.

Chukovsky, K. (1963) *From Two to Five*. Los Angeles, CA: University of California Press.

Clark, A. and Moss, P. (2001) *Listening to Young Children: The Mosaic Approach*. London: National Children's Bureau/Joseph Rowntree Foundation.

Clark, E.V. (1982) 'The young word maker: a case study of innovation in the child's lexicon', in E. Wanner and L.R. Gleitman (eds), *Language Acquisition: The State of the Art*. Cambridge: Cambridge University Press. pp. 390–425.

Clay, M.M. (1975) *What Did I Write?* London: Heinemann.

Collins, F. M. and Svensson, C. (2008) 'If I had a magic wand I'd magic her out of the book: the rich literacy practices of competent early readers', *Early*

Years, 28(1): 81–91.

Crystal, D. (1997) *The Cambridge Encyclopedia of Language*. Cambridge: Cambridge University Press.

Crystal, D. (1998) *Language Play*. Harmondsworth: Penguin.

Crystal, D. (2000) *Language Death*. Cambridge: Cambridge University Press.

Crystal, D. (2004) *The Stories of English*. London: Penguin.

Crystal, D. (2005) *How Language Works*. London: Penguin.

Crystal, D. (2008) *txtng. the gr8 db8*. Oxford: Oxford University Press.

Department of Education and Science (DES) (1975) *A Language for Life* (Bullock Report). London: HMSO.

Department of Education and Science (DES) (1988) *English for Ages 5–11: Proposals of the Secretaries of State* (Cox Report). London: NCC/HMSO.

Department for Children, Schools and Families (DCSF) (2007) *Confident, Capable and Creative: Supporting Boys' Achievements*. Norwich: DCSF Publications.

Department for Children, Schools and Families (DCSF) (2008) *The Early Years Foundation Stage: Setting the Standards for Learning, Development and Care for Children from Birth to Five*. Nottingham: DCSF Publications.

Department for Children, Schools and Families (DCSF) (2009) *Independent Review of the Primary Curriculum: Final Report*. Nottingham: DCSF Publications.

Department for Education and Skills (DfES) (2006) *Independent Review of the Teaching of Reading. Final Report* (Rose Review). Nottingham: DfES.

Department for Education and Skills (DfES) (2007) *Letters and Sounds: Principles and Practice of High Quality Phonics*. London: DfES.

Department of Education and Skills (DfES) and Sure Start Unit (2002) *Birth to Three Matters: A Framework to Support Children in their Earliest Years*. London: DfES.

Doherty, M. J. (2009) *Theory of Mind. How Children Understand Others' Thoughts and Feelings*. Hove: Psychology Press.

Dombey, H. (2006) 'How should we teach children to read?', *Books for Keeps*, 156: 6–7.

Doonan, J. (1993) *Looking at Pictures in Picture Books*. Stroud: Thimble.

Drummond, M.J. (1993) *Assessing Children's Learning*. London: David Fulton.

Drury, R. (2007) *Young Bilingual Learners at Home and School. Researching Multilingual Voices*. Stoke-on-Trent: Trentham Books.

Elfer, P., Goldschmied, E. and Selleck, D. (2003) *Key Persons in the Nursery: Building Relationships for Quality Provision*. London: David Fulton.

Engel, D.M. and Whitehead, M.R. (1993) 'More first words: a comparative study of bilingual siblings', *Early Years*, 14(1): 27–35.

Engel, D.M. and Whitehead, M.R. (1996) 'Which English? Standard English and language variety: some educational perspectives', *English in Education*, 30(1): 36–49.

Engel, S. (1995) *The Stories Children Tell: Making Sense of the Narratives of Childhood*. New York: W.H. Freeman.

Fabian, H. and Mould, C. (eds) (2009) *Development and Learning for Very Young Children*. London: Sage.

Featherstone, S. (ed.) (2006) *L is for Sheep. Getting Ready for Phonics*. Lutterworth: Featherstone Education.

Featherstone, S. and Featherstone, P. (eds) (2008) *Like Bees, not Butterflies*.

Child Initiated Learning in the Early Years. London: A & C Black/Featherstone Education.

Ferreiro, E. and Teberosky, A. (1982) *Literacy Before Schooling*. London: Heinemann.

Fox, C. (1993) *At the Very Edge of the Forest: The Influence of Literature on Storytelling by Children*. London: Cassell.

Freire, P. and Macedo, D. (1987) *Literacy: Reading the Word and the World*. London: Routledge and Kegan Paul.

Gamble, N. and Yates, S. (2008) *Exploring Children's Literature: Teaching the Language and Reading of Fiction*. 2nd edn. London: Sage.

Gardner, H. (1980) *Artful Scribbles: The Significance of Children's Drawings*. London: Jill Norman.

Gardner, H. (1983) *Frames of Mind: The Theory of Multiple Intelligences*. New York: Basic Books.

Gardner, H. (1991) *The Unschooled Mind: How Children Think and How Schools Should Teach*. London: Fontana.

Geekie, P. and Raban, B. (1993) *Learning to Write and Read Through Classroom Talk*. Warwick Papers on Education Policy No. 2. Stoke-on-Trent: Trentham Books.

Gentry, J.R. (1982) 'An analysis of developmental spelling in GNYS AT WRK', *The Reading Teacher*, November: 192–200.

Gerhardt, S. (2004) *Why Love Matters: How Affection Shapes a Baby's Brain*. Hove: Routledge.

Gillen, J. and Hall, N. (2001) '"Hiya, Mum!" An analysis of pretence telephone play in a nursery setting', *Early Years*, 21(2): 15–24.

Goldschmied, E. and Jackson, S. (2004) *People Under Three: Young Children in Day Care*. 2nd edn. London: Routledge.

Goleman, D. (1996) *Emotional Intelligence: Why It Can Matter More than IQ*. London: Bloomsbury.

Goodwin, P. (ed.) (2008) *Understanding Children's Books: A Guide for Education Professionals*. London: Sage.

Goouch, K. (2007) 'Parents' voices: a conversation with parents of pre-school children', in K. Goouch and A. Lambirth (eds), *Understanding Phonics and the Teaching of Reading*. Maidenhead: Open University Press.

Goouch, K. (2008) 'Understanding playful pedagogies, play narratives and play spaces', *Early Years*, 28(1): 93–102.

Gopnik, A., Meltzoff, A. and Kuhl, P. (1999) *How Babies Think: The Science of Childhood*. London: Weidenfeld and Nicolson.

Goswami, U. (2007) 'Learning to read across languages: the role of phonics and synthetic phonics', in K. Goouch and A. Lambirth (eds), *Understanding Phonics and the Teaching of Reading*. Maidenhead: Open University Press.

Goswami, U. (2008) *Cognitive Development: The Learning Brain*. Hove: Psychology Press.

Goswami, U. and Bryant, P.E. (1990) *Phonological Skills and Learning to Read*. Hove: Lawrence Erlbaum.

Graves, D. (1983) *Writing: Teachers and Children at Work*. London: Heinemann.

Graves, D. (1984) *A Researcher Learns to WRITE*. London: Heinemann.

Gregory, E. (2008) *Learning to Read in a New Language. Making Sense of Words and Worlds*. 2nd edn. London: Sage.

Gregory, E., Long, S. and Volk, D. (2004) *Many Pathways to Literacy: Young*

Children Learning with Siblings, Grandparents, Peers and Communities. London: Routledge.

Gregory, E., Arju, A., Jessel, J., Kenner, C. and Ruby, M. (2007) 'Snow White in different guises: interlingual and intercultural exchanges between grandparents and young children at home in East London', *Journal of Early Childhood Literacy,* 7(1): 5–25.

Gregory, R.L. (1977) 'Psychology: towards a science of fiction', in M. Meek, A. Warlow and G. Barton (eds), *The Cool Web: The Pattern of Children's Reading.* London: Bodley Head. pp. 393–8.

Griffiths, N. (1997) *Storysacks: A Starter Information Pack.* Swindon: Storysack National Support Project.

Hall, N. and Robinson, A. (2003) *Exploring Writing and Play in the Early Years.* 2nd edn. London: David Fulton.

Hall, N., Larson, J. and Marsh, J. (eds) (2003) *Handbook of Early Childhood Literacy.* London: Sage.

Halliday, M.A.K. (1975) *Learning How to Mean: Explorations in the Development of Language.* London: Arnold.

Hardy, B. (1977) 'Towards a poetics of fiction: an approach through narrative', in M. Meek, A. Warlow and G. Barton (eds), *The Cool Web: The Pattern of Children's Reading.* London: Bodley Head. pp. 12–23.

Harris, M. (1992) *Language Experience and Early Language Development.* Hove: Lawrence Erlbaum.

Heath, S.B. (1983) *Ways with Words: Language, Life and Work in Communities and Classrooms.* Cambridge: Cambridge University Press.

Hughes, T. (1988) 'Myth and education', in K. Egan and D. Nadaner (eds), *Imagination and Education.* Milton Keynes: Open University Press. pp. 30–44.

Hutchin, V. (1999) *Right from the Start: Effective Planning and Assessment in the Early Years.* London: Hodder.

Hutchin, V. (2007) *Supporting Every Child's Learning across the Early Years Foundation Stage.* London: Hodder.

Hymes, D.H. (1972) 'On communicative competence', in J.B. Pride and J. Holmes (eds), *Sociolinguistics.* Harmondsworth: Penguin.

Johnson, P. (1991) *A Book of One's Own.* London: Hodder and Stoughton.

Jones, R. (1996) *Emerging Patterns of Literacy: A Multidisciplinary Perspective.* London: Routledge.

Karmiloff, K. and Karmiloff-Smith, A. (2001) *Pathways to Language: From Fetus to Adolescent.* Cambridge, MA, and London: Harvard University Press.

Kenner, C. (2000) *Home Pages: Literacy Links for Bilingual Children.* Stoke-on-Trent: Trentham Books.

Kress, G. (1994) *Learning to Write.* 2nd edn. London: Routledge and Kegan Paul.

Kress, G. (1997) *Before Writing: Rethinking the Paths to Literacy.* London: Routledge.

Kress, G. (2000) *Early Spelling: Between Convention and Creativity.* London: Routledge.

Lambirth, A. (2007) 'Social class and the struggle to learn to read: using Bernstein to understand the politics of the teaching of reading', in K. Goouch and A. Lambirth (eds) *Understanding Phonics and the Teaching of Reading: Critical Perspectives.* Maidenhead: Open University Press.

Le Guin, U.K. (1981) 'It was a dark and stormy night: or why are we huddling about the camp fire?', in W.J.T. Mitchell (ed.), *On Narrative*. Chicago, IL: University of Chicago Press. pp. 187–95.

Lewis, D. (2001) *Reading Contemporary Picturebooks: Picturing Text*. London: Routledge Falmer.

Lierop, M. van (1985) 'Predisposing factors in early literacy: a case study', in M.M. Clark (ed.), *New Directions in the Study of Reading*. Lewes: Falmer. pp. 64–80.

Makin, L. and Whitehead, M. (2004) *How to Develop Children's Early Literacy: A Guide for Professional Carers and Educators*. London: Paul Chapman Publishing.

Mallett, M. (1999) *Young Researchers: Informational Reading and Writing in the Early and Primary Years*. London: Routledge.

Mallett, M. (2003) *Early Years Non-Fiction: A Guide to Helping Young Researchers Use Information Texts*. London: Routledge Falmer.

Marriott, S. (1991) *Picture Books in the Primary Classroom*. London: Paul Chapman Publishing.

Marsh, J. and Hallett, E. (eds) (2008) *Desirable Literacies: Approaches to Language and Literacy in the Early Years*. 2nd edn. London: Sage.

Matthews, J. (2003) *Drawing and Painting: Children and Visual Representation*. 2nd edn. London: Paul Chapman Publishing.

Meadows, S. (2006) *The Child as Thinker: The Development and Acquisition of Cognition in Childhood*. 2nd edn. London: Routledge.

Meek, M. (1988) *How Texts Teach What Readers Learn*. Stroud: Thimble.

Meek, M. (1996) *Information and Book Learning*. Stroud: Thimble.

Meyer, R. J. (2002) *Phonics Exposed. Understanding and Resisting Systematic Direct Intense Phonics Instruction*. Mahwah, NJ: Lawrence Erlbaum Associates.

Mudd, N. (1994) *Effective Spelling: A Practical Guide for Teachers*. London: Hodder and Stoughton.

Nelson, K. (1989) *Narratives from the Crib*. Cambridge, MA: Harvard University Press.

Newkirk, T. (1984) 'Archimedes' dream', *Language Arts*, 61(4): 341–50.

Nutbrown, C. (1997) *Recognising Early Literacy Development: Assessing Children's Achievements*. London: Paul Chapman Publishing.

Nutbrown, C. (2006) *Threads of Thinking: Young Children Learning and the Role of Early Education*, 3rd edn. London: Sage.

Nutbrown, C. and Page, J. (2008) *Working with Babies and Children: From Birth to Three*. London: Sage.

Nyland, B., Ferris, J. and Dunn, L. (2008) 'Mindful hands, gestures as language: listening to children', *Early Years*, 28(1): 73–80.

Olson, D.R., Torrance, N. and Hildyard, A. (eds) (1985) *Literacy, Language and Learning: The Nature and Consequences of Reading and Writing*. Cambridge: Cambridge University Press.

Ong, W.J. (1982) *Orality and Literacy: The Technologizing of the Word*. London: Methuen.

Opie, I. and Opie, P. (1980) *A Nursery Companion*. Oxford: Oxford University Press.

Paley, V.G. (1981) *Wally's Stories: Conversations in the Kindergarten*. Cambridge, MA: Harvard University Press.

Pawl, J. (2006) 'Being Held in Another's Mind', www.wested.org/online_pubs/ccfs-06-o1-chapter1.pdf

Payton, S. (1984) 'Developing awareness of print: a young child's first steps towards literacy', *Education Review Offset Publication, No. 2*, University of Birmingham.

Pennac, D. (2006) *The Rights of the Reader*. Trans. S. Adams. London: Walker.

Peters, M.L. (1985) *Spelling Caught or Taught? A New Look*. London: Routledge.

Piaget, J. (1926) *The Language and Thought of the Child*. London: Routledge and Kegan Paul.

Pinker, S. (1994) *The Language Instinct: The New Science of Language and Mind*. Harmondsworth: Allen Lane/Penguin.

Pinker, S. (2002) *The Blank Slate: The Modern Denial of Human Nature*. London: Allen Lane.

Pinker, S. (2007) *The Stuff of Thought: Language as a Window into Human Nature*. London: Penguin Books.

Read, C. (1986) *Children's Creative Spelling*. London: Routledge and Kegan Paul.

Reddy, V. (1991) 'Playing with others' expectations: teasing and mucking about in the first year', in A. Whiten (ed.), *Natural Theories of Mind*. Oxford: Blackwell. pp. 145–58.

Rich, D., Casanova, D., Dixon, A., Drummond, M. J., Durrant, A. and Myer, C. (2005) *First Hand Experience. What Matters to Children. An Alphabet of Learning from the Real World*. Woodbridge: Rich Learning Opportunities.

Rich, D., Drummond, M.J. and Myer, C. (2008) *Learning: What Matters to Children. An Alphabet of What Learners Do*. Woodbridge: Rich Learning Opportunities.

Riley, J. (2006) *Language and Literacy 3–7: Creative Approaches to Teaching*. London: Paul Chapman Publishing.

Ruby, M., Kenner, C., Jessel, J., Gregory, E. and Arju, T. (2007) 'Gardening with grandparents: an early engagement with the science curriculum', *Early Years*, 27(2): 131–44.

Sassoon, R. (1995) *The Acquisition of a Second Writing System*. Oxford: Intellect.

Sassoon, R. (2003) *Handwriting: The Way to Teach It*. 2nd edn. London: Paul Chapman Publishing.

Saussure, F. de (1974) *Course in General Linguistics*. Glasgow: Collins. (First published 1915, Paris: Payot.)

Saxe, R. and Baron-Cohen, S. (eds) (2007) *Theory of Mind*. Hove: Psychology Press.

Scollon, R. and Scollon, S.B.K. (1981) *Narrative, Literacy and Face in Interethnic Communication*. Norwood, NJ: Ablex.

Selinker, L. (1992) *Rediscovering Interlanguage*. London: Longman.

Sendak, M. (1977) 'Questions to an artist who is also an author', in M. Meek, A. Warlow and G. Barton (eds), *The Cool Web: The Pattern of Children's Reading*. London: Bodley Head. pp. 241–56.

Serpell, R., Baker, L. and Sonnenschein, S. (2005) *Becoming Literate in the City. The Baltimore Early Childhood Project*. Cambridge: Cambridge University Press.

Sheridan, D. (1979) '"Flopsy, Mopsy and Tooth": the storytelling of preschoolers', *Language Arts*, 56(1): 10–15.

Siraj-Blatchford, I. and Clarke, P. (2000) *Supporting Identity, Diversity and Language in the Early Years*. Buckingham: Open University Press.

Siraj-Blatchford, I. and Manni, L. (2008) '"Would you like to tidy up now?" An analysis of adult questioning in the English Foundation Stage', *Early Years. An International Journal of Research and Development*, 28(1): 5–22.

Siraj-Blatchford, I., Sylva, K., Muttock, S., Gilden, R. and Bell, D. (2002) *Researching Effective Pedagogy in the Early Years*. DfES Research Brief 356. London: DfES.

Siren Films (2004) *Attachment in Practice*. Newcastle Upon Tyne.

Smith, B. (1994) *Through Writing to Reading: Classroom Strategies for Supporting Literacy*. London: Routledge.

Smith, B.H. (1981) 'Narrative versions, narrative theories', in W.J.T. Mitchell (ed.), *On Narrative*. Chicago, IL: University of Chicago Press. pp. 209–32.

Smith, F. (1982) *Writing and the Writer*. New York: Holt, Rinehart and Winston.

Smith, F. (1988) *Joining the Literacy Club*. London: Heinemann.

Smith, F. (1994) *Understanding Reading: A Psycholinguistic Analysis of Reading and Learning to Read*. 5th edn. Hillsdale, NJ: Lawrence Erlbaum.

Snow, C.E. (1977) 'The development of conversation between mothers and babies', *Journal of Child Language*, 4: 1–22.

Snow, C.E., Barnes, W.S., Chandler, J., Goodman, I.F. and Hemphill, L. (1991) *Unfulfilled Expectations: Home and School Influences on Literacy*. Cambridge, MA: Harvard University Press.

Stephens, J. (1992) *Language and Ideology in Children's Fiction*. London: Longman.

Stern, D. (1977) *The First Relationship: Infant and Mother*. London: Fontana.

Styles, M. and Arizpe, E. (2002) *Children Reading Pictures: Interpreting Visual Texts*. London: Routledge Falmer.

Styles, M., Bearne, E. and Watson, V. (eds) (1992) *After Alice: Exploring Children's Literature*. London: Cassell.

Styles, M., Bearne, E. and Watson, V. (eds) (1994) *The Prose and the Passion: Children and their Reading*. London: Cassell.

Styles, M., Bearne, E. and Watson, V. (eds) (1996) *Voices Off: Texts, Contexts and Readers*. London: Cassell.

Tizard, B. and Hughes, M. (2002) *Young Children Learning*. 2nd edn. Oxford: Blackwell.

Trevarthen, C. (1993) 'Playing into reality: conversations with the infant communicator', *Winnicott Studies*, 7(Spring): 67–84.

Trevarthen, C. (2002) 'Learning in companionship', *Education in the North: The Journal of Scottish Education*, 10: 16–25.

Trudgill, P. (1994) *Dialects*. London: Routledge.

Trudgill, P. (2003) *The Norfolk Dialect*. Cromer: Poppyland Publishing.

Truss, L. (2003) *Eats, Shoots and Leaves. The Zero Tolerance Approach to Punctuation*. London: Profile Books.

Vygotsky, L.S. (1978) *Mind in Society: The Development of Higher Psychological Processes*. Cambridge, MA: Harvard University Press.

Vygotsky, L.S. (1986) *Thought and Language*. Revd and ed. by A. Kozulin. Cambridge, MA: MIT Press.

Wade, B. and Moore, M. (2000) 'A sure start with books', *Early Years*, 20(2): 39–46.

Watson, V. and Styles, M. (eds) (1996) *Talking Pictures: Pictorial Texts and Young Readers*. London: Hodder and Stoughton.

Weinberger, J. (1996) *Literacy Goes to School: The Parents' Role in Young Children's Literacy Learning*. London: Paul Chapman Publishing.

Weir, R.H. (1962) *Language in the Crib*. The Hague: Mouton.

Wells, G. (ed.) (1981) *Learning Through Interaction: The Study of Language Development*. Cambridge: Cambridge University Press.

West Yorkshire Playhouse (2000) *Imaginary Worlds: Creative Learning through Play*. Leeds: WY Playhouse AAS Development Unit.

Whalley, M. and Pen Green Centre Team (2007) *Involving Parents in their Children's Learning*. 2nd edn. London: Paul Chapman Publishing.

White, D. (1954) *Books before Five*. New Zealand: Council for Educational Research.

Whitehead, M.R. (2002) 'Dylan's routes to literacy: the first three years with picture books', *Journal of Early Childhood Literacy*, 2(3): 269–89.

Whitehead, M.R. (2007) *Developing Language and Literacy with Young Children*. 3rd edn. London: Paul Chapman Publishing.

Whitehead, M.R. (2009) *Supporting Language and Literacy Development in the Early Years*. 2nd edn. Maidenhead: Open University Press.

Winnicott, D.W. (1971) *Playing and Reality*. Harmondsworth: Penguin.

Wolf, M. (2008) *Proust and the Squid. The Story and Science of the Reading Brain*. Cambridge: Icon Books.

Worthington, M. and Carruthers, E. (2003) *Children's Mathematics: Making Marks, Making Meaning*. London: Paul Chapman Publishing.

DVDs AND USEFUL WEBSITES

www.booksforkeeps.co.uk – Books for Keeps.

www.booktrusted.com – the Book Trust.

www.clpe.co.uk – Centre for Literacy in Primary Education.

www.childrenslaureate.org – the Children's Laureate.

www.deni.gov.uk – Northern Ireland Department for Education.

www.ican.org.uk – ICAN, UK charity supporting children's talk and communication.

www.learning.wales.gov.uk – Welsh Department for Education and Training.

www.ncb.org.uk – National Children's Bureau.

www.primaryreview.org.uk – The Primary Review, University of Cambridge.

www.scotland.gov.uk – Learning and Teaching, Scotland.

www.signsforsuccess.co.uk – teaching signing.

www.singandsign.com – Felix, S. (2001) *Sing and Sign: Help your Baby to Communicate before Speech.*

www.sirenfilms.co.uk – Siren Films: Newcastle upon Tyne, NE1 4XF, tel: 0191 232 7900.

www.standards.dcsf.gov.uk/primaryframeworks/nationalstrategies – Department for Children, Schools and Families, England.

www.talktoyourbaby.org.uk – National Literacy Trust early language campaign.

INDEX